LEARN ITALIAN

TARGET:
LANGUAGES

LEARN ITALIAN

Beginner level
A2

Federico Benedetti

Adapted for English speakers
by Elise Bradbury

ASSIMIL®

THE TARGET: LANGUAGES SERIES

01

THE COMMON EUROPEAN FRAMEWORK OF REFERENCE FOR LANGUAGES

When, exactly, can someone say they "speak" a foreign language? When can they claim to speak it "correctly" and fluently? Language mastery is an issue that has long exercised educationalists and linguists. It might have remained a topic of academic debate, and language acquisition just another subject on the educational curriculum, were it not for the fact that today's learners need to demonstrate or prove the skills they have acquired, especially when working in a professional environment, applying for a job, or even migrating to another country.

Various systems and scales have been developed to measure language proficiency, including the International English Language Testing System (IELTS), the ALTE Framework and, in the United States, the ACTFL Proficiency Guidelines and the ILR Scale.

In the European Union, which has more than 20 official languages (among the 120 or so spoken throughout Europe as a whole), the assessment issue was a particularly critical question. That is why the Council of Europe in 2001 designed the Common European Framework of Reference for Languages (CEFRL). The main purpose of this initiative was to provide a method for learning, teaching and assessing that applies to all European languages so that they can be learned and practised more easily. Another of the original aims of the CEFRL, in addition to encouraging Europe's citizens to travel and to interact with each other, was to put some order into the multiple private assessment tests that were in use at the time and that, in most cases, were specific to just one language.

More than 15 years after the CEFRL was rolled out, it has proven hugely successful, not only in Europe but throughout the world. Now available in some 40 languages, the framework is widely used by educators, course designers, human resource managers and companies, who "find it advantageous to work with stable, accepted standards of measurement and format".[1]

---

[1] "Common European Framework of Reference for Languages: learning, teaching, assessment", Council of Europe, 2001

CEFRL LEVELS AND CATEGORIES

The Common European Framework comprises 3 broad categories and 6 common levels of competency:

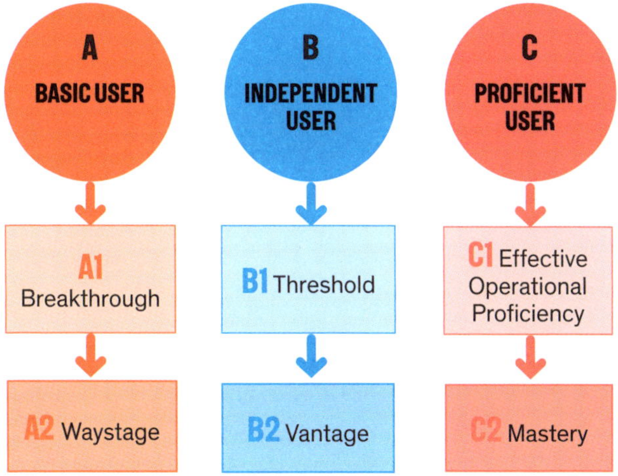

Each level of competency comprises detailed "descriptors" of language proficiency and communication:

- spoken and written production
- reception (listening and reading comprehension)
- spoken and written interaction
- spoken and written mediation
- non-verbal signals.

For this Target: Languages course, we have restricted the communication activities to reception and basic production. Interaction, mediation and non-verbal communication will be performed at a later stage by meeting and interacting with native speakers, either physically or online.

A2 LEVEL COMPETENCIES

At Level A2, the learner can:

- understand phrases and the highest frequency vocabulary
- read short texts and find information in simple materials
- understand short, simple personal letters
- communicate in simple, routine tasks

• describe in simple terms his/her family and other people, living conditions, educational background and job
• write short, simple notes and messages.

Most self-study methods refer to one of the CEFRL levels, generally B2, but few have been produced with those requirements specifically in mind. The Target: Languages series has been designed using the descriptors and competencies outlined in the reference framework. The content of the dialogues has been enhanced with respect to the baseline specifications in order to meet the real needs of today's users. And, faithful to the Assimil philosophy, every effort has been made to make the learning experience enjoyable.

A word of advice to learners

By listening carefully to the dialogues, reading and understanding the grammatical explanations, and completing all the exercises, you will reach Level A2. There is no specific timeframe, so you can choose the pace that you feel comfortable with. But when you reach the end of the course, that's when the work really begins! You must immerse yourself in the language, taking every opportunity to talk with native speakers, watch movies, read books, articles and blogs – in short, to take every opportunity for using the knowledge you have acquired. That is the first important step on the road to mastery – however it is officially measured!

* Comparative competency scales

CEFRL	ACTFL	ILR
A1	Novice Low Novice High	0 0+
A2	Intermediate Low Intermediate Mid	1
B1	Intermediate High	1+
B2	Advanced Advanced Plus	2 2+
C1	Superior	3 3+
C2	Distinguished	4 4+

Courtesy of The American University Center of Provence

LEARN ITALIAN

TOPICS

- PRONUNCIATION
- WORD STRESS AND ACCENTUATION
- REGIONAL VARIATIONS
- INTONATION IN STATEMENTS, EXCLAMATIONS AND QUESTIONS

02

PRONUNCIATION

Many people consider Italian one of the world's most beautiful languages and decide to learn it for this reason. Luckily, Italian pronunciation, apart from certain letter combinations, is not too difficult. The best way to pick up the pronunciation is to practice: as you work through the lessons, listen to the recordings of the dialogues and exercises and repeat them out loud as many times as you need to. Over time, this will increase both your fluency and your comprehension.

In general, Italian is highly phonetic: words are pronounced as they are written. Moreover, most of the letters are pronounced in a similar way to English. In this section, we explain only the letters and groups of letters that are pronounced differently, thus posing the main difficulties for English speakers. Most include a pronunciation exercise accompanied by a recording: listen to the audio and then repeat the phrases aloud. Pretend you're Italian – this will help you pick it up!

THE VOWELS

MAIN VOWEL SOUNDS

The key vowel sounds are as follows: **a** [ah] as in *fall*, **e** [ay] as in *say* or [eh] as in *bed*, **i** [ee] as in *tree*, **o** [oh] as in *no*, and **u** [oo] as in *food*. (Note that a final **e** is not silent in Italian: **cane** [kahneh] *dog*.)

Listen to and repeat the days of the week (which are not capitalized in Italian).
a. lunedì *(Monday)* **b. martedì** *(Tuesday)* **c. mercoledì** *(Wednesday)* **d. giovedì** *(Thursday)* **e. venerdì** *(Friday)* **f. sabato** *(Saturday)* **g. domenica** *(Sunday)*

VOWEL COMBINATIONS

Vowels that occur side by side are pronounced individually, but when spoken quickly they tend to blend together. Here are a few of the most common: **ai** [I] as in *aisle*, **ao, au** [ao] as in *now*, **ei** [ey] as in *achy* (without the 'ch'), **ia, ie, io, iu** [y] + vowel, **oi** [oy] as in *boy*, and **ua, ue, ui, uo** [w] + vowel.

Listen to and repeat these words.
a. mai *(never)* **b. autunno** *(autumn)* **c. lei** *(she)* **d. grazie** *(thank you)* **e. lezione** *(lesson)* **f. poi** *(then)* **g. quanto** *(how much)* **h. uomo** *(man)*

CONSONANTS AND LETTER COMBINATIONS

THE 'C' AND 'CH'

• The letter **c** is a hard [k] before the vowels **a, o, u**: **caffè** [kahf-fay] *coffee, café*, **cosa** [kosah] *thing*, **cura** [koorah] *care*.

• Before **e** and **i**, the **c** is pronounced [ch]: **piacere** [pyahchayray] *pleasure, delight*, **Sicilia** [seecheelyah] *Sicily*. This is the case even if the vowels **a, o, u** come after the **i**: **Ciao!** [chaao] *Hello!*

• A **ch** (before **e** and **i**) is pronounced [k]: **che** [kay] *that*, **chiodo** [kyohdoh] *nail*.

Listen to the recording and then read these words or phrases out loud.

a. Mi chiamo Chiara. *My name is Chiara.* **b. occhio** *eye* **c. Non mi è mai piaciuta la cioccolata.** *I have never liked chocolate.* **d. pacchetto** *packet, package* **e. parcheggio** *parking lot, car park* **f. Taci, per piacere!** *Be quiet, please!*

THE 'G' AND 'GH'

• The letter **g** is a hard [g] before the vowels **a, o, u**: **gatto** [gaht-toh] *cat*, **goccia** [goh-chah] *drop*, **gusto** [goostoh] *taste*.

• Before **e** and **i**, the **g** is pronounced [j]: **gelato** [jaylahtoh] *ice cream*, **Parigi** [pah-reejee] *Paris*. This is the case even if the vowels **a, o, u** come after the **i**: **Norvegia** [nohrvayjah] *Norway*, **giocare** [johkahray] *to play*, **giusto** [joostoh] *just, fair*.

• A **gh** (before **e** and **i**) is pronounced with a hard [g]: **colleghi** [kohl-layghee] *colleagues*, **funghi** [foonghee] *mushrooms*.

Listen to the recording and then read these phrases out loud.

a. i colleghi belgi *the Belgian colleagues* **b. il giorno di pioggia** *the rainy day* **c. le paghe dei giusti** *the wages of the righteous* **d. i gerani e i mughetti** *the geraniums and the lilies of the valley*

THE 'GLI' AND 'GN'

The **gli** is pronounced [ly] as in *million* (the **g** is silent): **famiglia** [fahmeelyah] *family*. The **gn** is pronounced [ny] as in *canyon* (the **g** is silent): **gnocchi** [nyohk-kee].

Listen to the recording and then read these words out loud.

a. figlio *son* **b. voglio** *I want* **c. migliore** *best* **d. paglia** *straw* **e. bagno** *bath, bathroom* **f. signore** *Mr, sir* **g. lasagne** *lasagne*

THE 'H'

Before a vowel, the letter **h** is always silent: **ho** [oh] *I have*.

THE 'QU'

The letter **q** is always followed by **u** and is pronounced [kw] + vowel: **quadro** [kwahdroh] *painting, square, chart.*

Listen to and repeat these words and phrases.

a. Pasqua *Easter* **b. i parchi acquatici** *the aquatic parks* **c. Quanti quaderni volete? – Quarantaquattro.** *How many notebooks do you want? – Forty-four.* **d. Vieni qui!** *Come here!*

THE 'R' AND 'RR'

The Italian **r** is rolled, a sound made by trilling the tip of the tongue against the roof of the mouth. A double **rr** is a longer trill than a single **r**.

Listen to and repeat these words.

a. rosso *red* **b. bere** *to drink* **c. forte** *strong* **d. burro** *butter* **e. guerra** *war*

THE 'SC'

• The **sc** is pronounced [sk] before the vowels **a, o, u**: **scala** [skahlah] *stairs*, **sconto** [skohntoh] *sale*, **scuola** [skwolah] *school*.

• Before **e** and **i**, the **sc** is pronounced [sh]: **pesce** [payshay] *fish*, **sci** [shee] *ski*. This is the case even if the vowels **a, o, u** come after the **i**: **lasciare** [lahshahray] *to leave,* **liscio** [leeshoh] *smooth*, **pastasciutta** [pahstahshoot-tah] *pasta*.

• A **sch** (before **e** and **i**) is pronounced [sk]: **affreschi** [ahf-frayskee] *frescoes*.

Listen to and repeat these sentences.

a. Peschiamo pesce a Scilla. *We fish the fish in Scilla.* **b. Lascia parlare gli sciocchi.** *Let the fools speak.* **c. Fischia quando la sciarpa è asciutta.** *Whistle when the scarf is dry.*

THE 'S' AND 'Z'

• The **s** is pronounced as in English unless it comes between two vowels or before the consonants **b, d, g, l, m, n, r** or **v**, in which case it is pronounced [z]: **casa** [kahzah] *house*, **smettere** [zmayt-tayray] *to stop*.

• The **z** is pronounced like [ds] or [ts]: **zero** [dsayro], **senza** [sayntsah] *without*.

Listen to and repeat these words.

a. rosa *pink* **b. sbadato** *careless* **c. importanza** *importance* **d. lezione** *lesson*

Now test yourself on some of these tricky pronunciations by ticking the box with the correct phonetic sound.

	[k]	[ch]	[sh]	[g]	[j]
parchi *parks*					
porci *pigs*					
giardino *garden*					
prosciutto *ham*					
fischiare *to whistle*					
piccolo *small*					
lasciare *to let*					
lanciare *to throw*					
lunghissimo *very long*					

DOUBLE CONSONANTS

In Italian words, double consonants are pronounced with more emphasis – almost as separate sounds with a slight pause between them. The effect is a bit like exaggerating the consonant. This distinction is important, because certain words can only be told apart by the difference between the single or double consonant: **sono** *I am* / **sonno** *sleep*; **nona** *ninth* (f.) / **nonna** *grandmother*. So when you're speaking or listening, don't confuse **la Nona di Beethoven** *Beethoven's Ninth* with **la nonna di Beethoven** *Beethoven's grandmother*!

Listen to and repeat these phrases.

a. Ho tanta sete. *I'm very thirsty.* / **ottantasette** *eighty-seven*

b. il tono di voce *tone of voice* / **il tonno in scatola** *canned tuna*

c. i tori di Siviglia *the bulls of Sevilla* / **le torri di Siviglia** *the towers of Sevilla*

d. Arriva! *He/she is coming!* / **a riva** *on the shore*

WORD STRESS

Italian is often described as a particularly musical language. Its lilting quality is largely due to the intonation and word stress (which syllable is emphasized in a word). When an Italian word is pronounced, one vowel is 'longer' than the others, giving it emphasis. While the stress is most often on the second-to-last syllable (**buongiorno** *good morning*), it is sometimes elsewhere in the word: you'll gradually pick up where the stress goes as you hear the words over time. As with double consonants, where the word stress is placed can change the meaning of a word. For example, **ancora** means *anchor*, while **ancora** means *again*; **perdono** means *pardon*, while **perdono** means *they lose*.

Italian words fall into the following categories depending on where the stress is placed. The terms for these are a bit strange!

- **parole piane** *level words*: in these words, the stress is on the second-to-last syllable: **amico** *friend* (m.); **mangiare** *to eat*.
- **parole sdrucciole** *slippery words*: the word stress is on the third-to-last syllable: **ultimo** *final*; **chiamali** *call them*.
- **parole bisdrucciole** *double slippery words*: the word stress is on the fourth-to-last syllable (this most often occurs with forms of verbs): **abitano** *they live*; **portacelo** *bring it to us*; **diteglielo** *tell him*.
- **parole tronche** *truncated words*: this term comes from the fact that what was formerly the final syllable has been lost over time. The word stress falls on what is now the last syllable and is indicated with a written accent: **città** *city*, **virtù** *virtue*.

Listen to these words and underline the syllable that is stressed.

Firenze *Florence*
canzone *song*
Federico *Frederic*
cantavano *they sang*
cantavamo *we sang*
felicità *happiness*
macchina *car*
fantastico *fantastic*
raccontatemelo *tell it to me* (speaking to a group)
raccontamelo *tell it to me* (speaking to one person)

REGIONAL VARIATIONS

It is important to point out that pronunciation varies from region to region in Italy. In some places, the **e** is more like that in *bed* than in *café* and the **o** is more like that in *hot* than in *bone*. The pronunciation of **s** and **z** can change particularly significantly depending on regional accent. The good news for learners is that this means you don't need to worry too much about the subtleties of pronouncing these letters!

While traditionally Tuscan (the language of Dante, the 14th-century poet) has been considered the linguistic benchmark for Italian, there is a wide diversity of regional dialects and accents, and pronunciation differences are commonly accepted. You might hear anyone from government ministers and academics to their less erudite compatriots speaking in their native regional accent. So in Tuscany or Bologna, the word **pesca** pronounced with an 'open' **e** as in *bed* [peskah] means *peach*, while pronounced with a 'closed' **e** as in *café* [payskah] it means *fishing*. However, in Lombardy and Veneto, both words are pronounced in the same way (with a 'closed' **e**), without causing too much confusion!

INTONATION IN STATEMENTS, EXCLAMATIONS AND QUESTIONS

When we think of Italian, one of the things that most comes to mind is how expressive it is. This is largely due to intonation and phrasal stress (which words or phrases are emphasized in a sentence). In English, we also use intonation to express meaning: for example, a rising intonation signals a question. Yet this is even more emphasized in Italian, a language in which intonation alone can differentiate the meaning of identically structured phrases:

Andiamo. *We're going.*
Andiamo! *Let's go!*
Andiamo? *Shall we go?*

Listen to these phrases and then repeat them, paying particular attention to the different intonations.

a. **Andiamo. / Andiamo! / Andiamo?**
b. **Dimmi quanto hai speso.** *Tell me how much you spent.*
   Dimmi: quanto hai speso? *So tell me: how much did you spend?*
   Quanto hai speso! *You spent so much!*
c. **Sei di Milano.** *You are from Milan.*
   Sei di Milano? *Are you from Milan?*
   Incredibile: sei di Milano! *It's amazing that you're from Milan!*
d. **Mangi più di me.** *You eat more than me.*
   Mangi più di me? *Do you eat more than me?*
   Mangi più di me! *You eat more than I do!*

I. FIRST CONTACT

II. EVERYDAY LIFE

III. JOBS & TASKS

IV. FREE TIME

I

FIRST CONTACT

1. INTRODUCTIONS AND GREETINGS

PRESENTAZIONI E SALUTI

AIMS

- INTRODUCING YOURSELF
- SAYING HELLO
- SAYING GOODBYE

TOPICS

- DEFINITE ARTICLES
- GENDER OF NOUNS
- FORMING THE PLURAL
- NOUNS AND ADJECTIVES ENDING IN -O
- THE SUBJECT PRONOUNS
- PRESENT TENSE OF THE VERB *ESSERE* ('TO BE')

THE NEW NEIGHBOUR (f.)

Carlo: Hi! I'm Carlo *(I myself I-call Carlo)*. What's your name *(And you how yourself you-call)*?

Luisa: Hello *(good-day)*! I'm Luisa. Nice to meet you *(pleasure)*!

Carlo: Are you the new neighbour (f.)?

Luisa: Yes, I've been living *(I-live)* here since yesterday. I come from Milan.

Carlo: Ah, you're from Milan.

Luisa: No, no, we are Sicilian (pl.), but my parents *(the mine)* have been working *(they-work)* in the north [of Italy] for years.

Carlo: As for me *(I on-the-other-hand)*, I'm from here, my family has been living *(it-lives)* in Bologna for generations and generations.

Luisa: It's a lovely city, isn't it *(true)*?

Carlo: Very beautiful! It's my city *(the mine)*! And it's full of young people!

Luisa: Well, I have to go to class now *(I now must go to lesson)*. My bus comes *(passes)* in two minutes. See you later *(us we-see)*!

Carlo: I'm also a student *(I'm student also-I)*, you know? So goodbye! See you soon *(at-the next)*! And ... careful not to miss the bus!

03 LA NUOVA VICINA

Carlo: Ciao! Io mi chiamo Carlo. E tu come ti chiami?

Luisa: Buongiorno! Io sono Luisa. Piacere!

Carlo: Sei la nuova vicina?

Luisa: Sì, abito qui da ieri; vengo da Milano.

Carlo: Ah, sei di Milano.

Luisa: No no, siamo siciliani, ma i miei lavorano nel nord da anni.

Carlo: Io invece sono di qui, la mia famiglia abita a Bologna da generazioni e generazioni.

Luisa: È una bella città, vero?

Carlo: Bellissima! È la mia! Ed è piena di ragazzi!

Luisa: Beh, io adesso devo andare a lezione. Il mio autobus passa tra due minuti. Ci vediamo!

Carlo: Sono studente anch'io, sai? Beh, arrivederci! Alla prossima! E… attenzione a non perdere l'autobus!

UNDERSTANDING THE DIALOGUE
GREETINGS

→ The polite standard greeting is **buongiorno** *good day* or **buonasera** *good evening*. The more informal **ciao** is used between friends and young people.
→ Another option is **Salve!**, which is between the two, but is better to reserve for people you're on familiar terms with.

INTRODUCING YOURSELF

→ To give one's name, the reflexive verb **chiamarsi** *to be called* is used: **Mi chiamo…** *My name is …* or literally, 'myself I-call'.
→ The reply is **Piacere!** *Nice to meet you!* This word literally means 'pleasure' and implies **È un piacere conoscerti!** *It's a pleasure to meet you!*

SAYING GOODBYE

The standard expression for *goodbye* is **arrivederci**. Other options are **ciao** *bye*, **alla prossima** *until next time* or **ci vediamo** *see you soon*.

CULTURAL NOTE

Immigration from the south to the north of Italy has been common since the end of World War II. Northern Italy is more economically developed, so it is easier to find work there, and whole families move as a result. For families in the north, however, it is not unusual to live in your hometown **da generazioni e generazioni…!**

GRAMMAR
AGREEMENT IN GENDER AND NUMBER

Every noun in Italian is either masculine or feminine, even those that don't refer to people: for example, **la città** *city* is feminine. This is important because other words that describe the noun (e.g. articles, pronouns and adjectives) change form to agree with its gender. So the adjective **bello** *beautiful* in the masculine becomes **bella** in the feminine. When an adjective describes a person, it needs to agree with the person's gender: **vicino** *neighbour* (male), **vicina** (female).

A noun and the words that modify it also change depending on whether it is singular or plural. In Italian, plurals are not formed by adding **-s**! The masculine singular ending **-o** changes to **-i**, and the feminine singular ending **-a** changes to **-e**: **ragazzo** *young man*, **ragazza** *young woman*, **ragazzi** *young men* (or a mixed group of young men and women), **ragazze** *young women*.

THE DEFINITE ARTICLE 'THE'

As a result, there are a number of ways to say *the* – not only are there different forms for masculine and feminine, singular and plural, but they also vary depending on what letter the following word starts with! The table below shows the different forms. Note that an apostrophe is used before a singular noun starting with a vowel: **l'amica** *friend* (f.).

	Masculine noun			Feminine noun	
	Starting with a consonant (but see column 2)	Starting with **s** + consonant, **gn, z, ps**	Starting with a vowel	Starting with a consonant	Starting with a vowel
SINGULAR	**il** **il mio autobus**	**lo** **lo studente**	**l'** **l'autobus**	**la** **la vicina**	**l'** **l'amica**
PLURAL	**i** **i miei**	**gli** **gli studenti, gli autobus**		**le** **le vicine, le amiche**	

NOUNS AND ADJECTIVES ENDING IN -O

Before you throw up your hands in despair at these complications, the good news is that many singular nouns and adjectives end in -**o** in the masculine and in **-a** in the feminine. As we've seen, the plural forms become **-i** (masculine) and **-e** (feminine):

	Masculine	Feminine
SINGULAR	**-o** **il siciliano bello**	**-a** **la siciliana bella**
PLURAL	**-i** **i siciliani belli**	**-e** **le siciliane belle**

THE SUBJECT PRONOUNS

The subject pronouns in Italian are **io** *I*, **tu** *you* (informal singular), **lui** *he*, **lei** *she*, **noi** *we*, **voi** *you* (informal plural) and **loro** *they*. When addressing someone formally, **Lei** *you* (singular) or **Loro** *you* (plural) are used. The subject pronouns are usually left out unless emphasis is necessary: for example, to show contrast or differentiate the speaker: **Io invece sono di qui.** *As for me, I'm from here.*

SOME PREPOSITIONS

• We've now seen two meanings for **da**. One is to indicate origin (*from*) **vengo da Milano** *I come from Milan*; another is to indicate the passage of time (*for, since*): **da generazioni** *for generations*.
• However, in **sei di Milano** *you're from Milan*, the preposition **di** *of* is used because the verb does not express movement ('you are of Milan').
• The preposition **tra** is used to express that something will happen within a period of time (*in*): **tra due minuti** *in two minutes*.

THE CONJUNCTION 'AND'

The one-letter word **e** means *and*. It becomes **ed** before a word starting with a vowel, although this is only strictly required before the vowel **e**: **ed è piena di ragazzi** *and it's full of young people.*

▲ CONJUGATION
THE PRESENT TENSE OF *ESSERE*

Introducing the present tense of the very useful verb **essere** *to be*, which is irregular. We've included the subject pronouns in the table below, but as we've mentioned, these are often left out since the conjugated verb indicates who the subject is.

(io) sono	*I am*	**(noi) siamo**	*we are*
(tu) sei	*you are* (informal sing.)	**(voi) siete**	*you are* (informal pl.)
(lui, lei, Lei) è	*he is, she is, you are* (formal sing.), also *it is*	**(loro, Loro) sono**	*they are, you are* (formal pl.)

⬢ EXERCISES

The exercises accompanied by audio are indicated with a speaker icon . In some cases, you need to listen to the recording first, and then answer the exercise questions; in other cases, you need to do the exercise first and then check your answers by listening to the audio. You'll find all of the answers in the 'Exercise answers' section at the end of the book.

VOCABULARY

abitare *to live* (in a place)
adesso *now*
anche *also, too* (**anch'io** *me too)*
l'anno *year* (**gli anni** *the years)*
l'autobus *bus*
bello/a *beautiful* (**bellissimo/a** *very beautiful)*
chiamarsi *to be called* (**chiamare** *to call)*
ciao *hi, hello*
la città *city*
come *how*
la famiglia *family*
la generazione *generation* (**le generazioni** *generations)*
ieri *yesterday*
invece *but, on the other hand, instead*
lavorare *to work*
la lezione *class, lesson*
ma *but*
il minuto *minute* (**i minuti** *minutes)*
nuovo/a *new*
passare *to pass*
perdere *to miss, to lose*
qui *here*
i ragazzi *young people* (**il ragazzo** *young man,* **la ragazza** *young woman)*
sapere *to know* (a fact or how to do something)
siciliano/a *Sicilian*
lo studente / la studentessa *student*
venire *to come*
il vicino / la vicina *neighbour*

1. USE THE CORRECT FORM OF DEFINITE ARTICLE FOR EACH NOUN.

a. .... città

b. .... studenti

c. .... vicino

d. .... università

e. .... siciliane

2. FILL IN THE TABLE WITH THE MISSING TERMS.

Masculine singular	Masculine plural	Feminine singular	Feminine plural
il vicino siciliano			
	i ragazzi belli		

03 3. LISTEN TO THE RECORDING AND THEN FILL IN THE MISSING WORD IN EACH SENTENCE.

a. Come ti chiami? Io mi .... Carlo.

b. Io .... Martina, ...

c. Abiti qui .... molto tempo?

d. .... qui da ieri.

e. Adesso devo andare; ....

f. Alla ....

4. FILL IN THE SENTENCES WITH THE CORRECT FORM OF THE VERB *ESSERE*.

a. I miei .... bolognesi da generazioni.

b. Noi invece .... siciliani.

c. Voi .... studenti.

d. Io .... di Milano e tu di dove ....?

e. Bologna .... molto bella.

2.
TALKING ABOUT YOURSELF

PARLARE DI SÉ

AIMS	TOPICS
• SAYING WHERE YOU'RE FROM • GIVING YOUR AGE • DESCRIBING WHAT YOU DO	• INDEFINITE ARTICLES • PRESENT TENSE OF THE VERB *AVERE* ('TO HAVE')

CLASSMATES *(companions of faculty)*

Solveig: Hi, can I sit *(seat-myself)* next to you? I've [only] been *(I-am)* here for a week, and in this course I don't know anyone *(not I-know no-one)*.

Albert: Of course! Have a seat *(Settle-yourself)*! There's a space *(place free)* right here!

Solveig: I'm Solveig. And *(you)* what's your name?

Albert: I'm Albert. I'm Belgian, born in Liège. You, however, with the name *(that)* you have, you are surely Scandinavian (f.).

Solveig: Yes, I'm from *(I-come from-the)* Norway. I'm here to learn Italian.

Albert: Me too, I need it for my job *(of-it I-have need for the my job)*.

Solveig: What do you do *(What work you-do)*?

Albert: I'm an *(I-do the)* engineer. In *(the)* my company we have relationships with countries around the world *(all the countries of-the world)*.

Solveig: So young [and] you're already [an] engineer? How old are you *(But how-many years you-have)*?

Albert: I'm 27 *(I-have twenty-seven years)*, and you?

Solveig: I'm 28 *(I of-them I-have twenty-eight)* and I'm still a student (f.)!

Albert: Everyone studies at their own pace *(In-the studies each has the his/her paces)*! And besides in *(in-the)* your country you (pl.) have *(of-the)* excellent schools, you (pl.) are really clever!

04 COMPAGNI DI FACOLTÀ

Solveig: Ciao, posso sedermi vicino a te? Sono qui da una settimana, e in questo corso non conosco nessuno.

Albert: Certo! Accomodati! C'è un posto libero proprio qui!

Solveig: Io mi chiamo Solveig, e tu come ti chiami?

Albert: Mi chiamo Albert, sono belga. Nato a Liegi. Tu invece, con il nome che hai, sei di certo scandinava.

Solveig: Sì, vengo dalla Norvegia, sono qui per imparare l'italiano.

Albert: Anch'io, ne ho bisogno per il mio lavoro.

Solveig: Che lavoro fai?

Albert: Faccio l'ingegnere, nella mia ditta abbiamo rapporti con tutti i paesi del mondo.

Solveig: Così giovane sei già ingegnere? Ma quanti anni hai?

Albert: Ho ventisette anni, e tu?

Solveig: Io ne ho ventotto e sono ancora una studentessa!

Albert: Negli studi, ognuno ha i suoi tempi! E poi nel tuo paese avete delle ottime scuole, siete bravissimi!

UNDERSTANDING THE DIALOGUE
INVITING SOMEONE TO SIT DOWN OR COME IN

Accomodati! (the underlined vowel is stressed) is an all-purpose invitation to come in, find a place, sit down: basically, to *Make yourself comfortable!*

TALKING ABOUT AGE

→ To ask how old someone is: **Quanti anni hai?** ('How-many years you-have?')
To say how old you are: **Ho ... anni.** ('I-have ... years.')

→ For the numbers, see lesson 7.

SAYING WHAT YOU DO

→ In everyday speech, someone might ask **Che lavoro fai?** *What do you do?* You might also hear **Che mestiere fai?** (**lavoro** *work, job* / **mestiere** *trade*). **Qual è la tua professione?** *What is your profession?* is more formal.

→ The most common reply uses the verb **fare** *to do*, with the definite article *the* rather than *a(n)*: **Faccio l'ingegnere.** *I'm an engineer.*

→ It is also possible to use **essere** *to be*, which is slightly more formal:
Sono medico. *I am a doctor*. (Note that no article is used before the noun.)
Some professions have a specific form for males and females: **avvocato / avvocatessa** *lawyer* (m./f.).

CULTURAL NOTE

Italian students finish secondary school at the age of 19 with **la maturità**, the equivalent of a *high school diploma*, with which they can apply to a university. The term for a university degree is **la laurea**. There are different levels: **la laurea breve triennale** (three years), a Bachelor's degree, which can be followed by **la laurea biennale** (two years), corresponding to a Master's degree. With another three years of study, a student can receive **il dottorato di ricerca** , a doctorate or PhD.

GRAMMAR
INDEFINITE ARTICLES

Like the definite article (*the*), there are different forms of the indefinite article (*a, an*). The form must agree with the gender of the noun, and also depends on the letter the noun starts with.

With a plural noun, the equivalent of the indefinite article *some* is formed by contracting the preposition **di** + the appropriate definite article (e.g. **degli** = **di** + **gli**). This is often left out with plural nouns, as in English: **avete ottime scuole** rather than **avete delle ottime scuole** *you have (some) excellent schools*; **abbiamo rapporti** rather than **abbiamo dei rapporti** *we have (some) relationships*. But as you may have noticed in the dialogues, articles are used in many contexts in Italian in which they are not used in English, so you'll have to get used to these differences!

	Masculine noun		Feminine noun	
	Starting with a consonant (but see column 2) or a vowel	Starting with **s** + consonant or **gn, z, ps**	Starting with a consonant	Starting with a vowel
SINGULAR	**un** **un posto** **un amico**	**uno** **uno studente**	**una** **una studentessa**	**un'** **un'amica**
	Starting with a consonant (but see column 2)	Starting with **s** + consonant or **gn, z, ps** or a vowel	Starting with a consonant or a vowel	
PLURAL	**dei** **dei colleghi**	**degli** **degli studenti** **degli amici**	**delle** **delle ottime scuole** **delle amiche**	

SOME PREPOSITIONS

The preposition **a** has several uses:

- it indicates direction towards a place: **Vado a Milano.** *I'm going to Milan.*
- it indicates proximity in the prepositional phrase **vicino a** *near to*:

Posso sedermi vicino a te? *Can I sit next to you?*

- it can also be used to convey being in a place, with no movement implied:

Sono nato a Liegi. *I was* ('I-am') *born in Liège.*

The term **con** means *with*: **con il nome che hai** *with the name that you have.*

Here's an easy one: **in** *in* (**in questo corso** *in this course*). However, when followed by a definite article, the contracted form is quite different: **nel tuo paese** *in* ('in-the') *your country* (**in + il = nel**). We'll look at contracted articles in the next lesson.

▲ CONJUGATION
THE PRESENT TENSE OF *AVERE* ('TO HAVE')

The very frequently used verb **avere** *to have* is irregular. Careful: the letter **h** before a vowel is silent in Italian, so it is not pronounced in the verb forms **ho** [oh], **hai** [I], **ha** [ah] or **hanno** [ahn-noh].

(io) ho	*I have*
(tu) hai	*you have* (informal singular)
(lui, lei, Lei) ha	*he has, she has, you have* (formal singular), also *it has*
(noi) abbiamo	*we have*
(voi) avete	*you have* (plural)
(loro, Loro) hanno	*they have, you have* (formal plural)

You have probably noticed that in contrast to English there are different forms of *you* in Italian, depending on whether the speaker is addressing one or more than one person, as well as on the level of politeness required (formal or informal). This affects both the pronoun and the conjugated form of the verb to use in specific situations.

⬢ EXERCISES

1. USE THE CORRECT FORM OF INDEFINITE ARTICLE FOR EACH NOUN.

a. .... città

b. .... lavori

c. .... studente

d. .... studentessa

e. .... ingegneri

f. .... scuole

2. FILL IN THE SENTENCES WITH THE CORRECT CONJUGATED FORM OF *AVERE*.

a. Io e Luisa .... una bella casa.

b. Carlo .... un ottimo lavoro.

c. Nel vostro paese .... ottime scuole.

d. Tu .... un nome bellissimo.

VOCABULARY

belga *Belgian* (m./f.)
bravo/a *good, clever, capable* (**bravissimo/a** *very good, clever, capable)*
conoscere *to know* (a person), *to meet*
così *so*
il bisogno *need, necessity*
il corso *course*
certo *of course, sure*
di certo *certainly*
la ditta *company, firm*
giovane *young*
imparare *to learn*
l'ingegnere *engineer*
l'italiano *Italian* (the language)
il lavoro *work, job*
libero/a *free, vacant*
il mondo *the world*
nessuno/a *no one*
il nome *first name*
ognuno *each*
ottimo/a *excellent*
il paese *country*
il posto *place, seat*
proprio *exactly, precisely*
sedersi *to sit down*
la settimana *week*
gli studi *studies (***lo studio** *study)*
il tempo *time, pace*
il rapporto *relationship*
scandinavo/a *Scandinavian*
la scuola *school*

04 ## 3. LISTEN TO THE RECORDING AND COMPLETE THE SENTENCES WITH THE MISSING WORD.

a. Posso sedermi vicino .... te?

b. Certo, ...!

c. Che .... fai?

d. .... l'ingegnere.

e. .... anni hai?

f. .... trent'anni.

4. COMPLETE THE TABLE WITH THE MISSING FORMS.

Masculine singular	Masculine plural	Feminine singular	Feminine plural
uno scandinavo			
	dei ragazzi bravissimi		

3.
ADDRESSING OTHERS (*TU* OR *LEI*)

DARE DEL TU E DARE DEL LEI

AIMS	TOPICS

AIMS

- USING FORMAL AND INFORMAL ADDRESS
- APOLOGIZING
- THANKING
- EXPRESSING POLITENESS

TOPICS

- NOUNS AND ADJECTIVES ENDING IN -E
- CONTRACTED PREPOSITION + ARTICLE
- REGULAR PRESENT TENSE OF *-ARE* VERBS (1ST GROUP)

I NEED SOME *(an)* INFORMATION

Linda: **Good morning, sir, I'm sorry to bother you** *(excuse if you [formal] I-bother)*. **I need some** *(I-have need of an)* **information.**

Traffic warden: **You're not bothering me** *(You [formal] not me bother by-no-means)* **at all, miss.**

Linda: **I would like to know what city we're in; I've** *(I-am)* **just arrived by car.**

Traffic warden: **We are in Scilla, a very beautiful city by the sea. People (sing.) come from all [over] the world for** *(the)* **our sea and** *(the)* **our excellent fish. Welcome (f.)!**

Linda: **Thank you very much** *(You [formal] I-thank much)*, **sir.**

Traffic warden: **Where are you from** *(Of where-are you [formal])*?

Linda: **I'm Canadian, I come from Montreal. I speak Italian quite well, but I have difficulty using Lei** *(I-make effort to give of-the Lei)*!

Traffic warden: **So let's use 'tu'** *(give-me of-the 'tu')*! **It's no** *(Not there-is)* **problem! What** *(work)* **do you do in Montreal?**

Linda: **I'm a teacher: I teach history and geography.**

Traffic warden: **So maybe you'd also like information** *(you-desire also informations)* **on the monuments to visit. Go to the tourist office right opposite** *(here of in-front)* **– they have brochures in English and in French.**

Linda: **Thank you so much** *(mister traffic-warden)*! **You** *[informal]* **are very kind! No, excuse me: you** *[formal]* **are very kind. I thank you.**

Traffic warden: **Don't mention it** *(Not there-is of what)*, **it's me who thanks you** *(thanks to you)*!

05 HO BISOGNO DI UN'INFORMAZIONE

Linda: Buongiorno, signore, scusi se La disturbo. Ho bisogno di un'informazione.

Vigile urbano: Lei non mi disturba affatto, signorina.

Linda: Vorrei sapere in che città siamo; sono appena arrivata in macchina.

Vigile urbano: Siamo a Scilla, una bellissima città sul mare. La gente viene da tutto il mondo per il nostro mare ed il nostro ottimo pesce. Benvenuta!

Linda: La ringrazio molto, signore.

Vigile urbano: Di dov'è Lei?

Linda: Sono canadese, vengo da Montréal. Parlo abbastanza bene italiano, ma faccio fatica a dare del Lei!

Vigile urbano: Allora dammi del tu! Non c'è problema! Che lavoro fai a Montréal?

Linda: Faccio l'insegnante, insegno storia e geografia.

Vigile urbano: Allora forse desideri anche informazioni sui monumenti da visitare; vai all'ufficio turistico qui di fronte, hanno depliant in inglese e in francese.

Linda: Grazie mille, signor vigile! Lei è molto gentile! No, scusa: tu sei molto gentile... Ti ringrazio.

Vigile urbano: Non c'è di che, grazie a te!

UNDERSTANDING THE DIALOGUE

USING *TU* AND *LEI*: THE INFORMAL AND FORMAL

In contexts that require a degree of formality, Italians **dare del Lei** ('give of-the Lei'). This involves using the feminine third-person pronoun to refer to *you* (an archaic reference to *His Lordship*, which is a feminine noun in Italian). The verb must also be conjugated in the third-person. But in many everyday contexts, you can **dare del tu** ('give of-the **tu**') and use the informal second-person *you*.

INFORMAL (**TU**)	FORMAL (**LEI**)
Scusa! *Excuse me!*	**Scusi!**
Accomodati! *Come in! Sit down!*	**Si accomodi!**
Come stai? *How are you?*	**Come sta?**
Come ti chiami? *What's your name?*	**Come si chiama?**
Di dove sei? *Where are you from?*	**Di dov'è Lei?**
Ti ringrazio. *I thank you..*	**La ringrazio.**
Arrivederci! *Goodbye!*	**ArrivederLa!**

THANKING

To emphasize **grazie** *thank you*, it can be followed by **mille** *thousand* or **tante** *many*, with **volte** *times* understood but not expressed: **grazie mille** or **grazie tante** *thank you so much*. A common reply is **Non c'è di che.** *Don't mention it.*

'JUST' + VERB

The adverb **appena** *just now* is used to describe an action that just happened. In the dialogue it appears in the present perfect **sono appena arrivata** *I* (f.) *have just arrived*, between the conjugated auxiliary verb **essere** *to be* and the past participle (in the feminine as the speaker is a woman). We'll be looking at this tense later, but for the moment just note that it is used to talk about a completed, one-off action in the past. The perfect tenses are usually formed with **avere** *to have* + past participle (as in English), but verbs of movement form the perfect tenses with **essere** *to be*.

CULTURAL NOTE

The **vigile urbano** is **un agente di polizia municipale** *a municipal police officer*: the former is a historical term that is still very commonly used. They are under the jurisdiction of the city government and their responsibilities include directing traffic, supervising civil and commercial activities (markets, etc.), and, of course, ensuring law enforcement in cooperation with the national police: **i carabinieri** (police with military and civil duties) and **la polizia** *the police force*.

GRAMMAR
NOUNS AND ADJECTIVES ENDING IN -E

A singular noun or adjective ending in **-e** is identical in both the masculine and the feminine. It only changes form in the plural, by replacing the final **-e** with **-i**. However, if an article is used with the noun, it has to be in the appropriate gender (and number), as shown in the table below.

	Masculine	Feminine
SINGULAR	**-e** **il canadese gentile**	**-e** **la canadese gentile**
PLURAL	**-i** **i canadesi gentili**	**-i** **le canadesi gentili**

SOME PREPOSITIONS

The preposition **in** can indicate (see also lesson 2):
• means: **Sono arrivata in macchina.** *I* (f.) *arrived by car.*
• language: **sia in inglese che in francese** *both in English and in French.*

Another use of **da** is to convey a final cause or function: **i monumenti da visitare** *monuments to visit*. Note the difference between **una tazza da caffè** *a coffee cup* ('a cup for coffee') and **una tazza di caffè** *a cup of coffee*.

The term **su** means *on, about*:
• for locations: **una città sul mare** *a city on the sea*
• to give the subject of something: **informazioni sui monumenti** *information on/ about the monuments.*

The examples **sul** and **sui** above are contracted articles, in which the preposition and the article are merged (see the table on the next page).

CONTRACTED ARTICLES

When the prepositions **a, di, da, in, con, su** are followed by a definite article, the two words form a contraction: These have the meaning *to the*, *at the*, *of the*, *for the*, *in the*, *with the*, *on the*, etc.

	il	lo	l'	la	i	gli	le
a	al	allo	all'	alla	ai	agli	alle
di	del	dello	dell'	della	dei	degli	delle
da	dal	dallo	dall'	dalla	dai	dagli	dalle
in	nel	nello	nell'	nella	nei	negli	nelle
con	col	collo	coll'	colla	coi	cogli	colle
su	sul	sullo	sull'	sulla	sui	sugli	sulle

For example: **su** *about* **+ i monumenti** *the monuments* = **sui monumenti** *about the monuments*, **su** *on* **+ il mare** *the sea* = **sul mare** *on the sea*.

In the case of the preposition **con** *with*, the contracted article is optional. So it is acceptable to say either **con il vigile** or **col vigile** *with the traffic warden*. But all the other prepositions + definite articles require the contracted form.

▲ CONJUGATION
THE REGULAR PRESENT TENSE OF *-ARE* VERBS (1ST GROUP)

There are three main types of Italian verbs, which conjugate in slightly different ways. The verbs in each group share the same conjugation pattern. The first group consists of verbs with an infinitive ending in **-are**. Here is its regular present tense:

parlare *to speak, to talk*	
(io) parlo	*I speak*
(tu) parli	*you speak* (informal singular)
(lui, lei, Lei) parla	*he, she speaks, you speak* (formal singular)
(noi) parliamo	*we speak*
(voi) parlate	*you speak* (plural)
(loro, Loro) parlano	*they speak, you speak* (formal plural)

Other **-are** verbs we've seen include: **disturbare** *to bother*, **desiderare** *to desire*, **arrivare** *to arrive*, **ringraziare** *to thank*, **dare** *to give*, **fare** *to do*, **visitare** *to visit*.

VOCABULARY

abbastanza *quite, rather*
affatto *absolutely, by all means / not at all, by no means*
benvenuto *welcome* (to a man) / **benvenuta** (to a woman)
canadese *Canadian* (m./f.)
il/i depliant *brochure(s)*
di fronte *opposite, across from*
dove *where*
la fatica *effort, hard work*
forse *maybe, perhaps*
il francese *French* (the language)
la gente *people* (careful, this word is singular in Italian)
gentile *kind, nice*
la geografia *geography*
l'informazione *information*
l'inglese *English* (the language)
l'insegnante *teacher*
insegnare *to teach*
la macchina *car*
il mare *sea, ocean*
il monumento *monument (***i monumenti** *monuments)*
il pesce *fish*
il problema *problem*
scusi (formal) / **scusa** (informal) *sorry, excuse me*
se *if*
signore *sir* / **signora** *madam* / **signorina** *miss*
la storia *history*
l'ufficio turistico *tourist office*
volere *to want*

EXERCISES

1. COMPLETE THESE SENTENCES WITH THE CORRECT PRESENT TENSE FORM OF THE VERB GIVEN IN PARENTHESES.

a. Buongiorno signorina, scusi se La ...., ho bisogno di un'informazione. (disturbare)

b. Che informazione ...., signore? (desiderare)

c. Tutti i turisti che .... di qua .... in macchina. (passare – arrivare)

d. Se .... delle informazioni, domandate al vigile urbano. (desiderare)

e. Io mi .... Giuseppe, e tu come ti .... ? (chiamare)

2. COMPLETE THE TABLE WITH THE MISSING FORMS.

Masculine singular	Masculine plural	Feminine singular	Feminine plural
l'insegnante canadese			
	i francesi gentili		

05 ### 3. LISTEN TO THE RECORDING AND FILL IN THE MISSING WORDS.

a. Lei di .... ?

b. .... canadese, vengo .... Montréal.

c. Scusi, ho .... di un'informazione.

d. Che informazione .... ?

e. La gente viene .... tutto il mondo per il nostro mare.

4. COMPLETE THESE SENTENCES WITH THE CORRECT CONTRACTED ARTICLE (CORRESPONDING TO THE ARTICLE + PREPOSITION GIVEN IN PARENTHESES).

a. Abito .... (**in+la**) città di Milano.

b. Ho bisogno di informazioni .... (**su + la**) città di Bologna.

c. Vengo .... (**da + l'**) università.

d. Domandiamo .... (**a + il**) vigile.

e. Arrivi .... (**con + la**) macchina di Piero.

4.
ASKING FOR INFORMATION AND EXPLANATIONS

CHIEDERE INFORMAZIONI E SPIEGAZIONI

AIMS	TOPICS

AIMS

- ASKING QUESTIONS
- SAYING THAT YOU HAVEN'T UNDERSTOOD
- EXPRESSING AGREEMENT OR DISAGREEMENT

TOPICS

- AGREEMENT OF NOUNS, ADJECTIVES AND ARTICLES
- FORMING QUESTIONS
- FORMING THE NEGATIVE
- THE PREPOSITION *A*
- REGULAR PRESENT TENSE OF *-ERE* VERBS (2ND GROUP)

THE CUSTOMER IS ALWAYS RIGHT

Karen: Good evening. Excuse me, how much are *(they-cost)* the black shoes *(that are)* in [the] window?

Clerk: I'm sorry *(to-me it-displeases)*, I didn't understand *(not I-have understood)*: which do you want to see? There are so many shoes in [the] window! The flat ones *(Those low)* or the ones with a heel?

Karen: The ones with a heel, please *(for favour)*.

Clerk: Yes, now I understand *(I've understood)*: there's only one pair with a heel. They are an excellent deal, ma'am. They are *(cost)* only 60 euros, and if you also take the flat ones, you can have them both for *(them I-sell together at)* 100 euros.

Karen: No, thank you, I'm only interested in *(to-me they-interest only)* the ones with a heel.

Clerk: Think it over *(About-it you-think well)*, miss, it's a real bargain, a really affordable price. What's more, personally I think *(I-find)* that for a young lady of *(the)* your age, flat shoes are better.

Karen: I'm sorry, but I don't agree *(not I-am of-agreement)*, and I want the ones with heels.

Clerk: Certainly, miss: 'the customer is always right *(has always reason)*!'

Karen: OK, I'm going to take a walk and think about it *(to-do a turn and about-it I-think a bit on)* … What time *(At what hour)* do you close?

Clerk: We close in an hour, you have *(all the)* time to think it over. The other shops close at *(the)* 7:00, but we stay open until *(at-the)* 8:00.

Karen: Can you repeat the price, please? I don't remember *(Not it I-remember)*, I've forgotten it *(it-I-have forgotten)*.

Clerk: 60 euros, and 100 euros if you get the others as well!

Karen: Thank you, see you later *(at more late)*.

Clerk: You've understood *(well)* our offer, miss, right?

Karen: I understand perfectly, thank you. Goodbye.

06 IL CLIENTE HA SEMPRE RAGIONE

Karen: Buonasera. Scusi, quanto costano le scarpe nere che sono in vetrina?

Commesso: Mi dispiace, non ho capito: quali vuole vedere? Ci sono tante scarpe in vetrina! Quelle basse o quelle col tacco?

Karen: Quelle con il tacco, per favore.

Commesso: Sì, ora ho capito: c'è un solo paio col tacco. Sono un'ottima occasione, signorina. Costano solo sessanta euro, e se prende anche quelle basse le vendo insieme a cento euro.

Karen: No, grazie, mi interessano solo quelle con il tacco.

Commesso: Ci pensi bene, signorina, è un vero affare, un prezzo davvero conveniente. E poi personalmente trovo che ad una ragazza della sua età stanno meglio le scarpe basse.

Karen: Mi dispiace ma non sono d'accordo, e voglio quelle col tacco.

Commesso: Certamente, signorina: "il cliente ha sempre ragione!"

Karen: Va bene, vado a fare un giro e ci penso un po' su… A che ora chiudete?

Commesso: Chiudiamo tra un'ora, ha tutto il tempo per riflettere. Gli altri negozi chiudono alle sette, ma noi rimaniamo aperti fino alle otto.

Karen: Può ripetere il prezzo, per favore? Non lo ricordo, l'ho dimenticato.

Commesso: Sessanta euro, e cento euro se prende anche le altre!

Karen: Grazie, a più tardi.

Commesso: Ha capito bene la nostra offerta, signorina, vero?

Karen: Ho capito benissimo, grazie. Arrivederci.

UNDERSTANDING THE DIALOGUE

SAYING THAT YOU HAVEN'T UNDERSTOOD

→ The verb **capire** *to understand* can be made negative in the present or the past: **Non capisco.** *I don't understand.* **Non ho capito.** *I didn't understand.* Either can optionally be preceded by **scusi** or **mi dispiace** *I'm sorry*.

ASKING SOMEONE TO REPEAT SOMETHING

→ **Può ripetere il prezzo, per favore?** *Can you repeat the price, please?*
→ Alternatively, you could say **Non ho capito.** or if the problem is to do with memory: **Non ricordo.** *I don't remember.* **Ho dimenticato.** *I've forgotten.*
→ If you'd like someone to say something more slowly, you can say: **Può ripetere lentamente, per favore?** *Can you repeat that slowly, please?*

C'È, CI SONO, CI

→ The contraction **c'è** (the adverb **ci** *there* + **è** *it is*) means *there is*: **c'è un solo paio** *there is only one pair*. The plural is **ci sono** *there are*: **ci sono tante scarpe** *there are so many shoes*.
→ The word **ci** can also be a pronoun meaning *about it/that* (note that object pronouns in Italian usually come before the verb): **ci penso** *I'm thinking about it*.

ASKING A PRICE, A TIME, WHICH ONE, ETC.

→ The dialogue includes several questions useful for everyday situations:
• To ask a price: **Quanto costa?** ('How-much it-costs?') *How much is it?* **Quanto costano?** ('How-much they-cost?') *How much are they?*
• To refer to an item: **Quale vuole?** (for one thing) *Which do you want?* **Quali vuole?** (for more than one thing) *Which ones do you want?*
• To ask what time something will happen: **A che ora chiudete?** ('At what hour you-close (pl.)?') *What time do you close?*

SAYING 'ONLY'

→ The term **solo** can be an adjective, in which case it needs to agree with the noun: **un solo paio** *a sole pair*, **la sola idea** *the only idea*, etc.
→ Or it can be an adverb, in which case it doesn't change form: **Costano solo sessanta euro.** *They only cost 60 euros.*

CULTURAL NOTE

Italy adopted the euro on 1 January 2002, rendering the former currency, the lira, obsolete. Many experienced the change negatively, equating it with an increase in prices, and even today many older Italians are still not happy about the euro. It is true that while officially €1 was the equivalent of almost 2000 lira (1936.27), in practice €1 has been rounded down to 1000 lira, and as a result the prices have doubled over time. But you can't fight progress! **Avanti!** *Forward!*

GRAMMAR
AGREEMENT OF NOUNS, ADJECTIVES AND ARTICLES

Don't forget that nouns and adjectives ending in **-o** have four forms: **il vicino** (m.), **la vicina** (f.) *neighbour*, **i vicini** (m.), **le vicine** (f.) *neighbours*. Whereas those ending in **-e** have two forms: **il/la cliente** *customer* (m./f.), **i/le clienti** *customers* (m./f.). Note that the article also needs to agree with the noun: **il vicino canadese** *the Canadian neighbour* (m.), **la perla nera** *the black pearl*, **i clienti canadesi** *the Canadian customers* (m.), **le scarpe nere** *the black shoes*.

FORMING QUESTIONS

The word order of a question is exactly the same as in a statement. The only difference is that the former is followed by a question mark when written, or pronounced with a rising intonation when spoken. **Ha capito.** *You have understood.* **Ha capito?** *Did you understand?*

FORMING THE NEGATIVE

To make a sentence negative, just place **non** before the verb: **Ho capito.** *I've understood.* **Non ho capito.** *I didn't understand.* **Non conosco nessuno.** *I don't know anyone.* **Non sono d'accordo.** *I don't agree.* If a pronoun is included in the sentence, the **non** comes before it: **Non lo ricordo.** *I don't remember (it).* **Non c'è problema.** *No problem.*

THE PREPOSITION *A*

The preposition **a** *in, on, to* (see p. 35) always becomes **ad** when it is used before a word starting with **a**. Before a word starting with any other vowel, this is optional: so either **ad una ragazza della sua età** or **a una ragazza** is possible.

DIFFERENCES IN TENSE USAGE

→ Tenses are not always used in the same way in different languages. For example, in Italian **ho capito** is in the present perfect (*I have understood*), conveying a completed action, while in English it would be more common to use the present tense in this case: *I understand*.

→ Another example of different tense usage is that the present tense in Italian sometimes translates to the present continuous (*to be ...-ing*) or the future in English. For example: **Vado a fare un giro.** *I'm going* ('I-go') *to take a walk.* **Ci penso un po'.** *I'll think* ('I-think') *about it a bit.*

▲ CONJUGATION
THE PRESENT TENSE OF REGULAR *-ERE* VERBS (2ND GROUP)

The second group of verbs in Italian has an infinitive ending in **-ere**. This infinitive ending is replaced with the conjugations below :

prendere *to take, to get*	
(io) prendo	*I take*
(tu) prendi	*you take* (informal singular)
(lui, lei, Lei) prende	*he, she takes, you take* (formal singular)
(noi) prendiamo	*we take*
(voi) prendete	*you take* (plural)
(loro, Loro) prendono	*they take, you take* (formal plural)

Some other regular **-ere** verbs seen in this lesson include: **vedere** *to see*, **vendere** *to sell*, **dispiacere** *to regret, to be sorry*, **chiudere** *to close*, **riflettere** *to consider, to reflect on*, **rimanere** *to remain, to stay*, **ripetere** *to repeat.*

⬢ EXERCISES

1. REWRITE THESE SENTENCES IN THE NEGATIVE.

Example: Parlo italiano. → Non parlo italiano.

a. Abitiamo a Bologna. → ....

b. Riflettete un po'. → ....

c. Vendono scarpe. → ....

VOCABULARY

l'affare *bargain, deal*
altro/a *other* (**gli altri** *the others*)
a più tardi *see you later*
basso/a *low, short*
bene *well* (**benissimo/a** *very well*)
buonasera *good evening*
capire *to understand*
certamente *certainly*
il/la cliente *customer*
il commesso / la commessa *salesperson, clerk*
conveniente *advantageous, affordable, cheap*
costare *to cost*
davvero *really, truly*
dimenticare *to forget*
l'età *age*
l'euro *euro*
il giro *turn, circle, walk*
insieme *together*
interessare *to interest*
il negozio *shop* (**i negozi** *shops*)
nero/a *black*
l'occasione *occasion, opportunity, bargain*
l'offerta *offer*
ora *now*
il paio *pair*
pensare *to think*
personalmente *personally*
un po' *a bit* (from **poco**: the shortened form ends in an apostrophe)
poi *then, furthermore*
il prezzo *price*
quanto/a *how much*
la ragione *reason* (**avere ragione** *to be right*)
ricordare *to remember*
la scarpa *shoe* (**le scarpe** *shoes*)
sempre *always*
stare meglio *to be better*
su *on, above*
il tacco *heel*
il tempo *time*
trovare *to find*
tutto/a *all*
il vero *truth, reality*
vero/a *true, real*
la vetrina *shop window*

06 ## 2. TURN EACH STATEMENT INTO A QUESTION AS SPOKEN ON THE RECORDING. REPEAT THE QUESTIONS OUT LOUD, PRACTICING THE INTONATION.

Example: Parli italiano. → Parli italiano?

a. Vuole vedere le scarpe nere. → ....

b. Hai capito la nostra offerta. → ....

c. C'è un posto libero vicino a te. → ....

3. REWRITE THESE PHRASES IN THE PLURAL.

a. il prezzo conveniente → ....

b. l'offerta eccezionale → ....

c. il cliente fortunato → ....

4. REWRITE THESE PHRASES IN THE FEMININE.

a. il cliente siciliano → ....

b. il commesso gentile → ....

c. il vicino canadese → ....

5. COMPLETE THE SENTENCES WITH THE CORRECT PRESENT TENSE FORM OF THE VERB GIVEN IN PARENTHESES.

Example: La commessa........................ scarpe. (vendere) →
La commessa vende scarpe.

a. A che ora .... i negozi? (chiudere)

b. Signorina, ... le scarpe nere in vetrina? (vedere)

c. Prima di parlare, di solito io .... (riflettere)
(Before speaking, usually I ...)

d. Noi per andare al lavoro .... l'autobus, e voi? (prendere)

5. ADMINISTRATIVE PROCEDURES

PRATICHE AMMINISTRATIVE

AIMS

- CARRYING OUT SIMPLE ADMINISTRATIVE PROCEDURES
- GIVING YOUR PERSONAL DETAILS
- TALKING ABOUT YOUR FAMILY OR FRIENDS
- SPELLING YOUR NAME

TOPICS

- THE ALPHABET
- SPELLING ALOUD
- SHOWING POSSESSION
- SPECIAL PLURAL AND FEMININE FORMS
- PRESENT TENSE OF REGULAR *-IRE* VERBS (3RD GROUP)
- VERBS ENDING IN *-CARE* AND *-GARE*

SIGNING UP FOR AN ITALIAN COURSE

Eleni: Excuse me, can I come in? Is it my turn *(It-touches to me)*?

Employee: Please, come in *(Yourself come-in by-all-means)*!

Eleni: Hello, I would like to sign up *(to-do the enrolment)* for the Italian course *(for foreigners)*.

Employee: Certainly! Many students learn Italian here with us. Do you have any identification with you?

Eleni: Yes, I'll check my handbag *(now it I-search in-the bag)* … No, I'm sorry, I don't have it.

Employee: It doesn't matter *(not it-makes nothing)*, we['ll] do [it by] self-certification. What's your name, miss? How old are you *(How-many years you-have)*? And what is *(the)* your nationality?

Eleni: My name is Eleni Dellis. I am 23 *(I-have twenty-three years)* and I'm Greek (f.), from Athens.

Employee: Excuse me, is Eleni written like this *(itself it-writes so)*: E like Empoli, L like Livorno, E like Empoli, N like Naples and I like Imperia ?

Eleni: Yes, exactly like that.

Employee: Do you have an address here in Perugia?

Eleni: Yes, 5 Garibaldi Street.

Employee: To establish *(decide)* the registration cost we need *(we-have need of-the)* your ISEE. Do you understand?

Eleni: No, what's *(what thing-it-is)* the ISEE?

Employee: It's a document that declares your *(the)* family income: basically *(in-short)*, the richer you are, the more you pay *(more you-are rich and more you-pay)* …

Eleni: We are not rich: my father is an office worker, my mother is [a] housewife, my brother is [a] student and my sister is unfortunately unemployed …

Employee: We also need *(they are necessary also)* two photos. [Will] you bring them to me *(to-me them you-bring)* tomorrow?

Eleni: Yes, okay.

Employee: You must pay the first instalment now in order to receive your school card *(the card of-the school)* at this address. If you prefer, you can pay everything right now, but the ISEE is required *(it is necessary the ISEE)* to work out the amount.

Eleni: No, I prefer to pay in instalments, thank you.

07 L'ISCRIZIONE AL CORSO DI ITALIANO

Eleni: Permesso, posso entrare? Tocca a me?

Impiegato: Si accomodi pure!

Eleni: Buongiorno, vorrei fare l'iscrizione al corso di italiano per stranieri.

Impiegato: Certamente! Tanti studenti e studentesse imparano l'italiano qui da noi. Ha un documento d'identità con Lei?

Eleni: Sì, ora lo cerco nella borsa… No, mi dispiace, non ce l'ho.

Impiegato: Non fa niente, facciamo l'autocertificazione. Come si chiama, signorina, quanti anni ha e qual è la sua nazionalità?

Eleni: Mi chiamo Eleni Dellis, ho ventitré anni e sono greca, di Atene.

Impiegato: Scusi, Eleni si scrive così: E come Empoli, L come Livorno, E come Empoli, N come Napoli e I come Imperia?

Eleni: Sì, proprio così.

Impiegato: Ha un indirizzo qui a Perugia?

Eleni: Sì, via Garibaldi 5.

Impiegato: Per decidere il costo dell'iscrizione abbiamo bisogno del suo ISEE. Capisce?

Eleni: No, che cos'è l'ISEE?

Impiegato: È un documento che certifica il reddito della famiglia, insomma più sei ricco e più paghi…

Eleni: Noi non siamo ricchi, mio padre fa l'impiegato, mia madre è casalinga, mio fratello è studente e mia sorella purtroppo è disoccupata…

Impiegato: Ci vogliono anche due foto. Me le porta domani?

Eleni: Sì, va bene.

Impiegato: Ora Lei deve pagare la prima rata per ricevere a questo indirizzo la tessera della scuola. Se preferisce può pagare tutto subito, ma ci vuole l'ISEE per decidere la somma.

Eleni: No, preferisco pagare a rate, grazie.

UNDERSTANDING THE DIALOGUE
ASKING IF YOU CAN COME IN, SIT DOWN, ETC.

The noun **permesso** *permission, authorization* is used as an interjection to ask if you can enter, sit down or squeeze past someone. In this case, its meaning corresponds to *Excuse me ...*. In an affirmative response, you may hear **pure** *by all means, please do*: **Si accomodi pure!** *Please come in!*

TOCCA A ME?

The way to ask if it's your turn, for example, in a queue or a game, is **Tocca a me?** ('It-touches to me?'). The affirmative reply is **Tocca a te!** *It's your turn!*

CE L'HO, NON CE L'HO

In everyday speech, sometimes **ce** is placed before the verb **avere** when the latter is preceded by the pronoun **l'**. In this case, **ce** isn't translated: **ce l'avete** *you have it*, **non ce l'ho** *I don't have it*, etc.

CI VUOLE, CI VOGLIONO

ci vuole + singular noun / **ci vogliono** + plural noun are impersonal expressions used to say that something is necessary. They can't be translated literally, but the meaning corresponds to *needs/need* or *is/are necessary*. They are always followed by a noun, and the verb is conjugated according to whether the noun is singular or plural: **ci vuole una foto** *a photo is required*; **ci vogliono due foto** *two photos are required*.

VA BENE

This expression literally means 'It goes well' and is used in a variety of ways: *all right*, *okay*, *all is well*.

THE ALPHABET AND SPELLING ALOUD

• To spell out a word, Italians use the names of cities in Italy to specify the letter, apart from the letter **h**, which is indicated by **hotel**.
• The letters **j, k, w, x, y** are only found in loan words and so are rarely used. The names of these letters are as follows: (j) **i lunga** [ee loongah], (k) **cappa** [kahp-pah], (w) **vu doppia** [voo dohp-pyah], (x) **ics** [eeks], (y) **ipsilon** [eepseelohn] or **i greca** [ee graykah].

A [ah]	**Ancona**	N [en-neh]	**Napoli**
B [bee]	**Bologna, Bari**	O [oh]	**Otranto**
C [chee]	**Como**	P [pee]	**Palermo, Padova**
D [dee]	**Domodossola**	Q [koo]	**Quarto**
E [ay]	**Empoli**	R [erreh]	**Roma**
F [ef-feh]	**Firenze**	S [esseh]	**Savona, Salerno**
G [jee]	**Genova**	T [tee]	**Torino, Taranto**
H [ahk-kah]	**hotel**	U [oo]	**Udine**
I [ee]	**Imola, Imperia**	V [vee]	**Venezia**
L [el-leh]	**Livorno**	Z [dseta]	**Zara**
M [em-meh]	**Milano**		

CULTURAL NOTE

Introduced in 1968 and expanded in 1997, **l'autocertificazione** *self-certification* allows Italians to declare their marital status, academic degrees and certain other personal information without having to provide official documents. The document known as the **ISEE** (**l'Indicatore della Situazione Economica Equivalente** *Index of Corresponding Economic Situation*) shows your family income.

GRAMMAR
SPECIAL PLURAL FORMS

• Nouns that end in an accented vowel (e.g. **la nazionalità**) do not change form in the plural: **l'università** *university*→ **le università** *universities*.

• Nouns ending in **-co** form the plural by adding an **h** before the **i** or **e** in order to retain the hard [k] sound. So a masculine ending **-co** becomes **-chi** (plural) and a feminine ending **-ca** becomes **-che** (plural): e.g. the adjective **ricco** *rich* [reek-koh] → **ricchi** [reek-kee] (m. pl.); **ricca** [reek-kah] → **ricche** [reek-kay] (f. pl.). There are some exceptions in the masculine: **greco** *Greek* → **greci** [graychee] *Greeks*, **amico** *friend* → **amici** [ahmeechee] *friends* , as well as words whose stress is on the third-to-last syllable, such as **simpatico** *nice* → **simpatici** [seempahtee-chee]. In the feminine, the rule is always respected: **greca** → **greche** [graykay], **amica** → **amiche** [ahmeekay], **simpatica** → **simpatiche** [seempahteekay].

• The same rule applies to words ending with **-go** (to retain the hard [g] sound) e.g. **lungo** [loongoh] *long* → **lunghi** [loonghee]; **lunga** [loongah] → **lunghe** [loongay].

SPECIAL FEMININE FORMS

• Some masculine nouns add **-essa** to form the feminine equivalent: e.g. **lo studente → la studentessa, il dottore → la dottoressa**. This is also the case for certain animals and noble titles: **il leone** *lion* → **la leonessa**; **l'elefante** *elephant* → **l'elefantessa**; **il conte** *count* → **la contessa, il principe** *prince* → **la principessa**.

SHOWING POSSESSION

In English, we often use nouns adjectivally to describe other nouns. In Italian, the equivalent construction is noun + **de** + article (or **di**) + noun: **la tessera della scuola** *school card*, **il costo dell'iscrizione** *enrolment fee*, **il reddito della famiglia** *family income*, **foto di vacanza** *holiday photo.*

In contrast to English, in Italian, possessive adjectives and pronouns must agree in gender and number with what is possessed. The following table shows the different forms of these possessives:

	OBJECT POSSESSED			
POSSESSOR	masc. sing.	fem. sing.	masc. pl.	fem. pl.
my/mine	**il mio**	**la mia**	**i miei**	**le mie**
your(s) (informal sing.)	**il tuo**	**la tua**	**i tuoi**	**le tue**
his/her(s)/its *your(s)* (formal sing.)	**il suo** **il Suo**	**la sua** **la Sua**	**i suoi** **i Suoi**	**le sue** **le Sue**
our(s)	**il nostro**	**la nostra**	**i nostri**	**le nostre**
your(s) (informal pl.)	**il vostro**	**la vostra**	**i vostri**	**le vostre**
their(s) *your(s)* (formal pl.)	**il loro** **il Loro**	**la loro** **la Loro**	**i loro** **i Loro**	**le loro** **le Loro**

Another difference with English is that the definite article is always used before the possessive adjective or pronoun, except when referring to family members. So it is **il mio amico** *my friend*, but **mio padre** *my father*, **mia madre** *my mother*, etc. However, the article is used with family members in the plural: **i miei fratelli** *my brothers*, **le mie sorelle** *my sisters*.

SOME PREPOSITIONS

• **da** can mean *at (someone's place)*: **Mangio da mia madre.** *I eat at my mum's.*
• **con** *with*: **Non ce l'ho con me.** *I don't have it with me.*

▲ CONJUGATION

THE PRESENT TENSE OF REGULAR *-IRE* VERBS (3RD GROUP)

• The third group of verbs in Italian has an infinitive ending in **-ire**. This infinitive ending is replaced with the conjugation endings below:

soffrire *to suffer*	
(io) soffro	*I suffer*
(tu) soffri	*you suffer* (informal singular)
(lui, lei, Lei) soffre	*he, she suffers, you suffer* (formal singular)
(noi) soffriamo	*we suffer*
(voi) soffrite	*you suffer* (plural)
(loro, Loro) soffrono	*they suffer, you suffer* (formal plural)

• Another verb with this conjugation pattern is **partire** *to leave*.

• However, many **-ire** verbs (e.g. **preferire** *to prefer*) have a spelling change in which **-isc-** is inserted between the verb stem and the conjugation ending in all persons except for the first- and second-person plural:

capire *to understand*	
(io) capisco	*I understand*
(tu) capisci	*you understand* (informal singular)
(lui, lei, Lei) capisce	*he, she understands, you understand* (formal singular)
(noi) capiamo	*we understand*
(voi) capite	*you understand* (plural)
(loro, Loro) capiscono	*they understand, you understand* (formal plural)

VERBS ENDING IN *-CARE* AND *-GARE*

These verbs have a spelling change in which an **h** is added after the **c** or the **g** when the conjugation ending begins with **e** or **i** in order to retain the hard [k] or [g] sound:

cercare *to look for*		**pagare** *to pay*	
(io) cerco	**(noi) cerchiamo**	**(io) pago**	**(noi) paghiamo**
(tu) cerchi	**(voi) cercate**	**(tu) paghi**	**(voi) pagate**
(lui, lei) cerca	**(loro) cercano**	**(lui, lei) paga**	**(loro) pagano**

EXERCISES

1. REWRITE THESE PHRASES IN THE PLURAL.

a. la mia amica greca → ....

b. la città ricca → ....

c. il tuo amico simpatico → ....

2. REWRITE THESE PHRASES IN THE FEMININE.

a. gli studenti simpatici → ....

b. il dottore canadese → ....

c. il principe siciliano → ....

3. COMPLETE THE SENTENCES WITH THE CORRECT PRESENT TENSE FORM OF THE VERB GIVEN IN PARENTHESES.

a. Siamo di Roma ma .... abitare a Milano. (preferire)

b. A che ora .... il tuo autobus? (partire)

c. Mia sorella non .... l'inglese. (capire)

d. Se .... ti porto *(you I take)* dal dottore. (soffrire)

4. FILL IN THE MISSING POSSESSIVES, INCLUDING THE DEFINITE ARTICLE WHERE NECESSARY.

a. Non siamo ricchi, ... padre fa l'impiegato.

b. Voi norvegesi siete bravissimi, ... scuole sono ottime!

c. Buongiorno signorina, ecco *(here is)* .... tessera.

d. Sei arrivato con .... macchina o con l'autobus?

07 ### 5. LISTEN TO THE RECORDING AND WRITE THE NAME THAT IS SPELLED OUT.

_ _ _ _ _ _ _

VOCABULARY

l'autocertificazione *self-certification*
la borsa *bag, handbag*
la casalinga *housewife*
cercare *to look for, to search*
certificare *to certify, to declare*
conoscere *to know, to be familiar with*
così *so, like this, like that*
il costo *cost*
decidere *to decide*
disoccupato/a *unemployed*
il documento *document*
domani *tomorrow*
entrare *to enter*
la foto *photo*
il fratello *brother*
greco/a *Greek*
imparare *to learn*
insomma *in short*
l'impiegato/a *employee*
l'indirizzo *address*
l'iscrizione *enrolment*
la madre *mother*
la nazionalità *nationality*
niente *nothing*
il padre *father*
pagare *to pay*
perché *why*
permesso *excuse me ...*
portare *to bring*
preferire *to prefer*
primo/a *first*
proprio *exactly, really*
purtroppo *unfortunately*
la rata *instalment, partial payment*
il reddito *revenue, income*
ricco/a *rich*
ricevere *to receive*
scrivere *to write*
la settimana *week*
la somma *amount, sum*
la sorella *sister*
straniero/a *foreign*
subito *immediately, right now*
tanto/a *many* (this is an adjective so must agree with the gender and number of the noun that follows it)
la tessera *card*
la via *street*

6. DESCRIBING PEOPLE

DESCRIVERE LE PERSONE

AIMS	TOPICS
• DESCRIBING PHYSICAL AND PERSONAL ATTRIBUTES • TALKING ABOUT CLOTHES • ASKING HOW SOMEONE IS AND WHAT'S BEEN HAPPENING	• SPECIAL PLURAL FORMS • DEMONSTRATIVE PRONOUNS AND ADJECTIVES • *ESSERE* AND *STARE*: 'TO BE' • ADJECTIVES AND WORD ORDER • SOME DIFFERENT USES OF VERBS • *-ARE* VERBS THAT ARE IRREGULAR IN THE PRESENT TENSE

HOLIDAY PHOTOS

Giulia: Hi, Carlo, how are you?

Carlo: I'm well, thanks, and you?

Giulia: Me too – I just came back *(I-am just returned* [f.]*)* from a fantastic holiday in Sardinia. If you want, I'll show you *(to-you I-make see)* the photos.

Carlo: Okay, but [can] you hand me *(to-me you-give the)* my glasses, please? They're [right] there, on that table.

Giulia: Look, here we are at the café: the one *(this)* in the foreground *(in first level)* is my husband, and the one *(that)* there at the *(in)* back on [the] right is my mother-in-law: decidedly much less photogenic, with that crooked nose and that huge mouth! And she is also a bit [of a] gossip ... The one *(This)* with the yellow shirt is my brother-in-law Filippo, and the lady with the white trousers next to him is his wife.

Carlo: Yes, I recognize them.

Giulia: Here, this is our group of *(the group of-the our)* friends: Luigi is the small one *(that small)* with *(the)* blond hair (pl.) and the red T-shirt, and to his left *(there)* is Mario, with the straw hat. Behind them *(Back of them there)* is Sandro, who is wearing a *(the)* sweater and *(the)* socks even though [it's] the middle of *(in full)* summer. Even when it's hot *(it-makes hot)*, he is *(has)* always cold.

Carlo: Really?

Giulia: Next to him *(there)* is his cousin (f.) Lara, with the long skirt. They are all close *(dear)* friends, we get along with them really well *(we-are very well with them)*. But *(the)* my favourites are Paolo and Luisa: here they are on the beach, at the seaside *(on shore at-the sea)*. See? He is thin and tall, and she is small and a bit plump. They are really extremely nice and also generous.

Carlo: What lovely photos! And what wonderful friends!

08 FOTO DI VACANZA

Giulia: Ciao, Carlo, come stai?

Carlo: Io sto bene, grazie, e tu?

Giulia: Anch'io, sono appena tornata da una bellissima vacanza in Sardegna. Se vuoi ti faccio vedere le foto.

Carlo: Va bene, ma mi dai i miei occhiali, per favore? Sono lì, su quel tavolo.

Giulia: Guarda, qui siamo al bar; questo in primo piano è mio marito, e quella là in fondo a destra è mia suocera, decisamente molto meno fotogenica, con quel naso storto e quella bocca enorme! Ed è anche un po' pettegola... Questo con la camicia gialla è mio cognato Filippo, e la signora con i pantaloni bianchi accanto a lui è sua moglie.

Carlo: Sì, li conosco.

Giulia: Ecco, questo è il gruppo dei nostri amici: Luigi è quello basso con i capelli biondi e la maglietta rossa, e alla sua sinistra c'è Mario, col cappello di paglia. Dietro di loro c'è Sandro, che porta il maglione e le calze anche in piena estate. Anche quando fa caldo, lui ha sempre freddo.

Carlo: Davvero?

Giulia: Vicino a lui c'è sua cugina, Lara, con la gonna lunga. Sono tutti cari amici, stiamo molto bene con loro. Ma i miei preferiti sono Paolo e Luisa, qui sono sulla spiaggia, in riva al mare. Vedi? Lui è magro e alto e lei è piccola e un po' grassa. Sono davvero molto simpatici e anche generosi.

Carlo: Che belle foto! E che begli amici!

UNDERSTANDING THE DIALOGUE

→ We've already seen the verb **essere** *to be*, which describes unchanging characteristics: **Sono Luisa, la nuova vicina.** *I'm Luisa, the new neighbour.* The verb **stare** also means *to be*, but is used to describe a temporary state or location: **Come stai?** *How are you?* **Sto bene.** *I'm fine.* **Stiamo molto bene con loro.** *We get on well with them.* **Sto a Milano.** *I live in Milan.*

→ Many prepositional phrases are formed with **a** (**accanto a** *next to*, **vicino a** *near to*, **in riva a** *on the shore/bank*, usually referring to a sea, lake or river) or **di** (**dietro di** *behind*, **a destra di** *on/to the right*, **a sinistra di** *on/to the left*.

→ When **bello** is used after a noun, it has the regular forms for an **-o** adjective (**bello/-a/-i/-e**). However, when it comes before a noun, its forms follow the same pattern as the definite article.

	Masculine noun			Feminine noun	
	Starting with a consonant (but see column 2)	Starting with **s** + consonant, **gn, z, ps**	Starting with a vowel	Starting with a consonant	Starting with a vowel
SINGULAR	**bel** **un bel maglione** *a nice sweater*	**bello** **un bello studente** *a good-looking student*	**bell'** **un bell'amico** *a handsome friend*	**bella** **una bella spiaggia** *a lovely beach*	**bell'** **una bell'amica** *a pretty friend*
PLURAL	**bei** **dei bei maglioni** *some nice sweaters*	**begli** **dei begli studenti** *some good-looking students* **dei begli amici** *some handsome friends*		**belle** **delle belle spiagge** *some lovely beaches* **delle belle amiche** *some pretty friends*	

CULTURAL NOTE

Italians love taking holidays, even during times of economic crisis. Almost everyone takes at least a week off in August. The most popular choice of vacation is to stay in a hotel on the seaside (a whopping 79% of Italians opt for this), with most (81%) staying in Italy. The most popular beaches are in the south of the country and on the Italian islands of Sicily and Sardinia. Italy is also a very popular destination for people from around the world: the tourism sector employs around 2.5 million Italians and represents almost 10% of the country's GDP.

GRAMMAR
SPECIAL PLURAL FORMS

• Shortened nouns don't change form in the plural: both the end of the word and the ending that would mark the plural are omitted: **la foto** *photo* → **le foto** *photos* (from **la fotografia** → **le fotografie**) or **la bici** *bike* → **le bici** (from **la bicicletta** → **le biciclette**) or **la moto** *motorcycle* → **le moto** (from **la motocicletta** → **le motociclette**). The shortened forms are by far the most common.
• Loan words from other languages don't change form in the plural either. So **il bar** *bar* → **i bar** *bars*, **il camion** *truck* → **i camion** *trucks* (from the French), as well as all words ending in a consonant, which have either been borrowed from Latin or from other languages: **l'autobus** *bus* → **gli autobus** *buses*.

DEMONSTRATIVE ADJECTIVES AND PRONOUNS

The term **questo** *this (one)* refers to a noun in proximity to the speaker or the person being spoken to; **quello** *that (one)* refers to something more distant. They can be used as pronouns or adjectives, and both have several forms in order to agree in gender and number with what is being referred to. While **questo** has the regular forms for an **-o** adjective (**questo/-a/-i/-e**), when **quello** is used as an adjective (i.e. before a noun), it changes form with the same pattern as **bello**:

	Masculine noun			Feminine noun	
	Starting with a consonant (but see column 2)	Starting with **s** + consonant, **gn, z, ps**	Starting with a vowel	Starting with a consonant	Starting with a vowel
SING.	**quel** **quel cappello** *that hat*	**quello** **quello studente** *that student*	**quell'** **quell'amico** *that friend*	**quella** **quella foto** *that photo*	**quell'** **quell'amica** *that friend*
PL.	**quei** **quei cappelli** *those hats*	**quegli** **quegli studenti** *those students* **quegli amici** *those friends*		**quelle** **quelle foto** *those photos* **quelle amiche** *those friends*	

When used as a pronoun, **quello** has just four forms (**quello/-a/-i/-e**): **Quello in primo piano è mio marito.** *The one in the foreground is my husband.* These terms are often used with **qui** *here* and **là** *there*: **Quella là in fondo a destra è mia suocera.** *The one there in the back at the right is my mother-in-law.*

ADJECTIVES AND WORD ORDER

By now you've probably noticed that usually an adjective is placed after a noun in Italian: **il naso storto** *crooked nose*, **la bocca enorme** *huge mouth*, **la camicia gialla** *yellow shirt*, **la gonna lunga** *long skirt*.

DIFFERENCES IN VERB USAGE

• This lesson has another example of the present perfect: **sono appena tornata** *I've* (f.) *just come back*. When the auxiliary verb is **essere**, the past participle agrees with the subject (in this example, the speaker is a woman).
• Note the verbs used in Italian for the expressions **fa caldo** *it's* ('it-makes') *hot* (from **fare** *to do, to make*), **ha freddo** *he/she is* ('has') *cold* (from **avere** *to have*).

▲ CONJUGATION
SOME COMMON IRREGULAR *-ARE* VERBS IN THE PRESENT

andare *to go*	
(io) vado	**(noi) andiamo**
(tu) vai	**(voi) andate**
(lui, lei, Lei) va	**(loro, Loro) vanno**

fare *to do, to make*	
(io) faccio	**(noi) facciamo**
(tu) fai	**(voi) fate**
(lui, lei, Lei) fa	**(loro, Loro) fanno**

dare *to give*	
(io) do	**(noi) diamo**
(tu) dai	**(voi) date**
(lui, lei, Lei) da	**(loro, Loro) danno**

stare *to be* (temporary state or location), *to remain*	
(io) sto	**(noi) stiamo**
(tu) stai	**(voi) state**
(lui, lei, Lei) sta	**(loro, Loro) stanno**

VOCABULARY

alto/a *tall*
basso/a *short*
bianco/a *white (***bianchi/e** (pl.)*)*
biondo/a *blond*
la bocca *mouth*
il caldo *heat (***caldo/a** *hot)*
le calze *socks*
la camicia *shirt*
i capelli *hair* (this is plural in Italian)
il cappello *hat*
caro/a *dear, cherished*
il cognato *brother-in-law /* **la cognata** *sister-in-law*
il cugino / la cugina *cousin*
davvero *really*
decisamente *decidedly, no doubt*
la destra *right* (direction, side)
enorme *huge*
l'estate *summer*
pieno/a *full*
fotogenico/a *photogenic*
il freddo *the cold (***freddo/a** *cold)*
generoso/a *generous*
giallo/a *yellow*
la gonna *skirt*
grasso/a *fat, plump, overweight*
il gruppo *group*
guardare *to look at, to watch*
lungo/a *long (***lunghi/e** (pl.)*)*
la maglietta *T-shirt*
il maglione *sweater, jumper*
magro/a *slender, thin*
il marito *husband*
meno *less*
la moglie *wife*
molto (adv.) *very, highly*
molto/a (adj.) *a lot, much (***molti/e** *many)*
il naso *nose*
gli occhiali *glasses, spectacles*
la paglia *straw*
i pantaloni *trousers*
pettegolo/a *gossipy*
il piano *flat surface, plane*
piccolo/a *small, little* (in size), *young* (in age)
portare *to wear*
preferito/a *favourite, preferred*
la riva *shore, bank, edge*
rosso/a *red*
simpatico/a *nice, likeable, pleasant*
la sinistra *left* (direction, side)
la spiaggia *beach*
storto/a *crooked, twisted*
il suocero *father-in-law /* **la suocera** *mother-in-law*
il tavolo *table*
tornare *to return, to come back*
la vacanza *vacation, holiday*

EXERCISES

1. REWRITE THESE PHRASES IN THE PLURAL.

a. la tua foto piccola → ....

b. questo maglione rosso → ....

c. quel bel bar → ....

d. quello studente magro → ....

e. il tuo cappello giallo → ....

f. quell'estate calda → ....

2. FILL IN THE SENTENCES WITH THE CORRECT FORM OF *QUESTO* OR *QUELLO*.

a. .... qui è mio marito, ... là in fondo è mia suocera.

b. .... casa là in fondo è la nostra.

c. Siamo appena arrivati in .... città.

d. Domani vado da .... mio amico.

3. COMPLETE THE SENTENCES WITH THE CORRECT FORM OF THE MOST APPROPRIATE VERB FROM THE FOLLOWING IRREGULAR *-ARE* VERBS (*ANDARE, DARE, FARE, STARE*).

a. Come .... signorina? – .... bene, grazie.

b. Gli italiani .... in vacanza al mare.

c. Sono troppo *(too)* grasso per portare questo maglione, lo .... a mio fratello perché *(because)* lui è magro.

d. Io .... una foto a mia moglie perché è molto fotogenica.

08 ### 4. LISTEN TO THE RECORDING AND FILL IN THE MISSING WORDS.

a. In estate fa .... non fa ....

b. In questa foto siamo sulla .... in riva al ....

c. In questa foto ci sono mio marito, sulla mia destra e mia suocera, alla mia ....

d. Ti .... vedere le foto della mia .... in Sardegna.

II

EVERYDAY LIFE

7.
DAILY ACTIVITIES

LE ATTIVITÀ DELLA GIORNATA

AIMS	TOPICS
• GIVING THE TIME • THE DAYS OF THE WEEK • THE MONTHS OF THE YEAR • THE SEASONS	• MAKING COMPARISONS • NUMBERS • SOME *-ERE* VERBS THAT ARE IRREGULAR IN THE PRESENT TENSE • REFLEXIVE VERBS

A NORMAL DAY *(days regular)*

Mario: Excuse me, Simona, what time is it *(what hours are-they)*?

Simona: It's 2:30 *(They-are the two and half)*, why?

Mario: This *(Today)* afternoon I have a work appointment that I can't miss. I must be in [the city] centre at *(the)* 4:00 sharp. In your opinion *(According-to you)*, what time should I leave *(from)* home?

Simona: [A] half-hour before, at 3:30.

Mario: Yes, but [what] if I happen to get stuck in *(by chance I-stay blocked in-the)* traffic? I want to leave earlier *(even early)*, at 3:15 *(three and a quarter)*. And if I arrive in advance, at 3:45 *(four less a quarter)*, oh well *(patience)*! I [will] sit in a café and drink something.

Simona: Maybe you're worrying a bit too much, don't you think?

Mario: You're right *(have reason)*, my day always has to be organized minute by minute: [in] the morning I wake up at 7:00, except [on] *(the)* Saturday and *(the)* Sunday. I take a *(do the)* shower and then I eat *(do)* breakfast at 7:30 in order to be at work at 8:30. I [eat] lunch at 12:30, [or] at the latest *(most late)* at 1:00, then I go back to the office at 2:00. [The] only exception [is] on Mondays *(the Monday)* [when] I go to [the] swimming pool during my *(the)* lunch break. Instead of eating lunch *(to-eat-lunch)*, [on] that day I have *(do)* a snack later. I finish work *(to-work)* at 6:00, and I eat dinner *(my dinner is)* at 7:30. [In] the evening I watch a bit of *(the)* TV and at 10:30 or, at the latest *(maximum)* 11:00, I go to bed.

Simona: At 11:00 *(At-the twenty-three)*! You eat dinner *(You-dine)* and go to bed very early! Don't you ever go out *(Not you-go-out never)*?

Mario: Yes, [on] Friday evening I go to the cinema, especially in [the] autumn and in [the] winter, because in [the] summer and [the] spring I like *(to-me it-appeals)* to do a walk. Of course, [at] the weekend *(end week)*, I go out with my friends all year [round].

Simona: You seem very home-loving, but in the end you go out more than me!

Mario: I'm more methodical than home-loving: I like to have a daily routine *(to-me they-appeal the hours regular)*.

09 GIORNATE REGOLARI

Mario: Scusa, Simona, che ore sono?

Simona: Sono le due e mezza, perché?

Mario: Oggi pomeriggio ho un appuntamento di lavoro che non posso mancare. Devo essere in centro alle quattro in punto. Secondo te a che ora devo partire da casa?

Simona: Mezz'ora prima, alle tre e mezza.

Mario: Sì, ma se per caso rimango bloccato nel traffico? Voglio partire ancora prima, alle tre e un quarto. E se arrivo in anticipo, alle quattro meno un quarto, pazienza! Mi siedo in un bar e bevo qualcosa.

Simona: Forse ti preoccupi un po' troppo, non credi?

Mario: Hai ragione, la mia giornata deve essere sempre organizzata minuto per minuto: la mattina mi sveglio alle sette, salvo il sabato e la domenica. Faccio la doccia e poi faccio colazione alle sette e trenta, per essere al lavoro alle otto e mezza. Pranzo a mezzogiorno e mezza, al più tardi all'una, poi ritorno in ufficio alle due. Sola eccezione: il lunedì vado in piscina durante la pausa pranzo. Invece di pranzare, quel giorno faccio una merenda più tardi. Finisco di lavorare alle sei, e la mia cena è alle sette e mezza. La sera guardo un po' la televisione e alle dieci e mezza o al massimo alle undici vado a letto.

Simona: Alle ventitrè! Ceni e vai a letto molto presto! Non esci mai?

Mario: Sì, il venerdì sera vado al cinema, soprattutto in autunno e in inverno, perché in estate e in primavera mi piace fare una passeggiata. Naturalmente il fine settimana esco con gli amici tutto l'anno.

Simona: Sembri molto casalingo, ma alla fine esci più di me!

Mario: Sono più metodico che casalingo, mi piacciono gli orari regolari.

UNDERSTANDING THE DIALOGUE
NUMBERS

→ The numbers from 1 to 20 are: *1* **uno,** *2* **due,** *3* **tre,** *4* **quattro,** *5* **cinque,** *6* **sei,** *7* **sette,** *8* **otto,** *9* **nove,** *10* **dieci,** *11* **undici,** *12* **dodici,** *13* **tredici,** *14* **quattordici,** *15* **quindici,** *16* **sedici,** *17* **diciassette,** *18* **diciotto,** *19* **diciannove,** *20* **venti**.
→ Counting by tens, 30 to 100 are: *30* **trenta,** *40* **quaranta,** *50* **cinquanta,** *60* **sessanta,** *70* **settanta,** *80* **ottanta,** *90* **novanta,** *100* **cento.**
→ The numbers in between are formed by ten + unit: *25* **venticinque,** *39* **trentanove**. If they end in 3, they have a written accent: *53* **cinquantatré**.
→ Numbers aren't hyphenated: *1946* **millenovecentoquarantasei**.

GIVING THE TIME

→ **Che ore sono?** ('What hours are-they?') or **Che ora è?** ('What hour is-it?') *What time is it?* (Note that the 24-hour clock is commonly used in Italy, especially in timetables, so don't be thrown by times from 13:00 to 24:00!)
→ **Sono le…** *It is…* (or **è** for 1:00 or a specific term such as midday or midnight)
→ 00:00 **è mezzanotte** ('it's midnight')**/sono le ventiquattro** ('they-are the 24')
→ 10:15 **sono le dieci e un quarto** ('they-are the ten and a quarter')
→ 10:30 **sono le dieci e mezza** ('they-are the ten and half')
→ 10:45 **sono le dieci e tre quarti** ('they-are the ten and three quarters') **/ sono le undici meno un quarto** ('they-are the eleven less a quarter')
→ 10:50 **sono le dieci e cinquanta/sono le undici meno dieci** ('eleven less 10')
→ 12:00 **è mezzogiorno** ('it's noon/midday')**/sono le dodici** ('they-are the 12')
→ 12:30 **sono le dodici e trenta** ('they-are the 12 and 30')
→ 13:00 *(1:00 pm)* **è l'una** ('it's the 1')**/sono le tredici** ('they-are the 13')
→ 15:25 *(3:25 pm)* **sono le quindici e venticinque** ('they-are the 15 and 25')

THE DAYS OF THE WEEK

Note that the days of the week are not capitalized in Italian: **lunedì** *Monday*, **martedì** *Tuesday*, **mercoledì** *Wednesday*, **giovedì** *Thursday*, **venerdì** *Friday*, **sabato** *Saturday*, **domenica** *Sunday.*

They are all masculine nouns, except for **domenica**: **un brutto lunedì di pioggia** *a nasty rainy Monday*, **una bella domenica di sole** *a lovely sunny Sunday*.

THE MONTHS OF THE YEAR

These are all masculine and are not capitalized.

gennaio *January*
febbraio *February*
marzo *March*
aprile *April*
maggio *May*
giugno *June*
luglio *July*
agosto *August*
settembre *September*
ottobre *October*
novembre *November*
dicembre *December*

THE SEASONS

la primavera *spring* (f.)
l'estate *summer* (f.)
l'autunno *autumn* (m.)
l'inverno *winter* (m.)

GIVING THE DATE

Che giorno è oggi? *What day is it today?*
Oggi è lunedì ventuno marzo, il primo giorno di primavera. *Today is Monday, 21 March, the first day of spring.*

CULTURAL NOTE

To preserve **il centro storico** *the historic centre*, most old towns are pedestrianized. Some 22,000 towns in Italy have historic monuments that date back to the Greeks, Etruscans, Romans or to the Middle Ages. These **zone a traffico limitato** are restricted to authorized vehicles. However, bans are rarely strictly applied in Italy …

◆ GRAMMAR
MAKING COMPARISONS

To form the comparative (the equivalent of *-er*), the construction is **più** *more* or **meno** *less* + adjective: **più caro** *more expensive,* **meno caro** *less expensive, cheaper.* If you want to add *than* something, this is formed by **di** (or **di** + definite article) + noun or pronoun or by **che** + adverb, verb or adjective or if the comparative is preceded by a preposition or indicates a quantity. Here are some examples:
Marzo è più lungo di febbraio. *March is longer than February.*
La tua casa è più grande della mia. *Your house is bigger than mine.*
Tu sei più fotogenico di me. *You are more photogenic than me.*
Mi piace di più dormire che lavorare. *I like sleeping more than working.*

Ottobre è più umido che freddo. *October is more wet than cold.*
A Milano fa meno caldo che a Roma. *In Milan it is less hot than in Rome.*
Mangiamo meno carne che pesce. *We eat less meat than fish.*

To say *as ... as*, **come** or (less commonly) **quanto** is placed before the second term being compared. **Gennaio è freddo come febbraio.** *January is as cold as February.*

▲ CONJUGATION
REFLEXIVE VERBS

These are verbs that include a reflexive pronoun (**mi, ti, si, ci, vi, si**) to indicate the subject is performing the action on itself (e.g. *I hurt myself, you hurt yourself*, etc.). When these verbs are conjugated, the pronoun must be included:

alzarsi *to get up* ('to-raise-oneself')	
mi alzo *I get up* ('myself I-raise')	**ci alziamo** *we get up*
ti alzi *you get up*	**vi alzate** *you* (pl.) *get up*
si alza *he, she, one gets up*	**si alzano** *they get up*

sedersi *to sit down* ('to-sit-oneself')	
mi siedo *I sit down* ('myself I-sit')	**ci sediamo** *we sit down*
ti siedi *you sit down*	**vi sedete** *you* (pl.) *sit down*
si siede *he, she, one sits down*	**si siedono** *they sit down*

SOME *-ERE* VERBS THAT ARE IRREGULAR IN THE PRESENT TENSE

Let's look at some irregular **-ere** verbs. These include **dovere** *to have to, 'must', 'should'*, **volere** *to want to* and **potere** *to be able to, 'can'.* These three verbs are usually followed by an infinitive: **Devo essere in centro.** *I have to be downtown.*

dovere *to have to*		**potere** *to be able to*	
devo *I must*	**dobbiamo**	**posso** *I can*	**possiamo**
devi	**dovete**	**puoi**	**potete**
deve	**devono**	**può**	**possono**

volere *to want to*		**bere** *to drink*	
voglio *I want to*	**vogliamo**	**bevo** *I drink*	**beviamo**
vuoi	**volete**	**bevi**	**bevete**
vuole	**vogliono**	**beve**	**bevono**

VOCABULARY

l'anticipo *advance*
l'appuntamento *appointment*
bloccato/a *blocked*
casalingo/a *home-loving*
il caso *chance, fate*
la cena *dinner*
cenare *to dine, to eat dinner*
il centro *town centre*
la colazione *breakfast*
credere *to believe*
la doccia *shower*
durante *during*
l'eccezione *exception*
la fine *end*
finire *to finish*
la giornata *day* (from morning to evening)
il letto *bed*
mancare *to miss*
la mattina *morning*
la merenda *snack*
metodico/a *methodical*
il minuto *minute*
naturalmente *naturally, of course*
oggi *today*
l'orario *schedule, timetable* (**gli orari** (pl.))
organizzato/a *organized*
la passeggiata *stroll, walk*
la pausa pranzo *lunch break*
Pazienza! *Oh well!*
piacere *to like, to please*
il pomeriggio *afternoon*
la piscina *swimming pool*
pranzare *to eat lunch*
il pranzo *lunch*
preoccuparsi *to be worried*
in punto *on the dot, sharp*
qualcosa *something, anything*
regolare *regular, normal*
salvo *except for*
secondo (te) *according to (you)*
la sera *evening*
svegliarsi *to wake up*
la televisione *television*
il traffico *traffic*
troppo *too much*
l'ufficio *office*
uscire *to go out*

rimanere *to stay, to remain*

rimango *I stay, remain*	**rimaniamo**
rimani	**rimanete**
rimane	**rimangono**

sapere *to know* (a fact or how to do something)

so *I know*	**sappiamo**
sai	**sapete**
sa	**sanno**

EXERCISES

09 ### 1. LISTEN TO THE RECORDING AND WRITE THE NUMBERS IN WORDS.

a. 404 → ....

b. 91 → ....

c. 1957 → ....

d. 22 → ....

e. 73 → ....

2. ANSWER THE QUESTIONS IN FULL, WRITING THE TIMES IN WORDS.

Example: A che ora ti alzi? (8:35) – Mi alzo alle otto e trentacinque.
A che ora pranzate? (12:45) – Pranziamo a mezzogiorno e tre quarti (alle dodici e quarantacinque)

a. A che ora cenano? (19:30) → ....

b. A che ora vi svegliate? (7:15) → ....

c. A che ora fai la doccia? (9:20) → ....

d. A che ora va in piscina, signora? (17:30) → ....

3. COMPLETE THESE SENTENCES WITH THE CORRECT PRESENT TENSE FORM OF THESE IRREGULAR *-ERE* VERBS.

a. Se parto da casa troppo tardi .... bloccata nel traffico. (rimanere)

b. Se arriviamo in anticipo, ... in un bar e .... qualcosa. (sedersi, bere)

c. Signorina, se ...., ... pranzare con noi. (volere, potere)

d. Signore, se non .... dov'è l'ufficio turistico, ... domandare al vigile urbano. (sapere, potere)

e. A che ora .... prendere l'autobus tu e tua sorella? (dovere)

4. COMPLETE THESE SENTENCES WITH *CHE, DI* OR *COME*.

a. In inverno fa più freddo .... in estate.

b. Modena è meno grande .... Milano.

c. In giugno fa caldo .... in luglio.

d. A Roma c'è più traffico .... a Venezia.

8.
LOOKING FOR AN APARTMENT

CERCARE UN ALLOGGIO

AIMS	TOPICS

AIMS

- DESCRIBING YOUR LIVING SITUATION
- EXPLAINING YOUR PLANS
- TALKING ABOUT ACCOMMODATION

TOPICS

- THE COMPARATIVE AND THE SUPERLATIVE
- NUMBERS: THOUSANDS
- ORDINAL NUMBERS
- SOME *-IRE* VERBS THAT ARE IRREGULAR IN THE PRESENT TENSE

AN APARTMENT FOR RENT

David: Hello. Excuse me, is this the estate agency 'Carulli'?

Carla: Absolutely! Hello!

David: Pleased to meet you. I'm David Cooper, I am *(come)* from the United States (pl.). I'm in Italy to study, and I'm looking for an apartment to *(for)* rent [that is] very inexpensive.

Carla: You've come at the right time *(You-arrive exactly at aim)*! We are the best agency in the city, and we have [some] really good-value flats. For example, we have this little apartment with *(of)* three rooms on the third floor: living room, bedroom, bathroom and a very small kitchen, on a very central street close *(at two steps)* to the university. We rent it every year to students, and they all say that it is excellent value for money *(a great relationship quality-price)*.

David: Yes, but I'm looking for something smaller, [as] I have to live on my own *(there I-must live of alone)*.

Carla: You're right, *(now)* we['ll] find something more suitable for *(adapted to)* you. We have more than 2000 apartments listed *(in-the our catalogue)*! For example, there is a studio on the 15th floor of the tallest high-rise building *(scrape-sky)* in the city.

David: Yes, but if the elevator breaks down *(it-is broken)*, what do I do? I have to go up 15 flights of stairs *(I-climb by feet 15 floors)*?

Carla: But that almost never happens *(not happens almost never)*!

David: When there's any type of bother *(a snag)*, it always happens *(arrives)* to me! I'd rather not *(I-prefer of no)*, thank you!

Carla: Then *(to-you)* I suggest another *(this-other)* possibility: a room in a flat shared with three other students. It is located *(Itself it-finds)* on the second floor: your room is the last [one] at the end of the hall, and of course all of you have use of the bathroom and kitchen. The rent for the apartment is *(of)* 1000 euros per month – given that there are four of you *(you-are in four)*, you *(of-it)* [would] pay only a quarter: that is, 250. What do you say *(What about-it you-say)*? This is the most suitable [option], isn't it?

David: I [would] say that if this is the least expensive of all [the options], I'll obviously have to take it *(I-accept by force)*!

10 UN APPARTAMENTO IN AFFITTO

David: Buongiorno; scusi, questa è l'agenzia immobiliare "Carulli"?

Carla: Certo, buongiorno!

David: Piacere, mi chiamo David Cooper, vengo dagli Stati Uniti, sono in Italia per studiare e cerco un appartamento in affitto molto economico.

Carla: Capita proprio a proposito! Siamo la migliore agenzia della città e abbiamo appartamenti davvero economicissimi. Per esempio, abbiamo questo appartamentino di tre stanze al terzo piano, soggiorno, camera da letto, bagno e una piccolissima cucina, in una via centralissima a due passi dall'università. Lo affittiamo tutti gli anni a studenti e tutti dicono che è un ottimo rapporto qualità-prezzo.

David: Sì, ma io cerco qualcosa di più piccolo, ci devo abitare da solo.

Carla: Ha ragione, ora troviamo qualcosa di più adatto a Lei. Abbiamo più di duemila appartamenti nel nostro catalogo! Per esempio, c'è un monolocale al quindicesimo piano del grattacielo più alto della città.

David: Sì, ma se l'ascensore è guasto che faccio? Salgo a piedi quindici piani?

Carla: Ma non succede quasi mai!

David: Quando c'è un guaio, capita sempre a me! Preferisco di no, grazie!

Carla: Allora Le propongo quest'altra possibilità: una camera in un appartamento condiviso con altri tre studenti. Si trova al secondo piano, la Sua camera è l'ultima in fondo al corridoio, e tutti avete naturalmente l'uso di bagno e cucina. L'affitto dell'appartamento è di mille euro al mese, siccome siete in quattro Lei ne paga solo un quarto, cioè duecentocinquanta. Che ne dice? Questo è il più conveniente, no?

David: Dico che se questo è il meno caro di tutti, accetto per forza!

UNDERSTANDING THE DIALOGUE

THE VERBS *SUCCEDERE* AND *CAPITARE*

→ These verbs share similar meanings. The more neutral is **succedere** *to happen, to occur*: **Non succede quasi mai!** *That almost never happens!* (Note that a double negative can be used in Italian: 'Not it-happens almost never!')

→ When used to mean *to happen*, **capitare** is often linked to something negative: **Quando c'è un guaio, capita sempre a me!** *When there's a hassle, it always happens to me!* But **capitare** can also mean *to end up* or *to turn up* somewhere.

THE PRONOUN *NE*

Be careful: the word **ne** is not used to form the negative! It is actually a pronoun that means *of it, about it*. Like other object pronouns, it is placed before the conjugated verb: **Ne paga solo un quarto.** *You pay only a quarter of it* (the rent). **Che ne dice?** *What do you say about it?*

A IN PREPOSITIONAL PHRASES OF PLACE

The preposition **a** is often used in phrases that describe locations: **in fondo al corridoio** *at the end of the corridor*, **di fronte a** *opposite, across from*, **di fianco a** *alongside*, **vicino a** *next to*, **in mezzo a** *in the middle of*, **intorno a** *around*.

IDIOMATIC USES OF PREPOSITIONS

Note the way the prepositions **da** and **in** are used in the following two idiomatic expressions. This usage is quite different from the English:

→ **Ci devo abitare da solo.** *I have to live on my own.*
Lo faccio da solo. *I will do it by myself.*

→ **Siete in quattro.** *There are four of you.*
In quanti venite? Veniamo in sei. *How many of you are coming? There will be six of us.*

CULTURAL NOTE

Around 70% of Italians own their home. Students make up the highest proportion of renters. Some come from abroad, but most are young Italians who have moved to another city to study. The latter represent approximately 20% of the students in Italian universities.

GRAMMAR
INTENSIFYING ADJECTIVES OR ADVERBS

→ One way to intensify an adjective or adverb in Italian is to add the suffix **-issimo** (which changes form to agree with the noun: **-issima, -issimi,-issime**):
Come stai/state? *How are you?* **Benissimo!** *Very well!* (a male speaking) **Benissima!** (a female speaking), **Benissimi!** (males or a mixed-gender group), **Benissime!** (females).

→ **molto** *very* can also be placed before an adjective or adverb: **molto economico** *very cheap*; **Molto bene!** *Very well!*

THE COMPARATIVE AND THE SUPERLATIVE

We've seen the way to make the comparative (lesson 7) with **più** (or **meno**) + adjective. The superlative (the equivalent of *the most/least* or *-est*) simply adds the definite article **il/la/i/le**: **il più conveniente** *the most suitable* (referring to a singular masculine noun), **i meno cari** *the cheapest* (referring to a masculine plural noun). The construction is definite article + noun + **più** or **meno** + adjective: **la ragazza più alta della scuola** *the tallest girl in the school*.

Some frequent comparatives have specific terms that are more commonly used than the regular comparative construction, although either is possible: e.g. **migliore** *better* or **più buono** ('more good').

ADJECTIVE	Comparative	Superlative	Intensified form
buono *good*	**migliore** *better*	**il migliore** *best*	**ottimo** *great*
cattivo *bad*	**peggiore** *worse*	**il peggiore** *worst*	**pessimo** *terrible*
grande *big*	**maggiore** *bigger*	**il maggiore** *biggest*	**massimo** *greatest*
piccolo *small*	**minore** *smaller*	**il minore** *smallest*	**minimo** *least, slightest*

Example: **la migliore agenzia della città** *the best agency in the city*.

ADVERB	Comparative	Intensified form
bene *well*	**meglio** *better*	**ottimamente, molto bene** *excellently, very well*
male *badly*	**peggio** *worse*	**pessimamente, molto male** *terribly, very badly*

MORE NUMBERS: THOUSANDS

The term **mille** is *1000*. Its multiples are formed by adding the suffix **-mila**: **duemila** *2000*, **tremila** *3000*, **centomila** *100,000*, **centosettantamila** *170,000*.

ORDINAL NUMBERS

The most common ordinal numbers are **primo** *first*, **secondo** *second*, **terzo** *third*, **quarto** *fourth*, **quinto** *fifth*, **sesto** *sixth*, **settimo** *seventh*, **ottavo** *eighth*, **nono** *ninth*, **decimo** *tenth*. After that, the construction is number (minus the final letter) + the suffix **-esimo**: e.g. **undicesimo (11°)** *eleventh*, **ventiquattresimo (24°)** *twenty-fourth*. Note that the ° symbol is used after a number to indicate an ordinal. Numbers ending in **-tre** or **-sei** add the suffix witihout omitting the final letter: **trentatreesimo** *thirty-third*, **cinquantaseiesimo** *fifty-sixth*. Because they are adjectives, ordinal numbers need to agree in gender and number with the noun. As in English, they are used for fractions: **un quarto** *one-fourth*.

▲ CONJUGATION

SOME *-IRE* VERBS THAT ARE IRREGULAR IN THE PRESENT

dire *to say, to tell*		
(io) dico	**(lui, lei, Lei) dice**	**(voi) dite**
(tu) dici	**(noi) diciamo**	**(loro, Loro) dicono**

salire *to climb, to go up, to get in*		
(io) salgo	**(lui, lei, Lei) sale**	**(voi) salite**
(tu) sali	**(noi) saliamo**	**(loro, Loro) salgono**

uscire *to exit, to leave, to go out, to come out*		
(io) esco	**(lui, lei, Lei) esce**	**(voi) uscite**
(tu) esci	**(noi) usciamo**	**(loro, Loro) escono**

venire *to come*		
(io) vengo	**(lui, lei, Lei) viene**	**(voi) venite**
(tu) vieni	**(noi) veniamo**	**(loro, Loro) vengono**

VOCABULARY

accettare *to accept*
adatto/a *adapted, suitable*
affittare *to rent*
l'affitto *rent* (noun)
l'agenzia immobiliare *(real) estate agency*
l'alloggio *lodging, accommodation*
a piedi *on foot* (**il piede** *foot* / **i piedi** *feet)*
l'appartamento *apartment, flat*
l'ascensore *elevator, lift*
il bagno *bathroom*
la camera (da letto) *bedroom* (**le camere** *rooms)*
caro/a *expensive*
centrale *central*
cioè *that is*
condiviso *shared* (past participle of the verb **condividere** *to share*)
il corridoio *corridor, hall*
la cucina *kitchen*
economico/a *inexpensive, good value, low-cost*
il grattacielo *skyscraper, high-rise building*
il guaio *snag, hassle, bother*
guasto/a *broken*
il letto *bed*
mai *never*
il mese *month*
il monolocale *studio flat*
il passo *step* (**i passi** *steps)*
per forza *by necessity* (**la forza** *force, strength)*
la possibilità *possibility*
il proposito *purpose, intention, aim*
proprio *exactly, really*
la qualità *quality*
il quarto *quarter*
quasi *almost*
salire *to climb, to go up*
siccome *given that, seeing that*
il soggiorno *stay, sojourn*
la stanza *room* (**le stanze** *rooms)*
ultimo/a *last, final*
l'uso *use, utilization*

ANOTHER IRREGULAR *-ERE* VERB

proporre *to suggest, to recommend, to propose*		
(io) propongo	**(lui, lei, Lei) propone**	**(voi) proponete**
(tu) proponi	**(noi) proponiamo**	**(loro, Loro) propongono**

Other verbs with an infinitive ending in **-rre** conjugate in the same way: **comporre** *to compose, to arrange*, **disporre** *to place, to put, to order*, **riporre** *to replace, to put away, to put back.*

EXERCISES

10 1. LISTEN TO THE RECORDING AND WRITE THE ORDINAL NUMBERS IN WORDS.

a. 44° → ....

b. 845° → ....

c. 5° → ....

d. 73° → ....

e. 16° → ....

2. COMPLETE THE SENTENCES WITH THE CORRECT FORM OF THE SUPERLATIVE OR INTENSIFIED ADJECTIVE.

a. Questa città mi piace molto, è .... (bella).

b. Prendo questo appartamento perché è .... (caro) di tutti.

c. La nostra agenzia è .... (buona) della città.

d. Voglio un appartamento .... (piccolo), ci devo abitare da solo.

3. COMPLETE THESE SENTENCES WITH THE CORRECT PRESENT TENSE FORM OF THE MOST APPROPRIATE IRREGULAR *-IRE* VERB (*DIRE, USCIRE, SALIRE, VENIRE*).

a. In inverno non .... quasi mai, ho troppo freddo.

b. Se .... con tuo fratello, preparo la cena per due.

c. I miei amici abitano al nono piano e .... sempre in ascensore.

d. Se .... all'agente immobiliare che cercate un appartamento, lui lo trova subito.

10 4. LISTEN TO THE RECORDING AND FILL IN THE MISSING WORDS.

a. Abito in un appartamento di tre .... al quarto ....

b. Questo appartamento è troppo grande, ... devo abitare da ....

c. La .... da letto è in .... al corridoio.

d. Le .... la possibilità di .... un appartamento con altri tre studenti.

9. ARRANGING TO MEET A FRIEND

DARE APPUNTAMENTO A UN AMICO

AIMS	TOPICS
• SUGGESTING AN ACTIVITY • GIVING A DATE OR A TIME • MAKING PLANS TO MEET SOMEONE	• SPECIAL PLURAL FORMS • SPECIAL FEMININE FORMS • THE PRESENT CONTINUOUS • TRANSLATING '-ING'

A DATE FOR THE CINEMA

Pietro: Hi, Rita! What are you doing *(you-do)* in these parts?

Rita: I'm doing a bit of shopping. Near your house there is one of the best clothes shops *(shops of clothing)* in the city, and today the sales start!

Pietro: How wonderful …

Rita: Seeing as your hands are free *(Seen that you-have hands free)*, help me carry a few *(of)* bags: they are very heavy and my arms are hurting *(to-me they-do badly to-the arms)*!

Pietro: Sure! Two pairs of arms *(of-it)* carry more than only one *(pair)*, right? However, I *(to-you)* suggest something much more interesting. I'm reading a fantastic book about Piero della Francesca, the great painter from the 15th century *(400)*. You know, the artist of the famous painting where there's an egg hanging *(hung)* in the centre of the scene, [as a] symbol of geometric perfection?

Rita: Listen, I eat eggs *(them I-eat to-the)* fried, I don't hang them *(at-all)* from the ceiling!

Pietro: You're incorrigible! In any case, at the Rivoli cinema, they're showing *(they-do)* a film about his life: it has *(there are)* excellent reviews in the press *(newspapers)*. They say that it's a true masterpiece.

Rita: What a bore! Another *(Again a)* film about a man, made by a man for men *(a public masculine)*! Why aren't there ever films about women painters, sculptors, writers, instead of always male painters, sculptors, and writers?

Pietro: So *(In-short)* do you want to come or not? That way *(Like-this)* at least you can grumble after the film.

Rita: OK, when *(there)* are we going?

Pietro: Can you next Monday?

Rita: What day is Monday? *(How-much of-it we-have Monday?)*

Pietro: Monday is the 12th.

Rita: The12[th] I have a commitment in the late *(in end)* afternoon; I can only [make it] in the evening.

Pietro: If you want, we [can] go to the showing at 10:00. [Shall] I come pick you up *(You I-come to take)* at your place at 9:30?

Rita: No, I['ll] come to yours, but come downstairs *(you descend)* as soon as I ring [the bell]. I don't want to wait a quarter of an hour on the sidewalk as *(to-the)* usual.

Pietro: Fine, [you old] grouch! [See you] on Monday at 9:30 – on time!

11 APPUNTAMENTO AL CINEMA

Pietro: Ciao, Rita, che fai da queste parti?

Rita: Sto facendo un po' di shopping. Vicino a casa tua c'è uno dei migliori negozi di abbigliamento della città, e oggi cominciano i saldi.

Pietro: Che meraviglia…

Rita: Visto che hai le mani libere, aiutami a portare un po' di borse, sono molto pesanti e mi fanno male alle braccia!

Pietro: Certo! Due paia di braccia ne portano più di un paio solo, vero? Io invece ti propongo qualcosa di molto più interessante. Sto leggendo un bellissimo libro su Piero della Francesca, il grande pittore del Quattrocento. Sai, l'autore del famoso quadro dove c'è un uovo appeso nel centro della scena, simbolo di perfezione geometrica?

Rita: Senti, le uova io le mangio al tegamino, non le appendo mica al soffitto!

Pietro: Sei incorreggibile! In ogni caso al cinema *Rivoli* fanno un film sulla sua vita: ci sono ottime recensioni sui giornali, dicono che è un vero capolavoro.

Rita: Uffa, ancora un film su un uomo fatto da un uomo per un pubblico maschile! Perché non ci sono mai film su pittrici, scultrici, scrittrici, invece che sempre su pittori, scultori e scrittori?

Pietro: Insomma, vuoi venire o no? Così almeno puoi brontolare dopo il film.

Rita: Va bene, quando ci andiamo?

Pietro: Lunedì prossimo, tu puoi?

Rita: Quanti ne abbiamo lunedì?

Pietro: Lunedì è il dodici.

Rita: Il dodici ho un impegno in fine pomeriggio, posso solo alla sera.

Pietro: Se vuoi andiamo allo spettacolo delle dieci. Ti vengo a prendere a casa tua alle nove e mezza?

Rita: No, vengo io da te, ma tu scendi appena suono il campanello, non voglio aspettare un quarto d'ora sul marciapiede come al solito.

Pietro: Va bene, brontolona! A lunedì alle nove e mezza, puntuale!

UNDERSTANDING THE DIALOGUE *DA QUESTE PARTI*

Note the use of the preposition **da** in the idiomatic expression **da queste parti** *in these parts*. In English, we use 'in' while the Italian uses **da**. If the area referred to is farther away, the demonstrative **quello** is used: **Non vado mai da quelle parti.** *I never go to those parts.* (i.e. that area).

DA TE OR *A CASA TUA*

There are two ways to say you're going *to someone's place*:

• **da** + a name or personal pronoun: **Vado da lui.** *I'm going to his [place].* or **Vado da Luigi.** *I'm going to Luigi's.*

• **a casa** + possessive adjective (or **di** + a name): **Vado a casa sua.** or **Vado a casa di Luigi**. If you're not talking about someone's home, but a shop, office, etc., you must use **da** (contracted with the article): **Vado dal dottore.** *I'm going to the doctor's.*

VERO?

The dialogue in this lesson includes several question tags used in Italian to seek confirmation from the other person in the conversation, though the question is purely rhetorical. We have many of these in English, and the Italians also use them frequently at the end of sentences: **no?** *isn't it?* **vero?** *right?*

THE CENTURIES: *IL QUATTROCENTO*

While the centuries can be referred to by the ordinal numbers, as in English (**il quindicesimo secolo** *the 15th century*), it is more common to use terms that refer to the hundreds within the dates the century contains: for example, **il Quattrocento** *the 15th century* ('the 400') since the years during this century contain the number 400 (e.g. *1459* **millequattrocentocinquantanove**). So **il Cinquecento** ('the 500') is *the 16th century*, **il Seicento** ('the 600') *the 17th century*, and so on.

GIVING THE DATE

To ask the date, the expression is **Quanti ne abbiamo oggi?** ('How-many of-it we-have today?') *What's the date today?* The reply is **Oggi ne abbiamo dodici.** ('Today of-it we-have twelve.') *Today is the 12th.*

MICA

The term **mica** *not ... at all* is an informal way to emphasize a negation in everyday speech: **Non ci credo mica!** *I don't believe that at all!* **Mica male!** *Not bad at all!*

SUBJECT-VERB WORD ORDER

Note the difference between **vengo da te** ('I-come to you') *I'll come to your place*, **io vengo da te** *as for me, I'll come to your place* (to emphasize what 'I' will be doing as opposed to anyone else), and **vengo io da te** *no, I'll come to yours* (to convey the contrary of what was suggested, i.e. 'I will do it rather than you').

CALLING SOMEONE'S ATTENTION TO SOMETHING

As in English, the imperative (command form) can be used to call someone's attention to what you're about to say: **senti** *listen* or **guarda** *look*. In the formal (**Lei** form), these become **senta** and **guardi**.

UFFA! HOW BORING!

This exclamation is accompanied by exhaling and blowing out one's cheeks, indicating boredom, impatience, displeasure or dissatisfaction. Learning another language includes knowing how to read body language!

CULTURAL NOTE

Italians are big fans of sales, especially for clothes: not surprising for a country famous for its sense of style ... The dates that shops can have sales are decided by the government and so occur at the same time nationwide. The winter sales start in the first week of January, and the summer sales in the first week of July. People may travel miles to other cities to take advantage of the discounted prices.

◆ GRAMMAR
SPECIAL PLURAL FORMS: MASCULINE SINGULAR -O → FEMININE PLURAL -A

Certain masculine singular words ending in **-o** change to feminine words ending in **-a** in the plural: **l'uovo** *egg* (masc.) → **le uova** *eggs* (fem.); **il paio** *pair* → **le paia** *pairs*; **il centinaio** *hundred* → **le centinaia** *hundreds*; **il migliaio** *thousand* → **le migliaia** *thousands*; **il braccio** *arm* → **le braccia** *arms*; **il riso** *laughter* → **le risa** *laughs*.

Some of these have two plural forms with different meanings: **il muro** *wall* → **i muri** *walls* (m.) or **le mura** *ramparts, fortified city walls* (f.).

SPECIAL FEMININE FORMS: MASCULINE ENDING *-TORE*, FEMININE ENDING *-TRICE*

→ The masculine suffix **-tore** is used to describe a person who does certain types of activities, similar to *-er/-or* in English. In the feminine it becomes **-trice**: **pittore** *painter* → **pittrice**; **scultore** *sculptor*→ **scultrice**; **scrittore** *writer* → **scrittrice**; **attore** *actor* → **attrice**; **lavoratore** *worker* → **lavoratrice**. There are some exceptions, including **dottore** *doctor* → **dottoressa**. These all form the plural in a regular way, with **-i** in the masculine and **-e** in the feminine.

→ While **la mano** *hand* ends in **-o**, it is feminine (plural: **le mani**).

▲ CONJUGATION
THE PRESENT CONTINUOUS

The present continuous (or the present progressive) tense is used to describe actions in progress, i.e. to be in the process of doing something. It is constructed with a conjugated form of **stare** *to be* + present participle. The present participle is formed simply by replacing the infinitive ending **-are** with **-ando** (**parlando** *talking*) or **-ere**/**-ire** with **-endo** (**partendo** *leaving*). There are only a few irregular present participles: **facendo** *doing* (from **fare**), **bevendo** *drinking* (from **bere**), **proponendo** *proposing* (from **proporre**), **dicendo** *saying* (from **dire**).

The present continuous is used in a similar way to English to describe something that is currently happening: **Che cosa stai facendo?** *What are you doing?* **Sto mangiando.** *I'm eating.* However, often Italian uses the simple present tense where in English the present continuous would be used: **Che fai?** *What are you doing?* In Italian, the present continuous more specifically conveys the idea of being right in the middle of doing something.

TRANSLATING '-ING'

While the Italian present participle is the equivalent of the *-ing* verb in continuous tenses, the English gerund (an *-ing* word used as a noun to describe a generalized action) is usually translated by an infinitive in Italian. We've seen this in many of the lesson titles: **dare appuntamento a un amico** *making* ('to-give') *a date with a friend,* **cercare un alloggio** *looking for* ('to-search') *an apartment.*

VOCABULARY

l'abbigliamento *clothing*
aiutare *to help*
almeno *at least*
appena *as soon as, only, just now*
appendere *to hang*
appeso/a *hung*
l'appuntamento *appointment, date*
aspettare *to wait*
brontolare *to grumble*
brontolone/a *grouchy, grumpy*
il campanello *doorbell*
il capolavoro *masterpiece*
il cinema *cinema, movie theatre*
come al solito *as usual*
così *like this, so, in this way*
dopo *after*
famoso/a *famous*
fare male *to hurt*
il film *film, movie*
geometrico/a *geometric*
il giornale *newspaper (***i giornali** *newspapers)*
l'impegno *commitment, errand, obligation, appointment*
incorreggibile *incorrigible, beyond correction*
interessante *interesting*
leggere *to read*
libero/a *free, available*
il libro *book*
mangiare *to eat*
il marciapiede *sidewalk, pavement*
maschile *masculine, manly (***femminile** *feminine)*
la meraviglia *marvel, splendour*
la perfezione *perfection*
pesante *heavy*
prossimo/a *next*
portare *to carry*
il pubblico *public, community*
puntuale *punctual, on time*
il quadro *painting, square*
la recensione *review (***le recensioni** *reviews)*
i saldi *sale, clearance* (pl.)
la scena *scene, setting*
scendere *to descend, to go down*
il simbolo *symbol*
il soffitto *ceiling*
lo spettacolo *show, performance*
suonare *to ring*
il tegamino (diminutive of **il tegame**) *pan, saucepan*
l'uomo *man (***la donna** *woman)*
venire a prendere *to pick someone up, to come get someone* ('to come to take')
visto che *seeing that*
la vita *life*

EXERCISES

1. COMPLETE THE TABLE WITH THE MISSING FORMS.

Masculine	Feminine
l'attore famoso	
	la scrittrice americana
il dottore simpatico	
i pittori milanesi	

2. COMPLETE THE TABLE WITH THE MISSING FORMS.

Singular	Plural
	le uova fresche
il mio braccio	
il muro della casa	
	le nostre mani

3. COMPLETE THESE SENTENCES WITH THE CORRECT FORM OF THE MOST SUITABLE VERB: *DOVERE, VENIRE, STARE, PROPORRE.*

a. Se hai bisogno di noi, ... da te oggi pomeriggio.

b. Questa agenzia .... appartamenti molto convenienti.

c. Quando fa caldo si .... bere molto.

d. Che cosa fate? – .... mangiando.

11 4. LISTEN TO THE RECORDING AND FILL IN THE MISSING PRESENT PARTICIPLES.

a. Che fate da queste parti? – Stiamo .... a fare shopping.

b. Sto .... l'italiano perché ne ho bisogno per il mio lavoro.

c. Che cosa stai ....? – Un libro sui pittori del Quattrocento.

d. A quest'ora mio fratello sta .... colazione.

10. ASKING FOR DIRECTIONS

CHIEDERE UN'INFORMAZIONE STRADALE

AIMS

- FINDING YOUR WAY AROUND
- EXPLAINING WHY YOU ARE GOING SOMEWHERE
- THANKING AND EXPRESSING GRATITUDE

TOPICS

- OBJECT PRONOUNS (WEAK FORMS)
- THE PRESENT PERFECT
- THE PAST PARTICIPLE OF REGULAR VERBS AND SOME COMMON IRREGULAR FORMS

HOW DOES ONE GET TO DELLA LUNA STREET?

Roberto: Hello, excuse [me] if I'm bothering you ... can you tell *(indicate to)* me the way *(street)* to get *(go)* to via della Luna, please? Earlier I asked *(to)* another gentleman, but perhaps I didn't understand his directions correctly *(well)* because I haven't found it.

Lady: Let's see *(Look)*, from here it's not very complicated, but it's a bit far. Do you see *(It you-see)* that traffic light over there, beside the red brick building?

Roberto: Yes, it's at the next intersection.

Lady: Well done! There you have to turn *(to)* right and go straight on *(always straight)* for about a kilometre, all the way to *(up-to)* a roundabout. After the traffic island you have to take the third *(to)* left, [which] is Mazzini Street. At the end of Mazzini Street, there is a square with the town hall, and you can't go any further *(cannot continue)*, you have no choice but to turn right. There you must keep on going *(continue again)* a little [way]: you [will] pass in front of a school, then a supermarket and a petrol station. After the petrol station, the first cross street that you find, to the right and the left, is via della Luna. But if you don't mind my asking *(excuse)*, what *(thing)* are you looking for on via della Luna?

Roberto: I would like to visit the archaeology museum; that's where it is *(it's there)*, isn't it?

Lady: No, not at all! It's a good thing I asked *(Less bad that it I-have done the question)*! The archaeology museum is on Della Luna Boulevard, not Della Luna Street! Now I am retired *(on pension)*, but I worked there all my *(the)* life as [a] security guard!

Roberto: And [so] how do I get to *(how one does to go to)* Della Luna Boulevard?

Lady: Luckily, it's even simpler *(again more simple)*. Della Luna Boulevard is precisely the tree-lined street where the town hall is. Does it seem clear to you now?

Roberto: Yes, now everything is clear.

Lady: Listen, perhaps I [could] go with you: that way you won't get lost *(not yourself you-lose)*.

Roberto: No, no, it's not necessary. This time I'll manage to get there on my own *(there it I-make alone)*!

12 COME SI FA PER ANDARE IN VIA DELLA LUNA?

Roberto: Buongiorno, scusi se La disturbo, mi può indicare la strada per andare in via della Luna, per favore? Prima l'ho chiesto ad un altro signore ma forse non ho capito bene le sue indicazioni, perché non l'ho trovata.

Signora: Guardi, da qui non è molto complicato, ma è un po' lontano. Lo vede quel semaforo laggiù, di fianco al palazzo di mattoni rossi?

Roberto: Sì, è al prossimo incrocio.

Signora: Bravo! Là deve girare a destra e andare sempre dritto per circa un chilometro fino a una rotatoria. Dopo la rotatoria deve prendere la terza a sinistra, è via Mazzini. In fondo a via Mazzini c'è una piazza con il municipio, e non può continuare, deve girare per forza a destra. Là deve continuare ancora un po', passa davanti a una scuola, poi a un supermercato e a un distributore di benzina. Dopo il distributore, la prima traversa che trova, a destra e a sinistra, è la via della Luna. Ma scusi, che cosa cerca in via della Luna?

Roberto: Vorrei visitare il museo archeologico; è lì, no?

Signora: No, per niente! Meno male che le ho fatto la domanda! Il museo archeologico è in viale della Luna, non in via della Luna! Ora sono in pensione, ma ci ho lavorato tutta la vita come custode!

Roberto: E come si fa per andare in viale della Luna?

Signora: Per fortuna è ancora più semplice. Il viale della Luna è proprio la strada alberata dove c'è il municipio. Le sembra chiaro adesso?

Roberto: Sì, ora è tutto chiaro.

Signora: Senta, magari L'accompagno io, così non si perde.

Roberto: No no, non è necessario, questa volta ce la faccio da solo!

UNDERSTANDING THE DIALOGUE
ASKING FOR DIRECTIONS

Two common ways to ask for directions are: **Come si fa per andare… ?** ('How one does to go …') *How does one get to …?* or **Mi può indicare** (or **dire**) **la strada per andare… ?** *Can you tell me the way to get* ('go') *to … ?* It never hurts to precede the question with **scusi** and follow it with **per favore**. Or if you're talking to someone you know or a young person in a more informal context you would say: **Scusa, mi puoi dire come si fa per andare in …, per favore?**

THE PREPOSITION *IN* IN AN ADDRESS

The preposition **in** is used in street addresses and directions: **Che cosa cerca in via della Luna?** *What are you looking for on via della Luna?* **Abito in piazza Italia 35.** *I live at 35 Italia Square.*

MENO MALE (OR *MENOMALE*) AND *PER FORTUNA*

There are two ways to say *fortunately, luckily*: **meno male** or **per fortuna**. **Che le ho fatto la domanda!** *Luckily I asked!* **Per fortuna sei arrivato in tempo!** *Fortunately you arrived in time!*

CE LA FACCIO

This expression corresponds to *to manage to do something*, in the sense of reaching an objective that takes a bit of effort. It includes the verb **fare**, so in the present tense: **ce la faccio** *I manage to*, **ce la fai** *you manage to*, **ce la fa** *he/she manages to*, **ce la facciamo** *we manage to*, **ce la fate** *you* (pl.) *manage to*, **ce la fanno** *they manage to*. In the present perfect, the past participle is in the feminine singular to agree with **la**: **ce l'ho fatta** *I managed it*, **ce l'hai fatta** *you managed it*, etc. You might also hear the negative **Non ce la faccio più.** *I can't handle it anymore*.

CULTURAL NOTE

Italians retire (**andare in pensione**) on average at the age of 66, but this depends on their profession, how long they've worked, and is also subject to changes in the laws that govern social security. The pension system is funded through taxes and managed by the **INPS (Istituto Nazionale di Previdenza Sociale)**, which also deals with unemployment benefits, health care, child benefits, etc.

GRAMMAR
OBJECT PRONOUNS (WEAK FORMS)

Object pronouns are pronouns that are acted upon by the verb. A direct object directly receives the action of the verb (*I see you*). An indirect object indicates to or for whom something occurs (*I give it to you*). In Italian, both types of object pronouns are the same in all persons except the third-person singular and plural:

Subject pronoun	Direct object	Indirect object
io *I*	**mi** *me*	**mi** *(to) me*
tu *you* (informal sing.)	**ti** *you*	**ti** *(to) you*
lui, lei *he, she, it* **Lei** *you* (formal sing.)	**lo** *him, it* (m.), **la** *her, it* (f.) **La** *you*	**gli** *(to) him, it* (m.), **le** *(to) her, it* (f.) **Le** *(to) you*
noi *we*	**ci** *us*	**ci** *(to) us*
voi *you* (pl.)	**vi** *you*	**vi** *(to) you*
loro *they*, **Loro** *you* (form. pl.)	**li** *them* (m.), **le** (f.)	**gli** *(to) them*

Remember that the third-person feminine singular (**Lei**) is used for the formal *you*, so the same applies for the object pronouns: **La vedo.** *I see her.* or *I see you* (formal). **Le parlo.** *I speak to her*. or *I speak to you* (formal).

The table above shows the 'weak' forms of the object pronouns, which are the most common. They are generally placed in front of the conjugated verb. There are also strong forms, which are used only for emphasis. More on this later!

CONJUGATION
THE PRESENT PERFECT

• As we've mentioned, the present perfect is used in Italian to describe a completed action or event in the past. Depending on context, it can translate to the simple past or the present perfect in English: **ho parlato** *I spoke* or *I have spoken*.
• As in English, the present perfect is usually formed with the auxiliary verb **avere** *to have* (conjugated in the present tense) + past participle: **ho mangiato** *I ate, have eaten*, **hai finito** *you finished, have finished*, **ha visto** *he/she saw, has seen*.
• However, with verbs that indicate movement and changes of state, **essere** *to be* is used as the auxiliary verb: **sono andato** *I* (m.) *went, have gone*, **sei partito** *you* (m.) *left, have left*. In this case, the past participle has to agree in gender and number with the subject: **sono venuto** *I came* (a male), **sono venuta** *I came* (a

female), **siamo venuti** *we came* (males or a mixed-gender group), **siamo venute** *we came* (females).

• The auxiliary verb **essere** is also used with reflexive verbs (**mi sono divertita** *I* (f.) *had fun*, from **divertirsi** *to enjoy oneself*) and with many intransitive verbs (verbs that can't be used with an object). However, a few of the latter take **avere**, such as **dormire** *to sleep*, **ridere** *to laugh* and **correre** *to run*.

• With the auxiliary verb **avere**, the past participle does not change form to agree with the subject unless the direct object comes before the verb. In this case, it does need to change: **Le sue indicazioni, non le ho capite.** *Your directions, I didn't understand them.* (**capite** is the feminine plural of the past participle **capito**).

• Note that the verb **piacere** forms the present perfect with **essere**: **Questa città mi è piaciuta molto.** ('This city to-me has appealed much.') *I liked this city a lot.*

• The verbs **avere** and **essere** form the present perfect with themselves as auxiliaries: **sono stato** *I* (m.) *was, have been*; **ho avuto** *I had, have had.*

THE PAST PARTICIPLE

• REGULAR FORMS

Infinitive ending in:	**-are**	**-ere**	**-ire**
Past participle ending:	**-ato**	**-uto**	**-ito**

Examples: **parlare** *to speak* → **parlato** *spoken*, **vendere** *to sell* → **venduto** *sold*, **finire** *to finish* → **finito** *finished*.

• IRREGULAR FORMS

Unfortunately, the majority of Italian verbs have an irregular past participle. Here are some of the most common:

• infinitives ending in **-are**: **fare** *to do, make* → **fatto** *done, made*.

• infinitives ending in **-ere**: **bere** *to drink* → **bevuto** *drunk*, **chiedere** *to ask* → **chiesto** *asked*, **chiudere** *to close* → **chiuso** *closed*, **correre** *to run* → **corso** *run*, **decidere** *to decide* → **deciso** *decided*, **dividere** *to divide, to share* → **diviso** *divided, shared*, **leggere** *to read* → **letto** *read*, **mettere** *to put* → **messo** *put*, **perdere** *to lose* → **perso** *lost*, **prendere** *to take* → **preso** *taken*, **ridere** *to laugh* → **riso** *laughed*, **scrivere** *to write* → **scritto** *written*, **vedere** *to see* → **visto** *seen*, **vivere** *to live* → **vissuto** *lived*.

• infinitives ending in **-ire**: **aprire** *to open* → **aperto** *opened*, **dire** *to say, to tell* → **detto** *said, told*, **venire** *to come* → **venuto** *come*.

VOCABULARY

accompagnare *to accompany, to go with*
alberato/a *tree-lined*
archeologico/a *archaeological*
la benzina *petrol, gasoline*
chiaro/a *clear*
chiedere *to ask*
il chilometro *kilometre*
complicato/a *complicated*
continuare *to continue*
il/la custode *guardian, security guard, custodian*
davanti *in front, forward*
il distributore di benzina *petrol/gas station*
la domanda *question*
dritto/a *straight*
fino a *until, up to*
girare *to turn*
l'incrocio *crossroads, intersection*
indicare *to indicate*
l'indicazione *indication, instruction, direction* (**le indicazioni** *directions*)
laggiù *over there, down there*
lontano/a *far, distant*
la luna *moon*
magari *possibly, perhaps*
il mattone *brick* (**i mattoni** *bricks*)
il municipio *town hall, city hall*
il museo *museum*
necessario/a *necessary*
il palazzo *building*
la pensione *retirement, pension*
perdersi *to get lost*
per niente *not at all, in no way*
la piazza *town square*
la rotatoria *roundabout, traffic island*
il semaforo *traffic light*
semplice *simple, easy*
la strada *street, road, way, route*
stradale (adj.) *to do with streets*
il supermercato *supermarket*
la traversa *cross street, side street*

EXERCISES

1. COMPLETE THESE SENTENCES WITH THE APPROPRIATE (WEAK) FORM OF THE OBJECT PRONOUN.

a. Quando ho incontrato *(I-have met)* Luisa, ... ho detto tutto.

b. Se .... racconti la tua situazione, forse posso fare qualcosa per te.

c. Carlo mi è molto simpatico, ma purtroppo *(unfortunately)* non .... vedo mai.

d. Gli spaghetti sono il mio piatto preferito, ... mangio spesso *(often)*.

2. REWRITE THESE PRESENT TENSE SENTENCES TO REFER TO SOMETHING THAT HAPPENED IN THE PAST USING THE PRESENT PERFECT.

a. Studio l'italiano per il mio lavoro.
→..

b. Luisa e Carla partono presto *(early)* per evitare *(avoid)* il traffico.
→..

c. Ringraziate *(thank)* il vigile per l'informazione.
→..

12 3. LISTEN TO THE RECORDING AND FILL IN THE MISSING FORMS OF THE PRESENT PERFECT.

a. In vacanza .... (leggere) quel libro, ma ora l'ho dimenticato.

b. La mia ditta *(company)* .... (essere) la più importante della città, ma non lo è più.

c. Ragazzi, ... (vedere) l'ultimo film di Sorrentino?

d. Io e mia sorella .... (chiedere) un'informazione a un vigile.

11. DOING THE SHOPPING

FARE LA SPESA

AIMS	TOPICS
• ASKING FOR INFORMATION WHEN BUYING SOMETHING • GOING TO THE MARKET OR SHOPS • TALKING ABOUT FOOD ITEMS	• OBJECT PRONOUNS (STRONG FORMS) • WORD ORDER AND OBJECT PRONOUNS (WEAK FORMS) WITH INFINITIVES AND THE PRESENT PARTICIPLE • THE IMPERFECT TENSE

AT THE SUPERMARKET

Ms Maluccelli: Excuse [me], can you tell me *(to-me you-know to-tell)* where the meat section *(section butcher)* is, please?

Clerk: Look, it's at the end of the third aisle, immediately on your right.

Ms Maluccelli: Do you know by any chance if they have pork sausage?

Clerk: I don't *(it)* know, ma'am, maybe you should go to a delicatessen ... here we only *(it)* have pork sausage at *(for)* Christmas. Here is my manager, you can speak with him, he *(it)* [will] certainly know.

Ms Maluccelli: No, I don't want to talk to *(with)* him, I don't find him courteous at all. The previous one was nicer *(He-was more nice that of before)*, don't you think?

Clerk: I don't know what to say *(to-you)*, ma'am. The one before lived a long way away *(far)* and asked for a *(the)* transfer.

Ms Maluccelli: Yes, it's true, hearing him speak I gathered *(one understood)* that he wasn't from here – he had a strange accent. But you, what *(thing)* do you sell, if you'll pardon me?

Clerk: I'm in charge of the fruit and vegetable section. Can I help you with anything *(be-to-you helpful in any thing)*, ma'am?

Ms Maluccelli: Of course! [Can you] give me a kilogram of potatoes, an onion and two or three hundred grams *(hectograms)* of carrots, please?

Clerk: Here you are, I put [it] all in three small sacks for you: *(and)* you have to go weigh them on the scale, then go *(pass)* to the check-out, if you don't mind *(not to-you it-displeases)*.

Ms Maluccelli: Oh yes, I know how it works *(how one does)*, I come to do my *(the)* shopping here *(at yours)* almost every day! I [can] find absolutely everything here: good bread like at the baker's, milk, biscuits, chocolate, cheese, meat, fish, fruit and vegetables (sing.), and even detergent and products for *(the)* cleaning *(of)* the house.

Clerk: Speaking of fruit, have you seen what excellent apples and what wonderful oranges we have?

Ms Maluccelli: Yes, but now I really must go *(away)*, possibly I [might] come back tomorrow. I like to come here *(To-me it-pleases to-come-here)* often in order to buy *(always)* fresh things, and then ... I chat with you sales clerks!

13 AL SUPERMERCATO

Signora Maluccelli: Scusi, mi sa dire dov'è il reparto macelleria, per favore?

Commesso: Guardi, è in fondo alla terza corsia, subito sulla Sua sinistra.

Signora Maluccelli: Sa se per caso hanno il cotechino?

Commesso: Non lo so, signora, forse deve andare in una salumeria, il cotechino qui lo abbiamo solo per Natale. Ecco il mio direttore, può parlare con lui, lo sa di sicuro.

Signora Maluccelli: No, con lui non voglio parlare, non lo trovo affatto gentile. Era più simpatico quello di prima, non trova?

Commesso: Non so che dirLe, signora. Quello di prima abitava lontano e ha chiesto il trasferimento.

Signora Maluccelli: Sì, è vero, sentendolo parlare si capiva che non era di qui, aveva uno strano accento. Ma Lei che cosa vende, scusi?

Commesso: Sono addetto al reparto ortofrutta. Posso esserLe utile in qualche cosa, signora?

Signora Maluccelli: Certo! Mi dà un chilo di patate, una cipolla e due o tre etti di carote, per favore?

Commesso: Ecco, Le metto tutto in tre sacchetti e deve andare Lei a pesarli alla bilancia, poi passare alla cassa, se non Le dispiace.

Signora Maluccelli: Sì sì, so come si fa, vengo a fare la spesa qui da voi quasi tutti i giorni. Ci trovo proprio tutto: il pane buono come dal fornaio, il latte, i biscotti, la cioccolata, il formaggio, la carne, il pesce, la frutta e la verdura, e persino il detersivo e i prodotti per la pulizia della casa.

Commesso: A proposito di frutta, ha visto che belle mele e che belle arance abbiamo?

Signora Maluccelli: Sì, ma adesso devo proprio andare via, magari torno domani. Mi piace venirci spesso per comprare sempre roba fresca, e poi… chiacchiero con voi commessi!

UNDERSTANDING THE DIALOGUE
AFFATTO

The adverb **affatto** reinforces a negation: **Non mi piace affatto.** *I don't like that at all*. The expression **niente affatto** (or **non ... per niente**) means *not at all, not in the slightest*: **Ti piace?** *Do you like it?* **Niente affatto.** *Not at all*.

WEIGHT MEASUREMENTS

The metric system is used in Italy, so weights are given in multiples of grams. While the term **un chilo** means *kilogram, kilo*, it is more common to use **un etto** (an abbreviation of **ettogrammo**) *hectogram, 100 grams*: so **due etti** *200 g*, etc. However, you may well hear **il mezzo chilo** *half kilogram* (500 g or 1 lb) rather than **cinque etti**. Some smaller weights include **un etto e mezzo** *150 g* and **mezzo etto** *50 g*. **Vorrei mezzo chilo di patate.** *I'd like a half kilo (1 lb) of potatoes*.

THE PREPOSITION *DA*

We've seen that **da** is used to say *to someone's place*. This is the case not only to talk about someone's home (**vengo da te** *I'll come to yours*), but for shops, restaurants, etc., in which case it contracts with the article: **dal fornaio** *to the bakery*.

VIA

The adverb **via** can be used with verbs of movement to convey a nuance of moving further away: **è andato via** *he went away*; **è scappato via** (from **scappare** *to escape, to run away*) *he ran far away*. In addition, **via** can be used in an exclamation to tell someone to get away from you, e.g. **Va' via!** *Go away!* Lastly, it is used to give the starting signal in a race: **Ai vostri posti, pronti? Via!** *On your marks, set? Go!*

CULTURAL NOTE

Let's talk about food! Italian food is known and loved internationally. But special lesser-known dishes appear at Christmas, such as **il cotechino** *pork sausage* and **lo zampone** *stuffed pig's trotter*, both holiday dishes from the north of Italy. Christmas desserts include **il panettone** (spiced brioche with dried fruit from Milan) and **il pandoro** (sponge cake from Verona). There are big differences between north and south: in the latter, the traditional Christmas meal includes **il cappone ripieno** *stuffed capon* (a castrated rooster) and **gli struffoli** (a sort of fritter).

GRAMMAR
OBJECT PRONOUNS (STRONG FORMS)

The strong forms of the object pronouns are less common than the weak forms. They are used to emphasize the object:

→ The strong forms of direct and indirect objects are identical. The only difference is that an indirect object pronoun is used after a preposition: **Parli a me?** *Are you talking to me?* (as opposed to someone else); **L'ho fatto per lei.** *I did it for her.*

→ Whereas the direct object comes directly after the verb: **Voglio te.** *I want you. It's you that I want.* (as opposed to someone else)

Subject pronoun	Direct/indirect object pronoun (strong form)
io *I*	**me** *me*
tu *you* (informal sing.)	**te** *you*
lui, lei *he, she* **Lei** *you* (formal sing.)	**lui** *him*, **lei** *her* **Lei** *you*
noi *we*	**noi** *us*
voi *you* (informal pl.)	**voi** *you*
loro *they*	**loro** *them*

Examples: **Speravo di vedere proprio voi.** ('I-was-hoping to see precisely you.') *You're just the person I was hoping to see.*
Parlo a lui ma mi rispondi tu. *I'm talking to him but you're the one answering me.*
Avvocato, sono venuto da Lei per un consiglio. *Attorney, I've* (m.) *come to you for some advice.*

WORD ORDER AND OBJECT PRONOUNS (WEAK FORMS) WITH INFINITIVES AND PRESENT PARTICIPLES

We saw the weak forms of the object pronouns in lesson 10. Typically, they are placed before a conjugated verb. With an infinitive (an unconjugated verb), the object pronoun can be attached as a suffix, with the infinitive losing its final vowel:
Voglio parlargli. *I want to speak to him.*
Dovevo immaginarlo! *I should have expected* ('imagined') *it!*
When an infinitive is used with another verb (as in the examples above), this construction is optional: the object pronoun can also be placed before the

conjugated verb. So either of the following is possible: **Mi sa dire... ?** or **Sa dirmi...?** *Can you* ('Do you know to') *tell me ...?* The same suffix construction is used with the impersonal pronouns **ci** (*here, there*) and **ne** (*of/about it*): **Mi piace venirci spesso.** *I like to come here often.* **Voglio parlarne.** *I want to talk about it.*

Aside from the infinitive, an object pronoun is also added to the end of a present participle (which doesn't lose its final vowel): **Sentendolo parlare, si capiva che non era di qui.** *Hearing him speak, I gathered that he wasn't from here.*

CONJUGATION
THE IMPERFECT

The imperfect tense is used to describe a regular, repeated action in the past. This can correspond to *used to* + infinitive or *was/were* + present participle, though in some cases it is used for situations in which the simple past could be used in English. Here are the regular conjugation endings for the three verb groups.

parlare *to speak*	**prendere** *to take*	**finire** *to finish*
parlavo *I was speaking, I used to speak* **parlavi** **parlava** **parlavamo** **parlavate** **parlavano**	**prendevo** **prendevi** **prendeva** **prendevamo** **prendevate** **prendevano**	**finivo** **finivi** **finiva** **finivamo** **finivate** **finivano**

There are only a few verbs that are irregular in the imperfect. Of these, of note is the very common verb **essere** *to be*: **ero** *I was*, **eri, era, eravamo, eravate, erano**. The verb stem changes in the imperfect for the verbs **fare**, **bere** and **dire**: **facevo** *I was doing*, etc. (**fare**), **bevevo** *I was drinking*, etc. (**bere**), **dicevo** *I was saying*, etc. (**dire**).

EXERCISES

1. COMPLETE THESE SENTENCES WITH THE APPROPRIATE STRONG OBJECT PRONOUN.

a. Ti trovo molto simpatico, mi piace lavorare con ....

b. Se ci dite la vostra situazione, forse possiamo fare qualcosa per ....

c. Conosciamo bene Laura e Claudio, siamo andati in vacanza con .... l'anno scorso *(last year)*.

d. Anch'io ho bisogno di parlare a Veronica, se vuoi andiamo insieme da ....

VOCABULARY

accanto *next to, beside*
addetto/a *responsible for, in charge of*
l'arancia *orange* (**le arance** *oranges*)
la bilancia *scale*
il biscotto *biscuit, cookie* (**i biscotti** *biscuits, cookies*)
la carne *meat*
la carota *carrot* (**le carote** *carrots*)
la cassa *check-out, cash register*
chiacchierare *to chat*
il chilo *kilogram*
la cioccolata *chocolate*
la cipolla *onion*
comprare *to buy*
la corsia *aisle*
il detersivo *detergent*
il direttore / la direttrice *director, manager*
di sicuro *certainly*
il formaggio *cheese*
il fornaio *baker's*
fresco/a *fresh*
la frutta *fruit*
il latte *milk*
la macelleria *butcher's*
la mela *apple* (**le mele** *apples*)
il Natale *Christmas*
ortofrutta *fruit and vegetables*
il pane *bread*
la patata *potato* (**le patate** *potatoes*)
pesare *to weigh*
prima *earlier, previously, before*
il prodotto *product* (**i prodotti** *products*)
la pulizia *cleaning, cleanliness*
la roba *things, stuff, goods* (colloquial collective noun)
il reparto *section*
il sacchetto *plastic/paper sack, carrier bag* (**i sacchetti** *sacks*)
la salumeria *delicatessen*
la spesa *shopping*
strano/a *strange, odd, unusual*
il trasferimento *transfer*
la verdura *vegetable, vegetables* (the latter is singular in Italian)

2. REWRITE THESE SENTENCES, CHANGING THE PRESENT PERFECT TO THE IMPERFECT TENSE. THEN TRANSLATE THEM.

a. Avete fatto la spesa al supermercato. → ....

Translation: ....

b. Hanno bevuto solamente acqua. → ....

Translation: ....

c. Non ha detto niente. → ....

Translation: ....

d. Sei stato a Firenze? → ....

Translation: ....

3. TRANSLATE THESE SENTENCES INTO ITALIAN.

a. You (informal sing.) were drinking. → ....

b. They were eating. → ....

c. You (informal pl.) were saying. → ....

d. We were taking. → ....

e. I was finishing. → ....

12. GOING TO THE DOCTOR

ANDARE DAL MEDICO

AIMS	TOPICS
• DESCRIBING YOUR PHYSICAL CONDITION • TALKING ABOUT YOUR HEALTH • ASKING FOR MEDICAL ADVICE	• THE IMPERATIVE (MAKING COMMANDS/REQUESTS) • WORD ORDER OF OBJECT PRONOUNS WITH THE IMPERATIVE

A TERRIBLE COLD

Doctor: Right this way, please *(yourself settle, come please-do forward)*. Come in! Tell me [what's wrong].

Steve: Hello, doctor. I have a terrible cold, and also a *(the)* cough. I'm blowing my nose all the time *(to-me I-blow always the nose)*, as soon as I breathe I start to cough, plus *(and)* my chest hurts *(to-me it-does badly the chest)*, as well as my *(the)* head.

Doctor: Let's take a look *(Now we-see)*. Sit down on the examination table and take off your *(the)* shirt. Breathe deeply a few *(many)* times, like this. Stick out your *(Stretch outside the)* tongue so I can look at your *(that it I-look the)* throat. Good, sit down and I'll write you a *(it I-do the)* prescription so [you can] go to [the] pharmacy.

Steve: Nothing *(of)* serious, I hope …

Doctor: No, don't worry *(not yourself you-worry)*, it's a bad *(big)* cold, but it should be treated *(one should cure)*, otherwise *(if not)* it might develop into *(become a)* bronchitis.

Steve: Excuse me, can we use *(give-ourselves)* 'tu'? I'm [still] learning *(the)* Italian, and I don't know [how] to use the polite form with 'Lei' very well yet.

Doctor: *(But)* Of course! You're *(You-have)* the [same] age as *(of)* my son! Come, sit down here and listen to me carefully: go to the pharmacy right away and get these medicines. *(But)* Go there immediately and take them *(already)* this evening, so that your cough doesn't get worse *(for not make worsen the cough)*. Tell me: you haven't had a *(the)* fever these [last] days, have you?

Steve: No, no, no *(nothing)* fever. Just a very sore throat *(Only so-much bad of throat)* when I cough.

Doctor: Fine, then a [cough] syrup will be enough *(enough the syrup)*: take *(take-of-it)* a spoon[ful] three times per day. I *(myself)* recommend [that you] do it: take care of yourself well, a *(the)* cold or cough can turn into something very serious, if they are not treated as is required. Therefore, don't take them *(to-the)* lightly. Don't neglect your health!

14 UN BRUTTISSIMO RAFFREDDORE

Dottoressa: Si accomodi, venga pure avanti. Entri! Mi dica.

François: Buongiorno dottore. Ho un bruttissimo raffreddore, e anche la tosse. Mi soffio sempre il naso, appena respiro comincio a tossire e mi fa male il petto, e anche la testa.

Dottoressa: Ora vediamo. Si sieda sul lettino e si levi la camicia. Respiri profondamente più volte, così. Tiri fuori la lingua che le guardo la gola. Bene, si sieda e le faccio la ricetta per andare in farmacia.

François: Niente di grave, spero…

Dottoressa: No, non si preoccupi, è un grosso raffreddore ma si deve curare, se no può diventare una bronchite.

François: Scusi, possiamo darci del tu? Sto imparando l'italiano, e non so ancora usare bene la forma di cortesia con il "lei".

Dottoressa: Ma certo! Hai l'età di mio figlio! Vieni, siediti qui e ascoltami bene: va' subito in farmacia e prendi queste medicine. Ma vacci subito e prendile già questa sera, per non fare peggiorare la tosse. Dimmi: non hai avuto la febbre in questi giorni, vero?

François: No no, niente febbre. Solo tanto mal di gola quando tossisco.

Dottoressa: Bene, allora basta lo sciroppo: prendine un cucchiaio tre volte al giorno. Mi raccomando, fallo: curati per bene, il raffreddore e la tosse possono diventare cose molto serie, se non sono curate come si deve. Dunque non prenderle alla leggera. Non trascurare la tua salute!

UNDERSTANDING THE DIALOGUE
REFLEXIVE VERBS WITH DIRECT OBJECTS

Some verbs and expressions include a reflexive verb as well as a direct object: we see this in **mi soffio il naso** *I blow my nose* ('myself I-blow the nose') and **mi levo la camicia** *I take off my shirt* ('myself I-take-off the shirt') and a similar case in **mi fa male la testa** *I have a headache* ('to-me it-does badly the head'). Note the expression **fare male** *to hurt, to ache*, in which the verb conjugates in the third-person singular or plural to agree with what hurts, accompanied by an indirect object pronoun referring to the person in pain: **il ginocchio e la mano mi fanno male** *my knee and hand hurt*. As you'll notice in these examples and in the dialogue, a definite article is usually used rather than a possessive adjective (*my, your*, etc.) to refer to body parts.

CULTURAL NOTE

The Italian medical system is overseen by **le Aziende Sanitarie Locali (A.S.L.)**, which replaced **le Mutue (Enti Mutualistici)** in 1980. The system guarantees universal health care to everyone (this was adopted in the Italian Constitution in 1948). Italians choose a GP from a list provided by their local **A.S.L**. and can go see their doctor at no charge. If they need to consult a specialist, they must go to their GP and ask for **un'impegnativa** *a referral*, which allows them to see a doctor that can treat the particular problem. This is either free or requires **il ticket** a *co-pay* or a medical charge paid by the patient, the amount of which can vary. It is also possible to go see any doctor and pay out of one's own pocket rather than rely on the public healthcare system. Many medicines prescribed by one's GP also require **il ticket** *a co-payment*, though some are free of charge or subsidized to keep the patient's costs low. Certain products are not reimbursed at all (**non mutuabili**). While Italians don't hold back when complaining about their country, they are generally satisfied with their health service.

CONJUGATION
THE IMPERATIVE

The imperative is the verb form used to make a command or a request (e.g. *Eat!*). The complication in Italian is that there are several different forms, depending on who is being addressed: *you* (informal singular: **tu**), *you* (formal singular: **Lei**), *we* (the equivalent to *Let's ...* or *Shall we ...?* **noi**), *you* (informal plural: **voi**) and *you* (formal plural: **Loro**). The following table shows the regular conjugations for these.

	-are verbs	**-ere** verbs	**-ire** verbs
Person addressed	**parlare**	**prendere**	**finire / partire**
(**tu**)	**parla!** *Speak!*	**prendi!** *Take!*	**finisci!** *Finish!* **/ parti!** *Leave!*
(**Lei**)	**parli!**	**prenda!**	**finisca! / parta!**
(**noi**)	**parliamo!**	**prendiamo!**	**finiamo! / partiamo!**
(**voi**)	**parlate!**	**prendete!**	**finite! / partite!**
(**Loro**)	**parlino!**	**prendano!**	**finano! / partano!**

• Note that the **tu**, **Lei** and **Loro** forms have a different vowel in the imperative conjugation ending than in the present tense conjugation.
• The negative **tu** imperative is formed with **non** + infinitive: **Non trascurare la tua salute!** *Don't neglect your health!* All other negative imperatives are formed by putting **non** in front of the affirmative command: e.g. **Non partite!** *Don't leave!* (pl.)
• If a verb is irregular in the present tense, the imperative uses the same irregular verb stem and then adds the conjugation ending: **Bevi!** *Drink!* (**tu** imperative of **bere** *to drink*), **Beva!** (**Lei** imperative), **Beviamo!** *Let's drink!* (**noi** imperative), etc.
• There are five single-syllable **tu** imperatives that are useful to know as they are very frequently used in everyday life: **dai** or **da'** *Give!* (from **dare**), **di'** *Tell!* (from **dire**), **fai** or **fa'** *Do!* (from **fare**), **stai** or **sta'** *Be!* (from **stare**), and **vai** or **va'** *Go!* (from **andare**). The forms with a final apostrophe indicate that the final vowel is omitted.

◆ GRAMMAR
WORD ORDER OF OBJECT PRONOUNS WITH THE IMPERATIVE

When an object pronoun is used with an imperative, it is attached to the end of the verb, forming a single word: **Ascoltami!** *Listen to me!* **Prendile!** *Take them!* (both of these are **tu** imperatives). The same is true with reflexive verbs: **Siediti!** *Sit down! Have a seat!* **Curati ...** *Take care of yourself.* The same rule applies to **ci** *here, there* and **ne** *about/of it*: **Prendine!** *Take some* ('of-it')*!* **Vacci!** *Go there!* (Note that the original word stress in the verb remains on the same syllable, regardless of the addition of the object pronouns).

However, in the **Lei** imperative, object and reflexive pronouns are usually placed before the verb: **Mi dica!** *Tell me!* **Si sieda!** *Have a seat!*

With the one-syllable **tu** imperatives, the first letter of the pronoun is doubled: **Dimmi!** *Tell me!* **Fallo!** *Do it!* **Vacci!** *Go there!* (except for **gli**: e.g. **Digli!** *Tell him!*)

EXERCISES

1. COMPLETE THE SENTENCES WITH THE CORRECT FORM OF THE IMPERATIVE.

a. Ho trovato questo per te, ... (prendere)

b. .... se no perdiamo il treno! (andare)

c. Signora, ... a cena da noi domani! (venire)

d. Ragazzi, ... quello che ho da dirvi. (sentire)

e. Se non vuoi, non .... quel libro. (leggere)

2. TRANSLATE THESE COMMANDS INTO ITALIAN.

a. Let's go there. → ....

b. Take three of them. (**tu**) → ....

c. Don't do it. (**tu**) → ....

d. Do it. (**tu**) → ....

3. REWRITE THESE SENTENCES IN THE PRESENT PERFECT AND THE IMPERFECT.

a. Mia sorella va in vacanza al mare.

→ ....

b. Beviamo caffè per non dormire.

→ ....

c. Marco e Luca si preoccupano troppo.

→ ....

d. Prendi la mia macchina ogni *(every)* mattina.

→ ....

14 4. LISTEN TO THE RECORDING AND FILL IN THE MISSING WORDS.

a. Le faccio la ricetta per andare in farmacia a comprare le ....

b. Prenda un .... di sciroppo tre volte al giorno.

c. Se non la curi, la tosse può ....

VOCABULARY

ascoltare *to listen*
la bronchite *bronchitis*
brutto/a *bad, rotten, ugly, nasty* (**bruttissimo/a** *very nasty*)
la camicia *shirt*
come si deve *as is required*
cominciare *to begin, to start*
il cucchiaio *spoon, tablespoon, spoonful*
curare *to treat, to cure, to take care of*
diventare *to become*
la farmacia *pharmacy*
la febbre *fever*
il figlio *son* (**la figlia** *daughter*)
il ginocchio *knee*
la gola *throat*
grave *serious, grave*
grosso/a *large, big, major, serious*
il lettino *examination table, child's cot* ('little bed')
levare *to remove, to lift, to raise*
la lingua *tongue*
mal di gola *sore throat*
la mano *hand* (note that this word is feminine)
la medicina *medicine* (**le medicine** *medicines*)
il naso *nose*
peggiorare *to worsen, to get worse*
per bene /perbene *well, properly*
il petto *chest*
prendere alla leggera *to take lightly*
preoccuparsi *to worry, to fret*
profondamente *deeply* (**profondo/a** *deep*)
raccomandare *to recommend*
il raffreddore *cold* (the illness)
respirare *to breathe*
la ricetta *prescription*
la salute *health*
lo sciroppo *syrup*
serio/a *serious, earnest*
soffiare *to blow*
la testa *head*
tirare fuori *to take something out of somewhere*
la tosse *cough* (noun)
tossire *to cough*
trascurare *to neglect*
la volta *time, occasion* (**le volte** *times*)

III

JOBS & TASKS

13. GOING TO THE BANK

ANDARE IN BANCA

AIMS

- TALKING ABOUT EVENTS IN THE FUTURE
- DEALING WITH BANKS AND MONEY

TOPICS

- THE FUTURE TENSE
- THE FUTURE OF VERBS ENDING IN *-CARE* AND *-GARE*
- SOME COMMON VERBS THAT ARE IRREGULAR IN THE FUTURE TENSE

OPENING A BANK ACCOUNT

Susan: I would like to open an account in this branch *(agency)*. I come from the United States and I will be working in Italy for at least a year, so I will need *(to have)* an account here in order to withdraw cash (pl.), write *(issue)* cheques and use a credit card.

Employee: Certainly, miss, we will do everything necessary. You will of course need to have your salary credited here *(You-will-have-to naturally make-resident here your salary)*. To do *(For)* this, it will suffice to give *(communicate)* your international bank account number to your employer *(giver of work)*. That way, they will transfer *(he by-means-of bank-transfer will-deposit)* the amount of your *(the)* salary directly into your *(on-the)* account.

Susan: Of course. Additionally, I will also pay all my bills from *(on)* this account.

Employee: For this as well, if you give *(will-communicate)* your account number to the various service providers *(suppliers)*, you will be able to *(indeed)* pay [the] electricity *(light)*, gas, water and telephone [bills] through your bank, obviously without ever [needing] to trouble yourself: we do everything! Moreover, all of your operations can be done *(you-will-be-able to-do)* via online banking, at [your own] home with your computer or mobile phone: bank transfers, telephone top-ups *(recharging telephone)*, TV licence fee [and] payment of *(the)* taxes.

Susan: I'll also need *(I-will-have also need of)* a credit card.

Employee: We will provide *(make)* you both a credit card, which charges *(with debit of)* all your expenses the following month *(the month subsequent)*, and a debit card, which allows you to make *(you will-serve for the)* withdrawals. For purchases in shops, however, with the debit card the charge is immediate.

Susan: Okay, we'll go over *(we-will-see)* all these questions when my first salary is deposited *(will-be credited)*. For now, prepare all the documents for me to sign for tomorrow morning. I'll come by around 8:30, before going to work. Will you (pl.) already be open at that time?

Employee: Of course, we open at 8:00 every morning.

15 APRIRE UN CONTO BANCARIO

Susan: Vorrei aprire un conto in questa agenzia. Vengo dagli Stati Uniti e lavorerò in Italia per almeno un anno, dunque dovrò avere un conto qui, per prelevare contanti, emettere assegni, e usare una carta di credito.

Impiegato: Certo, signorina, faremo tutto il necessario. Dovrà naturalmente domiciliare qui il Suo stipendio. Per questo basterà comunicare il suo IBAN al suo datore di lavoro, così lui tramite bonifico verserà l'importo dello stipendio direttamente sul conto.

Susan: Certamente, poi pagherò anche tutte le mie bollette su questo conto.

Impiegato: Anche per questo, se comunicherà l'IBAN ai vari fornitori, potrà appunto pagare luce, gas, acqua e telefono attraverso la Sua banca, ovviamente senza scomodarsi mai: facciamo tutto noi! Del resto, tutte le Sue operazioni, le potrà fare tramite l'*home banking*, da casa con il Suo computer o col cellulare: bonifici, ricariche telefoniche, canone RAI, pagamento delle tasse.

Susan: Avrò anche bisogno di una carta di credito.

Impiegato: Le faremo sia la carta di credito, con addebito di tutte le Sue spese il mese successivo, sia un bancomat, che Le servirà per i prelievi. Per gli acquisti in negozio, però, con il bancomat l'addebito è immediato.

Susan: Va bene, vedremo tutte queste questioni quando il primo stipendio sarà accreditato. Per ora mi prepari tutti i documenti da firmare per domattina. Passerò verso le otto e trenta, prima di andare in ufficio. Sarete già aperti a quell'ora?

Impiegato: Certamente, apriamo alle otto tutte le mattine.

UNDERSTANDING THE DIALOGUE

TRAMITE

→ As a preposition, this term translates to *by means of, through*: **L'ho conosciuto tramite un collega.** *I met him through a colleague.*

→ As a noun, **tramite** refers to *means, vehicle, channel*: **Ha fatto da tramite tra la mia ditta e la tua.** *He was the go-between between my company and yours.*

→ In many contexts, it translates to *by, via*: **tramite bonifico** *via bank transfer.*

SCOMODARSI

→ The adjective **comodo/a** means *comfortable* as well as *convenient, practical:* **Questa poltrona è davvero comoda.** *This armchair is really comfortable.* **Cerco un treno con un orario comodo per andare a Roma.** *I'm looking for a train with a convenient schedule to go to Rome.*

→ Its opposite is **scomodo/a** *uncomfortable, inconvenient*: **C'è un treno alle sei del mattino, ma è un orario un po' scomodo.** *There's a train at 6:00 in the morning, but it's a time that's a bit inconvenient.* The verb **scomodare** *to inconvenience, to disturb* derives from this word; its reflexive form is **scomodarsi** *to go out of one's way, to put oneself out*: **Si è scomodato venendo fin qui.** *He went out of his way to come* ('coming') *all the way here.*

THE PREPOSITION *DA*: CONVEYING FINALITY

Among its many uses, **da** is employed to indicate finality, i.e. the destination of an object or the final goal of an action, as in **i documenti da firmare** *the documents to sign* (i.e. that must be signed); **Queste non sono cose da dire.** *These are not things one should say.*

SE + FUTURE

In contrast to English, the future tense can be used in a **se** *if* clause in Italian (we use the present tense in this context): **Se domani farà bello, andremo al mare.** ('If tomorrow it-will-make beautiful, we-will-go to-the sea.') *If it is nice tomorrow, we'll go to the sea.* **Se comunicherà l'IBAN ai vari fornitori, potrà appunto pagare.** ('If you-will-communicate the-IBAN to-the various suppliers, you-will-be-able-to quite-so pay.') *If you give your IBAN to the various service providers, you can pay that way.* In lesson 27, we'll see that this is one of the ways to form conditional sentences.

CULTURAL NOTE

If you'll be staying in Italy for a longer period than a holiday, you may want to open a bank account there. Most transactions in Italy these days are done electronically: employees receive their salaries by bank transfer, and **le bollette** *bills* for regular monthly services are typically paid by direct debit or **bonifico automatico** *automatic bank transfer*. To withdraw money from an ATM or pay for purchases, **il bancomat** *debit card* is the usual option – the payment is immediately debited from one's account. The term **il bancomat** is also used to refer to a *cash machine, ATM*. As for **la carta di credito** *credit card*, this payment method is mostly used for buying things online. Banks are typically open Monday to Friday from 8:30 to 1:30 and then after lunch from 3:00 to 4:30. However, today there are far fewer bank branches in cities than formerly, as most customers do their banking transactions online.

▲ CONJUGATION
THE FUTURE TENSE

To describe an event that is going to happen at a later date, the future tense is used: **Andrò in Italia.** *I will go to Italy.* (However, if an event is definitely going to happen in the near future, the present tense is usually used in Italian: **Vado in Italia domani.** *I'm going to Italy tomorrow.*)

For verbs that are regular in the future tense, the first group (**-are**) and second group (**-ere**) have the same conjugation. The third group (**-ire**) varies slightly, as the conjugation ending starts with an **i**. Here are the regular future conjugations:

	-are verbs	**-ere** verbs	**-ire** verbs
	parlare *to speak*	**prendere** *to take*	**finire** *to finish*
io	**parlerò** *I will speak*	**prenderò**	**finirò**
tu	**parlerai** *you will speak* (informal sing.)	**prenderai**	**finirai**
lui, lei, Lei	**parlerà** *he/she will speak, you will speak* (formal sing.)	**prenderà**	**finirà**
noi	**parleremo** *we will speak*	**prenderemo**	**finiremo**
voi	**parlerete** *you will speak* (plural)	**prenderete**	**finirete**
loro, Loro	**parleranno** *they will speak, you will speak* (formal pl.)	**prenderanno**	**finiranno**

THE FUTURE TENSE OF VERBS ENDING IN *-CARE* AND *-GARE*

As we saw for the present tense, verbs ending in **-care** and **-gare** insert an **h** before a conjugation ending beginning with an **-i** in order to retain the hard [k] or [g] sound. In the future tense, the same thing occurs before the conjugation endings beginning with an **-e**. So the future forms of the verb **scaricare** *to download* are as follows: **scaricherò** *I will download*, **scaricherai, scaricherà, scaricheremo, scaricherete, scaricheranno**. The future of **pagare** *to pay* is **pagherò** *I will pay*, **pagherai, pagherà, pagheremo, pagherete, pagheranno.**

SOME COMMON VERBS THAT ARE IRREGULAR IN THE FUTURE

In the future tense, any irregularities occur in the verb stem – the conjugation endings are always regular. The irregularity in the stem is found in all persons, so that simplifies things. Here are some of the most frequently used verbs that are irregular in the future tense given in the first-person singular:
andrò *I will go* **(andrai** *you will go*, **andrà** *he/she/it will go*, etc.**) (andare); darò** *I will give* **(dare); farò** *I will do, make* **(fare); starò** *I will be* **(stare); berrò** *I will drink* **(bere); proporrò** *I will suggest, propose* **(proporre); rimarrò** *I will stay, remain* **(rimanere); saprò** *I will know* **(sapere); terrò** *I will hold, grasp* **(tenere); vedrò** *I will see* **(vedere); vivrò** *I will live* **(vivere); verrò** *I will come* **(venire)**.

Note that in Italian the modal auxiliary verbs (*must, should, can*) also conjugate in the future tense: **dovrò avere un conto** *I will need to have an account*, **le potrà fare tramite l'*home banking*** *you will be able to do it via online banking*. These verbs are also irregular in the future tense. Here they are in the first-person singular: **dovrò** *I will have to* **(dovere); potrò** *I will be able to* **(potere); vorrò** *I will want to* **(volere)**.

EXERCISES

1. COMPLETE THE SENTENCES WITH THE CORRECT FORM OF THE FUTURE TENSE.

a. Al nostro arrivo *(arrival)* in Italia .... un conto bancario. (aprire)

b. Signora, domattina .... i documenti che ho preparato per Lei? (firmare)

c. Questo negozio .... alle diciannove e trenta. (chiudere)

d. I miei genitori *(parents)*...................................... la settimana prossima. (arrivare)

VOCABULARY

accreditare *to credit*
l'acqua *water*
l'acquisto *purchase*
(**gli acquisti** *purchases)*
l'addebito *debit, charge*
appunto *indeed, exactly, quite so*
l'assegno *cheque*
(**gli assegni** *cheques)*
avere bisogno di *to need*
la banca *bank*
bastare *to suffice*
la bolletta *bill* (**le bollette** *bills)*
il bonifico *bank transfer*
il canone *TV licence fee*
il cellulare *mobile phone*
il computer *computer*
comunicare *to communicate, to convey, to transmit*
i contanti *cash*
il conto bancario *bank account*
il datore di lavoro *employer*
direttamente *directly*
i documenti *documents, identification*
domattina *tomorrow morning*
domiciliare *to establish legal residence* (**il domicilio** *domicile, residence)*
dunque *so, therefore*
emettere *to emit, to issue*
firmare *to sign*
il fornitore *supplier*
(**i fornitori** *suppliers)*
il gas *gas*
immediato/a *immediate*
l'importo *amount*
la luce *light, electricity*
l'operazione *operation*
(**le operazioni** *operations)*
il pagamento *payment*
prelevare *to withdraw, to get*
il prelievo *withdrawal* (also *blood sample*) (**i prelievi** *withdrawals)*
preparare *to prepare*
la questione *question, problem, matter, issue*
(**le questioni** *issues, matters)*
la ricarica telefonica *telephone top-up (for prepaid phone cards)*
sia... sia *both ... and, whether ... or*
la spesa *expense, cost, purchase* (also *grocery shopping*)
(**le spese** *expenses)*
lo stipendio *salary*
successivo/a *next, subsequent, following*
la tassa *tax* (**le tasse** *taxes)*
il telefono *telephone*
usare *to use*
versare *to deposit* (also *to pour*)
verso *towards, close to*

2. COMPLETE THESE SENTENCES WITH THE CORRECT FORM OF THE FUTURE TENSE (THESE ARE IRREGULAR VERBS).

a. Se vieni da me, ... conoscere la mia famiglia. (potere)

b. Se posso, domattina .... a firmare quei documenti. (venire)

c. Per ricevere il vostro stipendio, ... aprire un conto bancario. (dovere)

d. Durante le nostre prossime vacanze, ... molte città italiane. (vedere)

3. TRANSLATE THESE SENTENCES INTO ITALIAN.

a. We will speak to him. → ....

b. You (pl.) will go there. → ....

c. You will sign it, sir. → ....

d. They will have to do it. → ....

15 4. LISTEN TO THE RECORDING AND FILL IN THE MISSING WORDS.

a. Con il bancomat potrà .... contanti.

b. Venga domattina a .... i documenti che Le ho preparato.

c. Ho appena ricevuto la .... della luce: è altissima!

14. MAKING A CLAIM (AT THE POST OFFICE)

FARE UN RECLAMO (ALL'UFFICIO POSTALE)

AIMS	TOPICS
• MAKING A CLAIM OR COMPLAINT	• WORD ORDER OF OBJECT PRONOUNS USED TOGETHER
• CLARIFYING A MISUNDERSTANDING	• SPECIAL FORMS OF THE FEMININE
• THANKING SOMEONE FOR THE QUALITY OF THE SERVICE	• TALKING ABOUT AN IMMINENT ACTION

A REGISTERED LETTER

Francesco: Hello, ma'am. I need to make a claim.

Employee: What kind of claim, may I ask?

Francesco: It's for a registered [letter] that was never *(has never been)* delivered to the addressee.

Employee: Excuse me, but who told you *(to-you-it-has told)* that it was this counter?

Francesco: Your colleague at window 12 *(it has)* told me. Why? It's not here?

Employee: No, but it's okay, I'll handle it *(of-it I-think me)*. Do you have the receipt of the registered [letter]?

Francesco: Here it is.

Employee: Give it to me, please, so I [can] check if there has been a problem. (…) No, I'm sorry, it's not in *(among)* the unsent letters *(the post not sent)*. Please fill in this form, and I hope that in a few days we will be able to give you a response.

Francesco: Thank you so much. *(Seen)* As you are so nice, I also *(would)* need to do another operation. I have to send a couple of letters overseas. Can you weigh them for me?

Employee: Of course! *(You-do a)* Registered or [shall] we send them by first-class post?

Francesco: One is a registered [letter] with advice of receipt *(receipt of return)*; the other, let's go ahead and send it by ordinary post, it's nothing important.

Employee: Fine *(Yes)*, however, I advise you to write the address of the sender on the envelope, one never knows …

Francesco: Do I need to buy the stamps and stick them on myself?

Employee: No, no, we will postmark [them] *(there we-put a postmark)* and they will be dispatched *(they-leave)* immediately.

Francesco: Ah, I was about to forget *(I-was to forget)* something very important: I also need *(to-make)* a money order. I have to pay a fine ...

Employee: We'll do this as well *(Now we-do also this)*.

Francesco: You are really very nice! I will never again *(more)* speak badly about post offices and postal workers!

Employee: Good for you, give us some *(of-it make a bit of)* good publicity, we need it *(of-it we-have need)*! Here we hear all kinds of things *(Here to-us about-it they-say everything of all the colours)*!

16 UNA LETTERA RACCOMANDATA

Francesco: Buongiorno, signora, devo fare un reclamo.

Impiegata: Che tipo di reclamo, scusi?

Francesco: È per una raccomandata che non è mai stata recapitata al destinatario.

Impiegata: Ma chi Gliel'ha detto, scusi, che era a questo sportello?

Francesco: Me l'ha detto la Sua collega dello sportello dodici. Perché? Non è qui?

Impiegata: No, ma va bene, ci penso io. Ha la ricevuta della raccomandata?

Francesco: Eccola qui.

Impiegata: Me la dia, per favore, così verifico se c'è stato un problema. (…) No, mi dispiace, non è tra la posta non inoltrata. Per favore, compili questo modulo, e spero che tra qualche giorno potremo darLe una risposta.

Francesco: Grazie mille. Visto che è così gentile, dovrei fare anche un'altra operazione. Devo spedire un paio di lettere all'estero. Me le può pesare?

Impiegata: Certo! Fa una raccomandata o le mandiamo in posta prioritaria?

Francesco: Una è una raccomandata con ricevuta di ritorno; l'altra mandiamola pure in posta ordinaria, non è nulla di importante.

Impiegata: Sì, però Le consiglio di scrivere l'indirizzo del mittente sulla busta, non si sa mai…

Francesco: Devo comprare i francobolli e incollarceli io?

Impiegata: No no, ci mettiamo un timbro noi e partono subito.

Francesco: Ah, stavo per dimenticare una cosa importantissima: devo anche fare un vaglia. Devo pagare una multa...

Impiegata: Adesso facciamo anche questo.

Francesco: Lei è davvero gentilissima! Non parlerò mai più male delle poste e dei postini!

Impiegata: Bravo, ci faccia un po' di buona pubblicità, ne abbiamo bisogno! Qui ce ne dicono tutti di tutti i colori!

UNDERSTANDING THE DIALOGUE
ECCO WITH OBJECT PRONOUNS

Object pronouns (the weak forms) can be attached to **ecco**, an adverb that means *here* or *there* and is also used as an exclamation that can mean *Here it is! Here you are! That's it!* etc. For example: **Eccomi!** *Here I am!* **Eccoti qui!** *Here you are!* **Eccola qui.** *Here it is.* (referring to the feminine noun **la ricevuta** *receipt*). Don't forget that an object pronoun needs to agree with the gender of the noun it refers to.

C'È, CI SONO IN THE PRESENT PERFECT

A reminder that **c'è** *there is* and **ci sono** *there are* are formed with **ci** + the verb **essere** in the third-person singular or plural. So in the present perfect, they become **c'è stato** (m.) / **stata** (f.) *there was, there has been* and **ci sono stati** (m.) / **state** (f.), *there were, there have been.* The verb **essere** forms the present perfect with itself, and as you know this auxiliary verb requires the past participle to agree with the subject: **C'è stato un problema.** *There has been a problem.* **Ci sono stati dei problemi.** *There have been some problems.* **C'è stata una festa.** *There was a party.* **Ci sono state delle feste.** *There were some parties.*

UN PAIO

While **un paio** means *a pair*, it is often used in the sense of *a couple*: **un paio di lettere** *a couple of letters*, **un paio di giorni** *a couple of days*.

CULTURAL NOTE

A letter sent **posta prioritaria** *priority* or *first-class post* is supposed to arrive 24 hours after it is sent. In fact, this is the standard, so it is essentially the same thing as sending a letter by **posta ordinaria** *regular post*. Like anywhere, next-day delivery is not always guaranteed!

GRAMMAR
WORD ORDER OF OBJECT PRONOUNS USED TOGETHER

• When an indirect and direct object pronoun are used together, the indirect object (usually a person) or reflexive pronoun always comes first. In addition, its final **-i** becomes **-e** in this case: **Mi dici questo.** ('To-me you-tell this.) *You tell me this.* → **Me lo dici.** ('To-me it you-tell.) *You tell it to me.*

• The same thing occurs if the direct object is **ne** *of it*: **mi dai** *you give me* → **me ne dai** *you give me some of it*.

• When the indirect object pronoun is **gli** *to him, to them*, the direct object pronoun is attached to it with the letter **e** inserted between them: **Gliene diamo.** *We give some of it to him/them.* But note that when the feminine **le** and the formal **Le** are paired with a direct object pronoun, they also become **gli**, so this same form is used whoever the indirect object is: **Glielo diciamo.** *We tell it to him/to her/to them/to you* (formal).

• The same change from **-i** to **-e** occurs with **ci** when it means *there*: **Ce li incollo io?** ('There them I-stick me?') *It's up to me to stick them on?* **Devo incollarceli io?** *Do I need to stick them on myself?*

• Here are all the combinations:

Indirect object or reflexive pronouns	Direct object pronouns				
	lo	**la**	**li**	**le**	**ne**
mi	**me lo**	**me la**	**me li**	**me le**	**me ne**
ti	**te lo**	**te la**	**te li**	**te le**	**te ne**
gli, le, Le	**glielo**	**gliela**	**glieli**	**gliele**	**gliene**
si	**se lo**	**se la**	**se li**	**se le**	**se ne**
ci	**ce lo**	**ce la**	**ce li**	**ce le**	**ce ne**
vi	**ve lo**	**ve la**	**ve li**	**ve le**	**ve ne**
gli	**glielo**	**gliela**	**glieli**	**gliele**	**gliene**

Remember that when a direct object is placed before the verb, the past participle needs to agree with it in number and gender: **Ce li hai dati.** *You have given them* (m.) *to us.* **Ce le hai date.** *You have given them* (f.) *to us.* The same is true with the direct object **ne** *of it, of them*, which can refer to a singular or plural, masculine or feminine noun: **Ti abbiamo chiesto delle patate e ce ne hai date.** *We asked you for potatoes and you have given us some* (f.). **Ti abbiamo chiesto dei biscotti e non ce ne hai dati.** *We asked you for biscuits and you didn't give us any* (m.).

SPECIAL FEMININE FORMS

Some masculine nouns end in **-a** – these don't change in the feminine: **il / la collega** *colleague*. This is the case for professions ending in **-ista**, such as **il/la giornalista** *journalist*, **il/la fisioterapista** *physical therapist*. However, while the singular form is the same, the plural forms are different: **i colleghi, le colleghe** *colleagues* (m./f.).

▲ VERBS
TALKING ABOUT AN IMMINENT ACTION

As we've seen, in Italian the present tense is often used to talk about an action that is expected to definitely occur in the near future. In this lesson's dialogue, there are two ways to express an imminent action (*to be about to* or *now let's ...*) .

→ **stare** (conjugated) + **per** + infinitive *to be about to do something*: **Stiamo per arrivare.** *We're about to arrive.* **Sto per perdere la pazienza.** *I'm about to lose my patience.*

→ **adesso** or **ora** (*now*) + verb conjugated in the present tense: **Adesso facciamo anche questo.** *Let's do that now as well.*

⬢ EXERCISES

1. REWRITE THESE SENTENCES, REPLACING THE NOUNS/PRONOUNS WITH THE CORRECT OBJECT PRONOUN COMBINATION (SEE THE TABLE ON PAGE 139).

Example: Leggo un libro a mio figlio. → Glielo leggo.

a. Avete mandato *(sent)* un pacco *(package)* a noi. → ....

b. Signora, chiedo a Lei questa informazione. → ....

c. Parliamo a voi di questo problema. → ....

d. Verseranno lo stipendio agli impiegati. → ....

2. REWRITE THESE PRESENT OR IMPERFECT TENSE SENTENCES TO CONVEY AN IMMINENT ACTION (USING *STARE PER*).

Examples: Partivo per la Francia. Stavo per partire per la Francia.
Prendo la macchina di tuo fratello. Sto per prendere la macchina di tuo fratello.

a. Faccio un lavoro difficile.
→ ....

b. Mi spieghi *(explain)* la tua situazione.
→ ....

c. Arrivavamo a casa sua.
→ ....

d. Vanno a lavorare.
→ ....

VOCABULARY

la busta *envelope*
il/la collega *colleague*
il colore *colour (***i colori** *colours)*
compilare *to fill in (a form)*
la cosa *thing*
il destinatario /la destinataria *addressee, recipient*
l'estero *overseas, abroad* (**estero/a** *foreign)*
il francobollo *postage stamp* (**i francobolli** *stamps)*
incollare *to stick*
inoltrare *to send, to convey*
la lettera *letter*
mandare *to send*
il mittente *sender*
il modulo *form*
la multa *fine, ticket*
non si sa mai *one never knows*
nulla *nothing, none, any*
l'operazione *operation*
ordinario/a *ordinary, regular*
il pacco *package, packet*
la posta *mail, post, postal service, post office*
il postino / la postina *postman, postwoman* (**i postini** *postal workers)*
la pubblicità *publicity, advertising*
prioritario/a *priority, first class* (adj.)
la raccomandata *registered letter, recorded delivery*
recapitare *to deliver (letters)*
il reclamo *claim, complaint*
la ricevuta *receipt*
la ricevuta di ritorno *advice of receipt (***il ritorno** *return)*
la risposta *response, reply, answer*
spedire *to send, to mail, to ship*
spiegare *to explain*
lo sportello *counter, window*
il timbro *postmark, rubber stamp*
il tipo *type, kind, sort*
il vaglia *money order*
verificare *to verify, to check*

3. TRANSLATE THESE SENTENCES INTO ITALIAN.

a. He hasn't said it (m.) to me.
→ ....

b. You (pl.) put them (m.) there.
→ ....

c. They have spoken to you (pl.) about it (m.).
→ ....

d. We will buy it (m.) from them.
→ ....

4. REWRITE THESE PRESENT-TENSE SENTENCES IN THE PRESENT PERFECT. (REMEMBER THAT THE PAST PARTCIPLE HAS TO AGREE WITH THE DIRECT OBJECT!)

a. Ce li danno. → ....

b. Ve le prendono. → ....

c. Glieli leggono. → ....

d. Me la comprano. → ....

15. A JOB INTERVIEW

IL COLLOQUIO DI LAVORO

AIMS

- TALKING ABOUT YOUR JOB EXPERIENCE
- DESCRIBING WHAT A JOB ENTAILS
- USING BASIC BUSINESS VOCABULARY

TOPICS

- WORD ORDER OF OBJECT PRONOUNS WITH AN IMPERATIVE, INFINITIVE OR PRESENT PARTICIPLE
- THE FUTURE PERFECT
- THE FUTURE USED TO EXPRESS DOUBT OR PROBABILITY

A FAMILY BUSINESS

Mr Bandini: Welcome, miss, to the company Bandini Ltd. I am very happy to meet *(receive)* you.

Simona: The pleasure is mine, sir *(doctor)*.

Mr B: We've read your CV in detail *(with much attention)*, and it seems to correspond exactly to what we're looking for *(to-us it-has seemed in everything corresponding to our research)*.

Simona: I'm happy to hear it *(To-me it-makes much pleasure)*. I find the job profile that you are offering very interesting as well.

Mr B: You haven't been *(You not are)* here in Varese for long, have you?

Simona: Uh, I've been living here for three years *(they-are three years that here I-live)*. Before I was in Mantua.

Mr B: Ah, it's true, excuse me. [As I was] saying it to you, I realized *(myself I-am given account)* that I was *(to-you)* speaking *(a)* nonsense. It's written in your CV!

Simona: Yes, I used to work for a very large firm, but *(too)* big companies are *(do)* not for me.

Mr B: Then ours will suit you perfectly *(will-do exactly the case)*: we are a typical long-standing family business *(of old date)*. My father wanted to entrust it to me when he retired *(has gone on pension)*. When you see *(will-have seen)* how we work *(one works)* here, you will fall in love with us!

Simona: And if I may ask, what salary are you offering for this *(my)* post of accountant?

Mr B: Well, on hiring we offer average salaries – not very high – but that can progress *(evolve)* with one's *(the)* career.

Simona: And the *(as)* hours?

Mr B: The office opens at 8:00 and closes at 6:00 *(18)*, with a break [for] lunch in the middle. Here we clock in *(one stamps the timecard)*, so [what's] important is to do your 40 weekly hours … and [that] the work [is] done well! We aim *(hold)* to have flexible hours: *(a)* part of an afternoon free is *(does)* always useful. Holidays, however, *(at ours)* are in August.

Simona: The ad in the newspaper didn't specify if it is *(was)* a short-term or permanent contract *(time fixed or indeterminate)*.You'll understand, sir, that a permanent *(fixed)* position is attractive *(makes gluttony)* to everyone …

Mr B: At the beginning, of course, it will be short-term, but when you *(will)* have completed *(done)* the trial period, if we're satisfied with you, you will be promoted to a permanent position.

17 UN’AZIENDA FAMILIARE

Signor Bandini: Benvenuta, signorina, alla ditta “Bandini S.p.A.”, sono davvero lieto di riceverLa.

Simona: Il piacere è mio, dottore.

Signor Bandini: Abbiamo letto il Suo curriculum vitae con molta attenzione, e ci è sembrato del tutto corrispondente alla nostra ricerca.

Simona: Mi fa molto piacere. Anche il profilo del posto che offrite, lo trovo molto interessante.

Signor Bandini: Lei non sta qui a Varese da molto, vero?

Simona: Beh, saranno tre anni che ci abito. Prima stavo a Mantova.

Signor Bandini: Sì, è vero, mi scusi. DicendoGlielo, mi sono reso conto che Le dicevo una sciocchezza. È scritto nel Suo curricolo!

Simona: Sì, lavoravo in un gruppo molto importante, ma le imprese troppo grandi non fanno per me.

Signor Bandini: Allora la nostra farà proprio al caso Suo, noi siamo una classica azienda familiare di vecchia data. Mio padre ha voluto affidarmela quando è andato in pensione. Quando avrà visto come si lavora qui, si innamorerà di noi!

Simona: E scusi, che stipendio proponete per il mio posto di ragioniera?

Signor Bandini: Beh, all’assunzione proponiamo stipendi medi, non altissimi, che però potranno evolvere con la carriera.

Simona: E come orari?

Signor Bandini: L’ufficio apre alle otto e chiude alle diciotto, con una pausa pranzo in mezzo. Qui si timbra il cartellino, quindi l’importante è fare le Sue quaranta ore settimanali… e il lavoro ben fatto! Teniamo ad avere orari flessibili: un pezzo di pomeriggio libero fa sempre comodo. Le ferie, invece, da noi sono in agosto.

Simona: L’annuncio sul giornale non specificava se era un contratto a tempo determinato o indeterminato. Lei capirà, dottore, che il posto fisso fa gola a tutti…

Signor Bandini: All’inizio naturalmente sarà determinato, ma quando avrà fatto il periodo di prova, se siamo soddisfatti di Lei, passerà a tempo indeterminato.

UNDERSTANDING THE DIALOGUE
APPROPRIATE LANGUAGE FOR FORMAL CONTEXTS

In a job interview, the register is more formal than in everyday situations, right from the outset: **Sono lieto/a di riceverLa.** *I'm* (m./f.) *glad you could make it.* The polite reply is: **Il piacere è mio.** *The pleasure is mine.* As you'll have noticed in the lessons, it is still common to use titles such as **signore** and **signora** in Italy. The titles **dottore/dottoressa** are used for anyone who has a university degree, not just for those with a medical degree.

SOME IDIOMATIC EXPRESSIONS

→ **Mi fa molto piacere.** ('To-me it-does much pleasure.') *I'm very happy to hear it.*

→ The way to say you have been doing something for a period of time is constructed with the present tense (rather than the present perfect) in Italian: **Saranno tre anni che ci abito.** ('They-are three years that here I-live.') *I've been living here for three years.*

→ The equivalent of *to realize* is **rendersi conto di** ('to give-oneself account of'). So in the past this would be, for example: **mi sono reso conto** *I realized.*

→ **fare per** + pronoun is the equivalent of *to suit someone,* i.e. to correspond with their wishes, personality or tastes: **Questo lavoro non fa per me.** *This work is not for me.* (in the sense of not being suitable).

→ In a similar way, **fare al caso** + possessive means *to be just what is needed, to be perfectly suitable*: **Questo attrezzo fa al caso mio.** *This tool is just what I need.* Another similar expression is **fare comodo a qualcuno** *to be useful to someone*: **Un po' di soldi prima delle vacanze fanno sempre comodo.** *A little money* (pl.) *before a vacation is always handy.* **Dici questo solo perché ti fa comodo.** *You say that only because it suits you.*

→ The principal meaning of the verb **tenere** is *to hold, to keep*, but **tenere a** means *to attach importance to, to care about, to be keen on*: **teniamo ad avere** *we consider it important to have* (remember that **a** → **ad** before a vowel).

→ The expression **fare gola** (literally, 'to make greedy') means *to be tempting, to be attractive.*

TIMBRARE IL CARTELLINO

This is the Italian expression for *to punch the clock*: **timbrare il cartellino** ('to stamp the timecard') (today these are usually swipe cards).

CULTURAL NOTE

Youth unemployment is one of the most concerning aspects of Italian society today: since 2010, the number of those under the age of 30 without work has increased to over a million. One of the worst impacts is that the lack of job offers has led to a dramatic drop in the hopes of many young people of ever finding a decent job, with the result that nearly 20% are neither studying nor looking for work. This situation particularly affects young people without a secondary school diploma in the south of Italy, but the outlook is not much brighter for those with a **laurea** *university degree*, many of whom emigrate not only to find a job, but to obtain a salary that corresponds to their level of education. Some 13,000 **laureati** *degree holders* have gone abroad since 2013, or a total of 82,000 young Italians with all types of educational backgrounds.

GRAMMAR
WORD ORDER OF OBJECT PRONOUNS WITH THE IMPERATIVE, INFINITIVE AND PRESENT PARTICIPLE

As we've seen, object pronouns (weak forms) are attached to the end of an imperative, infinitive or a present participle. The word order remains the same: the indirect object always comes before the direct object:

→ Imperative: **Diglielo.** ('Say to-him it.') *Say it to him* (or *her* or *them*). (**tu** imperative) **Ditemelo.** *Say it to me.* (**voi** imperative). However, in the formal (**Lei**) imperative, the object pronouns come before the verb: **Me lo dica.** *Say it to me.* With single-syllable **tu** imperatives, the pronoun's first consonant is doubled (except for **gli**): **Dimmelo.** *Say it to me.* **Faccelo.** *Do it for us.*

→ Infinitive (note that the infinitive loses its final vowel when the pronoun is attached to it): **Ha voluto affidarmela.** *He wanted to entrust it* (f.) *to me.* However, when two verbs are used together (as in the example above), the position of the object pronouns is optional: these can either be attached to the infinitive or placed before the conjugated verb: **Ha voluto affidarmela.** or **Me l'ha voluta affidare.** *He wanted to entrust it* (f.) *to me*. **Voglio parlargliene.** or **Gliene voglio parlare.** *I want to talk to him/her/them/you* (formal) *about it.*

→ Present participle: **dicendoglielo** *saying it to him/her/them/you* (formal). Note that the addition of the object pronoun(s) doesn't change the original word stress of the verb: in **dicendo** → **dicendoglielo**, the stress remains on **cen**. The same is true for infinitives and imperatives: **Parlate!** *Speak!* (pl.) → **Parlatemene!** *Speak to me about it!* **Andatevene!** *Go away!* (pl.)

▲ CONJUGATION
THE FUTURE PERFECT

The future perfect is used to describe a completed action or event that will have occurred at an earlier point than a future time being spoken about. It is formed with the auxiliary verb **avere** (or with certain verbs, **essere**) conjugated in the future tense + past participle: **Prima di domani, avrò finito il libro.** *Before tomorrow, I will have finished the book.* **A che ora sarà arrivata?** *What time will she have arrived?*

Note that in Italian, the future perfect is used in *after*... and *when*... clauses, whereas in English the present perfect is used in this case: **Dopo avrò finito di lavorare, andrò al cinema.** *After I've* ('will-have') *finished working, I'll go to the cinema.* **Quando avrà visto come si lavora qui...** *When you've* ('will-have') *seen how we work here....*

THE FUTURE USED TO EXPRESS DOUBT OR PROBABILITY

The future is often used in Italian to convey uncertain information or to make a guess, contexts in which *must, might* or *could* would be used in English: **Che ore saranno?** *What time could it be?* **Saranno le tre.** *It might be 3:00.* **Sarà stanco dopo ieri sera.** *He must be tired after last night.*

If talking about uncertain information in the past, the future perfect would be used: **Non so, saranno state le tre.** *I don't know, it must have been 3:00.*

⬢ EXERCISES

1. REWRITE THESE SENTENCES, REPLACING THE NOUNS/PRONOUNS WITH THE CORRECT OBJECT PRONOUN COMBINATION (SEE THE TABLE ON PAGE 139).

Example: Devi portare questo libro ai tuoi colleghi. Devi portarglielo.

a. Voglio parlare a te di questo problema. Voglio ....

b. Non possiamo chiedere questa informazione a voi. Non possiamo ....

c. Mi piace preparare questa specialità a te. Mi piace ....

d. Portate a noi quei documenti. ....

VOCABULARY

affidare *to entrust*
altissimo/a *very high*
l'annuncio *advertisement*
l'assunzione *hiring, employment*
l'attenzione *attention*
l'azienda *company, business, firm*
ben fatto/a *well done, properly done*
la carriera *career*
il cartellino *timecard*
il caso *case, instance*
il contratto *contract*
corrispondente *corresponding*
il curricolo / il curriculum vitae *CV, resumé*
la data *date (calendar)*
determinato/a *determined, fixed*
la ditta *company, firm*
evolvere *to evolve, to develop, to progress*
familiare *family, domestic* (adj.)
fare piacere *to please, to make happy (***il piacere** *pleasure)*
le ferie *holidays, vacation time, leave from work* (pl.)
fisso/a *fixed, unmovable, steady, permanent*
flessibile *flexible*
il giornale *newspaper*
l'impresa *company, business, firm (***le imprese** *companies)*
indeterminato/a *indeterminate, unspecified*
l'inizio *beginning, start*
innamorarsi *to fall in love*
lieto/a *happy, content*
medio/a *average (***medi, medie** (m. pl., f. pl.)*)*
offrire *to offer*
il periodo di prova *trial period (***la prova** *test, trial)*
un pezzo *piece, part*
il posto *position, job*
il profilo *profile*
raccontare *to tell, to recount*
il ragioniere / la ragioniera *accountant*
rendersi conto *to realize*
la ricerca *research*
ricevere *to receive*
la sciocchezza *slip-up, foolishness, stupidity*
sembrare *to seem*
settimanale *weekly*
soddisfatto/a *satisfied*
specificare *to specify*
stanco/a *tired (***stanchi/e** (pl.)*)*
tornare *to return, to come back*
vecchio/a *old*

2. REWRITE THESE SENTENCES USING THE FUTURE TO CONVEY THAT THE INFORMATION IS UNCERTAIN.

Examples: Forse sono le quattro. → Saranno le quattro.

Forse erano le quattro. → Saranno state le quattro.

a. A quest'ora forse dormono. → ....

b. Forse è gia arrivata a casa. → ....

c. Forse hai preso il raffreddore.→ ....

d. Forse non parlano italiano. → ....

3. TRANSLATE THESE PHRASES INTO ITALIAN.

a. Tell it (m.) to him. (**tu**) → ....

b. Put it (m.) on. (**voi** imperative of **mettersi**) → ....

c. Saying it (m.) to you ... (**tu**) → ....

d. Give it (f.) to them. (**tu**) → ....

4. COMPLETE THE SENTENCES WITH THE CORRECT FORM OF THE FUTURE PERFECT OF THE VERB GIVEN IN PARENTHESES.

a. Ti racconterò tutto quando .... (tornare) dalle vacanze. (a male speaking)

b. Apriremo un conto bancario quando .... (ricevere) il primo stipendio.

c. Vi inviteranno quando .... (trovare) un appartamento più grande.

d. Cercherete un lavoro quando .... (finire) l'università.

16. ATTENDING A WORK MEETING

PARTECIPARE A UNA RIUNIONE DI LAVORO

AIMS

- PARTICIPATING IN A WORKPLACE CONVERSATION
- BUSINESS VOCABULARY

TOPICS

- RELATIVE PRONOUNS
- THE PASSIVE VOICE
- THE IMPERSONAL *SI*

THE BOARD OF DIRECTORS

Ms Luchetti: Mr Volpi, you know, don't you, that this afternoon *(there)* is the meeting of the board of directors *(council of administration)* in which the balance sheet will be approved *(one will-approve the balance)*? As [the] new manager of the sales division *(sector)*, you are expected *(held)* to participate *(there)*. The CEO *(delegated administrator)* will describe the commercial strategy that is going to be *(will-go)* followed in the coming months.

Mr Volpi: Of course, Ms Luchetti, I have already noted *(signalled)* it in [my] agenda.

Ms L: The new products to be launched on the market next season [and] the domestic appliances that I spoke to you about yesterday will also be presented. This presentation of the new catalogue is *(comes)* done each year in May, for the launch in October, although *(even if)* certain years it is done later.

Mr V: How many will we be at the meeting?

Ms L: There will surely be Mr Sani, the CEO, the chairman of the board, the vice-chairman and the managing director, [and] then the different board members *(councillors)*, and the directors in charge of *(the sectors)* purchasing, personnel, marketing and media, and, of course, you for sales. I advise you to read the minutes from the previous meeting: many issues that were discussed in that [meeting] will be taken up again *(retaken)* tomorrow.

Mr V: Do you remember which topics were discussed?

Ms L: Well, many things were discussed, now I can't remember *(not myself I-recall)* exactly: we *(one)* must have talked about marketing, the profitability of the branches, turnover ... the usual things!

Mr V: Will the problem that you spoke to me about last week, the merger with Eurodomestici, be dealt with *(confronted)* as well?

Ms L: I don't *(about-it)* have the slightest idea, nothing has been said concerning that *(to this purpose)*.

Mr V: You don't seem very interested in business activity *(life)*, or am I mistaken *(myself I-make-mistake)*?

Ms L: That's exactly right *(Just so)*!

18 IL CONSIGLIO DI AMMINISTRAZIONE

Signora Luchetti: Signor Volpi, sa, vero, che oggi pomeriggio c'è la riunione del consiglio di amministrazione in cui si approverà il bilancio? Come nuovo responsabile del settore vendite, Lei è tenuto a parteciparvi. L'amministratore delegato illustrerà la strategia commerciale che andrà seguita nei prossimi mesi.

Signor Volpi: Certamente, dottoressa, l'avevo già segnato in agenda.

Signora Luchetti: Saranno anche presentati i nuovi prodotti da lanciare sul mercato nella prossima stagione, gli elettrodomestici di cui Le ho parlato ieri. Questa presentazione del nuovo catalogo viene fatta ogni anno in maggio, per il lancio in ottobre, anche se certi anni si è fatta più tardi.

Signor Volpi: In quanti saremo alla riunione?

Signora Luchetti: Di sicuro ci saranno il dottor Sani, l'amministratore delegato, il presidente, il vice-presidente e il direttore generale, poi i diversi consiglieri, e i dirigenti responsabili dei settori acquisti, personale, comunicazioni e media, e naturalmente Lei per il settore vendite. Le consiglio di leggere il verbale della riunione precedente, molte questioni di cui si è parlato in quella saranno riprese domani.

Signor Volpi: Si ricorda quali argomenti si sono discussi?

Signora Luchetti: Mah, si sono discusse molte cose, ora non mi ricordo di preciso: si sarà parlato di marketing, di redditività delle filiali, di fatturato... le solite cose!

Signor Volpi: Sarà affrontato anche il problema del quale mi ha parlato la settimana scorsa, la fusione con l'"Eurodomestici"?

Signora Luchetti: Non ne ho la minima idea, non è stato detto niente a questo proposito.

Signor Volpi: Lei non sembra molto interessata alla vita aziendale, o mi sbaglio?

Signora Luchetti: Proprio così!

UNDERSTANDING THE DIALOGUE
VI INSTEAD OF *CI*

The pronoun **ci** with the meaning *there* is sometimes replaced with **vi**: e.g. **parteciparvi** *to participate in it* ('there'). So you might hear **vi sono** rather than **ci sono** *there is*, although **ci** is more common.

GRAMMAR
RELATIVE PRONOUNS

A relative pronoun is used to introduce a clause that gives more information about something previously mentioned in the main clause (e.g. *that, who, which*, etc.). The most common relative pronoun in Italian is **che**. If the relative pronoun follows a preposition, **cui** is used. In more formal contexts, the longer **il quale**, etc. is used.

EVERYDAY SPEECH	MORE FORMAL*
che *that, which, who, when*, etc.	**il quale** (referring to a masc. sing. noun)
preposition + **cui** *of/to/for/with which, whom*, etc.	**la quale** (referring to a fem. sing. noun) **i quali** (referring to a masc. pl. noun) **le quali** (referring to a fem. pl. noun)

* If these forms are used after a preposition, the preposition and the article are contracted.

Here are some examples of relative pronouns you're most likely to hear in everyday speech. Note that in English, in many contexts relative pronouns are omitted (or sentences are rephrased to avoid them), but they are required in Italian.

La persona che parla. *The person who speaks.*
La persona che vedi. *The person that you see.*
La persona a cui abbiamo parlato. *The person to whom we have spoken.*
La persona per cui sono venuto. *The person for whom I have come.*
La persona con cui siamo venuti. *The person with whom we have come.*
La persona di cui ti abbiamo parlato. *The person we spoke to you about* ('about whom to-you we-have spoken').

The more formal option is mainly used in writing.

La persona alla quale abbiamo parlato. *The person to whom we spoke.*
La persona per la quale sono venuto. *The person for whom I came.*
La persona con la quale siamo venuti. *The person with whom we came.*
La persona della quale ti abbiamo parlato. *The person we spoke to you about.*

▲ CONJUGATION
THE PASSIVE VOICE

• In the passive voice, the sentence is constructed so that the subject receives the action of the verb. This can be used to avoid having to identify 'who' is doing the action: for example, if what receives the action is more important than who is doing it (Active: *We discuss the issues.* → Passive: *The issues are being discussed.*). As in English, the passive voice is formed using a conjugated form (in the appropriate tense) of **essere** *to be* + past participle:

Il bilancio è approvato. *The balance sheet is approved.* (present tense of **essere** + past participle of **approvare**: passive voice in the present)

Il bilancio sarà approvato. *The balance sheet will be approved.* (future tense of **essere** + past participle of **approvare**: passive voice in the future)

• The passive voice can also be used in any other tense:

Il bilancio è stato approvato. *The balance sheet has been approved.* (present perfect of **essere** + past participle: passive voice in the present perfect)

Il bilancio sarà stato approvato. *The balance sheet will have been approved.* (future perfect of **essere** + past participle: passive voice in the future perfect)

• In the passive voice, the past participle must agree with the subject:

La direttiva è stata approvata. *The directive has been approved.*

• To indicate who the 'agent' of the action is, the preposition **da** *by* (contracted with the article if there is one) is used: **Il bilancio è stato approvato dal consiglio d'amministrazione.** *The balance sheet has been approved by the board.*

VARIANTS OF THE PASSIVE VOICE

→ In some passive sentences, **venire** *to come* can be used instead of **essere** *to be*: **La presentazione del nuovo catalogo viene fatta in maggio.** *The presentation of the new catalogue is* ('comes') *done in May.* However, if the conjugated form is a compound verb (consisting of more than one verb), **essere** must be used: **La presentazione del nuovo catalogo è stata fatta in maggio.** *The presentation of the new catalogue was done in May*.

→ Another passive construction is formed with the auxiliary verb **andare** *to go*, which is used to express obligation (*to have to be, to need to be*): **La presentazione va fatta / andava fatta in maggio.** *The presentation must be done / had to be done in May.* **Le compresse vanno prese due volte al giorno.** *The tablets must be taken twice a day.*

THE IMPERSONAL *SI*

The impersonal pronoun **si** *one* is another way to avoid specifying exactly who carried out the action, translating in English to the passive voice: **Si fa la presentazione del nuovo catalogo.** *The new catalogue is presented.* ('One it-does the presentation of-the new catalogue.'). In this construction, the verb conjugates in the third-person singular if what receives the action is singular, and in the third-person plural if what receives the action is plural: **Quali argomenti si sono discussi?** *What topics are being* ('they-are') *discussed?* Also note that the past participle functions as an adjective in these cases, so it needs to agree in gender and number with the noun: **Si sono discusse molte cose.** *Many things were discussed.* (**discusse** agrees with the feminine plural **cose**).

The reflexive can also be used in a passive sense, conveying that an action happened to the subject: **Dove si sono nascosti questi biglietti?** *Where are those tickets hidden?* (from the reflexive verb **nascondersi** *to hide oneself*).

Sometimes the impersonal **si** is used before the reflexive pronoun **si**, in which case the former becomes **ci**: **Ci si alza presto.** ('One oneself wakes early.) *One wakes up early.* If the impersonal **si** is used before **ne** *of/about it*, it becomes **se**: **Se ne parla molto.** *People are talking about it a lot.* (In English, it is more common to use the general 'people' than the impersonal pronoun 'one'.)

EXERCISES

1. FORM COMPLETE SENTENCES FROM THE CLAUSES PROVIDED, USING A RELATIVE PRONOUN TO LINK THEM.

Example: Ecco la persona – ti ho parlato di questa persona. →
Ecco la persona di cui ti ho parlato.

a. Ti spiego il problema – sono venuto per questo problema.

→ ....

b. Ti ho portato il libro – mi avevi prestato questo libro.

→ ....

c. Voglio vedere il lavoro – mi avete tanto parlato di questo lavoro.

→ ....

VOCABULARY

affrontare *to confront, to tackle, to deal with*
l'agenda *agenda, work diary*
l'amministratore / l'amministratrice *administrator*
l'amministratore delegato / l'amministratrice delegata *CEO (chief executive officer)*
l'amministrazione *administration*
approvare *to approve*
l'argomento *topic, subject* (**gli argomenti** *topics*)
il bilancio *balance sheet*
il catalogo *catalogue*
commerciale *commercial (having to do with commerce)*
il consigliere / la consigliera *councillor, advisor* (**i consiglieri / le consigliere** *councillors*)
il consiglio di amministrazione *board of directors*
il consiglio *advice, counsel*
delegato/a *delegated*
il direttore generale /la direttrice generale *managing director*
il/la dirigente *director, manager* (**i/le dirigenti** *directors*)
discutere *to discuss*
l'elettrodomestico *domestic appliances*
il fatturato *turnover, revenue*
la filiale *branch, subsidiary*
la fusione *merger*
l'idea *idea*
illustrare *to illustrate, to describe*
lanciare *to launch*
il lancio *launch*
il mercato *market*
minimo/a *smallest, slightest, least*
partecipare *to participate*
precedente *previous, preceding*
presentare *to present*
la presentazione *presentation*
il presidente / la presidentessa *president, chairperson*
il proposito *purpose, intention, aim, subject, topic*
la redditività *profitability*
il/la responsabile *person in charge, manager* (**i/le responsabili** *managers*)
ricordarsi *to remember*
riprendere *to resume, to get back to, to take up again*
la riunione *meeting*
sbagliarsi *to make a mistake*
segnare *to signal, to mark, to highlight, to indicate*
seguire *to follow, to continue*
il settore *sector*
solito/a *usual*
la stagione *season*
la strategia *strategy*
la vendita *sale, trade* (**le vendite** *sales*)
il verbale *minutes (of a meeting), memo*

2. REWRITE THESE SENTENCES IN THE PASSIVE VOICE.

Example: Accompagno mio figlio a scuola. →
Mio figlio è accompagnato a scuola da me.

a. Turisti francesi hanno affittato *(rented)* la mia casa in montagna.

→ ....

b. Molti parlano l'inglese.

→ ....

c. Turisti di tutto il mondo visitano Roma.

→ ....

3. TRANSLATE THESE SENTENCES INTO ENGLISH.

a. Questo lavoro va fatto.

→ ....

b. Non se n'era parlato.

→ ....

c. Si dorme poco.

→ ....

d. È una città da vedere (che va vista).

→ ....

4. COMPLETE THE SENTENCES WITH THE CORRECT FORM OF THE VERB IN THE PASSIVE VOICE IN THE PRESENT PERFECT.

Example: Il bilancio .... (approvare) dal consiglio d'amministrazione.
→ Il bilancio è stato approvato dal consiglio d'amministrazione.

a. La recensione *(review)* al mio libro .... (scrivere) da un famoso giornalista.

b. La mia ditta .... (fondare) da mio nonno *(grandfather)*.

c. Quando è uscito *(came out)*, quel film non .... (capire) da nessuno.

17. ON THE PHONE

AL TELEFONO

AIMS	TOPICS
• MAKING A PHONE CALL • ASKING SOMEONE ABOUT THEIR ACTIVITIES • RESOLVING A MISUNDERSTANDING • SAYING WHAT HAS TO BE DONE	• QUESTION WORDS • EXCLAMATIONS • LOCATING EVENTS IN TIME • EXPRESSING OBLIGATION AND NECESSITY ('TO HAVE TO', 'MUST')

SWAPPING SHIFTS *(exchange of shift)*

Paola: Hello (on phone), who is it *(who speaks)*?

Luca: Hi, it's *(I-am)* Luca.

P: Sorry, I can't hear you very *(not you I-hear)* well. Speak louder!

L: Luca, Luca Medi, don't you recognize me? We work together at the post office!

P: Ah yes! Sorry, Luca, I didn't recognize *(hadn't recognized)* you. I have an old phone that doesn't work very well, and every so often the line cuts off. What *(For what thing)* are you calling about? It's been *(It's)* a while *(piece)* since we've seen each other *(that not each-other we-see)*!

L: Yes, I changed [my] shift a month ago. This week, for example, I'm doing the afternoon, and you're working the morning [shift], right?

P: Yes, but why *(how ever)* did you change shift(s)?

L: I sort of had to *(I've been a bit obligated)*.

P: What? It's not possible! You need *(It's-necessary)* to protest, one mustn't accept everything! You need *(of-it it-is-wanted)* a bit more nerve!

L: No, *(but)* what have you understood? No one made *(has obligated)* me, it was just a manner of speaking! It's because of *(by way of)* my basketball practice *(trainings of basketball)* that they changed [my] schedule.

P: Jeez, what [a] misunderstanding! So *(But)* you play *(at)* basketball? Since when *(For how-much time)*?

L: Since *(From when)* I was little.

P: And how many practices do you have *(do)* per week?

L: Three practices plus a *(the)* game on Saturday or Sunday.

P: What commitment! And how many hours you must devote to it – my goodness!

L: What can I say *(What thing you-want)*, it's my passion!

P: You must be really good then!

L: Well, I manage alright *(myself it I-get-out)*, but unfortunately I haven't succeeded in becoming [a] professional. That requires *(of-it they-are-wanted)* training, perseverance *(constancy)*, and above all a lot of luck!

P: Yes, then perhaps one needs to have natural talents as well … Excuse me *(so much)*, but I can't stay on the phone long because I have to make an important call soon *(within little)*. Could *(Perhaps)* I hang up and call you back in a bit?

L: No, no, I'm also waiting for a call, so *(for that)* I can't leave the phone busy *(occupied)* for long. I just *(simply)* wanted to ask you if you could swap *(do an exchange of)* shift[s] with me Monday: I need the afternoon [off] to go to practice.

P: Oh sure, that's fine, there's no problem: but we need *(it-is-needed)* to tell *(it to)* the boss right away.

L: No, it's not important to tell *(it)* him immediately, I'll send him an email. Thank you so much!

19 SCAMBIO DI TURNO

Paola: Pronto, chi parla?

Luca: Ciao, sono Luca.

Paola: Scusi, non La sento bene. Parli più forte!

Luca: Luca, Luca Medi, non mi riconosci? Lavoriamo insieme all'ufficio postale!

Paola: Ah sì! Scusa, Luca, non ti avevo riconosciuto. Ho un vecchio telefono che non funziona tanto bene, ed ogni tanto cade la linea. Per che cosa mi chiamavi? È un pezzo che non ci vediamo!

Luca: Eh sì, ho cambiato turno un mese fa; questa settimana per esempio io faccio il pomeriggio, e tu lavori di mattina, vero?

Paola: Sì, ma come mai hai cambiato turno?

Luca: Sono stato un po' obbligato.

Paola: Cosa? Non è possibile! Bisogna protestare, non bisogna accettare tutto! Ci vuole un po' più di coraggio!

Luca: No, ma che hai capito? Nessuno mi ha obbligato, era solo un modo di dire! È per via dei miei allenamenti di pallacanestro che hanno cambiato orario.

Paola: Accidenti, che malinteso! Ma tu giochi a pallacanestro? Da quanto tempo?

Luca: Da quando ero piccolo.

Paola: E quanti allenamenti fai alla settimana?

Luca: Tre allenamenti più la partita al sabato o alla domenica.

Paola: Che impegno! E quante ore devi dedicarci, mamma mia!

Luca: Che cosa vuoi, è la mia passione!

Paola: Sarai bravissimo allora!

Luca: Beh, me la cavo, ma purtroppo non sono riuscito a diventare professionista. Ci vogliono allenamento, costanza, e soprattutto tanta fortuna!

Paola: Sì, poi magari bisogna avere anche delle doti naturali... Scusami tanto, ma non posso stare al telefono a lungo perché devo fare una telefonata importante fra poco. Magari riattacco e ti richiamo fra un po'.

Luca: No, no, anch'io aspetto una chiamata, per cui non posso lasciare il telefono occupato a lungo. Volevo semplicemente chiederti se puoi fare uno scambio di turno con me lunedì, ho bisogno del pomeriggio per andare all'allenamento.

Paola: Ah sì, va bene, non c'è nessun problema, ma bisogna dirlo subito al principale.

Luca: No, non importa dirglielo subito, gli mando io una mail. Grazie mille!

UNDERSTANDING THE DIALOGUE

TALKING ON THE TELEPHONE

Here is some useful vocabulary for phone conversations. When someone answers the phone they say **Pronto!**, which literally means *ready*. Another alternative is **Pronto, chi parla?** *Hello, who is it?* The caller replies **Sono ...** *It's* ... ('I-am') and then says who it is: **Sono Carlo.** or **Sono il signor Rossi.** or **Sono io.** *It's me*. While **riattaccare** means *to hang up (the phone)*, the colloquial term for this is **mettere giù** *to put down*. If a call is cut off, the expression is **cadere la linea** ('to-fall/crash the line'): **Scusa, non ti sentivo più, è caduta la linea.** *Excuse me, I couldn't hear you anymore, the line was cut off.*

ASKING 'WHY?' AND THE REPLY

The options for asking the reason for something include **Perché?** *Why?* **Per che cosa?** ('For what thing?') and **Come mai?** ('How ever?'). The latter is often used in the sense of *Why on earth?*

The reply most commonly starts with **perché...** *because*. In the dialogue, we also see **per via di**, which generally means *on account of*. **Perché hai cambiato turno?** *Why have you changed your shift?* **È per via dei miei allenamenti.** *It's on account of my practices.*

LOCATING EVENTS IN TIME

- → To indicate the frequency of an activity, **a** is often used: **tre allenamenti alla settimana** *three practices per week*, **tre volte al giorno** *three times a day*, **una volta al mese** *once a month*.
- → **fa** means *ago*: **10 anni fa** *ten years ago*, **Quanto tempo fa?** *How long ago?*
- → In contexts that would require *since* with the present perfect in English, the present tense is used in Italian: **È un pezzo che non ci vediamo.** *It's been* ('it is') *a while since we've seen* ('that we don't see') *each other.* (Note that the reflexive pronoun can be used to mean *each other.*)

CAVARSELA

This idiom (based on **cavare** *to get out, to extract*) means *to manage, to cope*: **Me la cavo.** *I'm getting on*. **Se l'è cavata bene.** *He/she coped quite well with it*.

CULTURAL NOTE

In Italy today, there are more mobile phones than there are people! Italians more often use their mobile phones than fixed landlines to make phone calls, and smartphones are also becoming the key device for going online.

GRAMMAR
SOME QUESTION WORDS

Let's look at some of the main question words in Italian.

• **Che?** *What? Which?*
Che città italiane hai visitato? *Which Italian cities have you visited?*
Che vuoi? / Che cosa vuoi? *What do you want?*

• **Quale?** (sing.) / **Quali?** (pl.) *What? Which? Which one(s)?*
(This needs to agree with the noun it refers to.)
Quale libro (m.) **/ borsa** (f.)**?** *Which book / bag?*
Quali libri (m.)**/ borse** (f.)**?** *Which books / bags?*

• **Quanto?** / **Quanta?** / **Quanti?** / **Quante?** *How much/many?*
(This needs to agree if used before a noun; before a verb, **quanto** is used.)
Quanti allenamenti fai alla settimana? *How many practices do you have a week?*
Quanto costano questi occhiali? *How much do these glasses cost?*

• **Chi?** *Who?*
Pronto, chi parla? *Hello, who's speaking?*

• All of these can be preceded by a preposition:
In che città abita? *In which city do you live?*
Con chi sei venuto? *With whom have you come?*
Da quante persone è composta la tua famiglia? ('Of how many people is composed your family?') *How many people are in your family?*

MAKING EXCLAMATIONS

The words above can also be used in exclamations:
Che malinteso! *What a misunderstanding!* (note the lack of indefinite article)
Quante ore devi dedicarci! *How many hours you must devote to it!*
Questo cappello costa trecento euro. *This hat costs 300 euros.* **Quanto!** *That much!* (literally, 'How much!')

▲ VERBS
EXPRESSING OBLIGATION AND NECESSITY ('TO NEED TO', 'MUST')

In Italian, *to need to, to have to* is usually conveyed with an impersonal expression (i.e. *to be necessary, to be required*) rather than with an active subject.

• One impersonal construction uses the third-person singular of **bisognare** *to be necessary* + verb:
Bisogna avere pazienza. *It is necessary to have patience.*

• Another is **ci vuole** + singular noun / **ci vogliono** + plural noun:
Ci vuole un po' più di coraggio. *A bit more nerve is necessary.*
Ci vogliono allenamento e costanza. *Practice and perseverance are required.*

• These expressions can be used in different tenses:
Ci è voluto molto coraggio. *A lot of courage was needed.* (Note that the verb **volere** forms the perfect tenses with the auxiliary verb **essere**.)
Bisognerà lavorare molto. *It will be necessary to work a lot.*

• In the dialogue we also see a way to express the opposite of something being necessary: **Non importa.** *It's not important. It doesn't matter.* This comes from the verb **importare** *to be important, to matter* and is very frequently used.
Bisogna dirlo subito al principale. *It's necessary to tell the boss right away.*
Non importa dirglielo subito. *It's not important to tell him immediately.*

EXERCISES

19 1. WRITE THE QUESTION THAT CORRESPONDS TO EACH RESPONSE USING THE QUESTION WORDS ON PAGE 163, AND THEN LISTEN TO THE RECORDING.

Example: Questa camicia costa quaranta euro.
→ Quanto costa questa camicia?

a. L'autobus arriva alle dodici e un quarto.

→ ....

b. Vogliamo mangiare la pizza.

→ ....

c. Le mie città preferite sono Siena e Firenze.

→ ....

VOCABULARY

accettare *to accept*
Accidenti! *Jeez! Darn!*
l'allenamento *training, exercise* (**gli allenamenti** *workouts*)
cadere *to fall, to crash*
cambiare *to change*
cavarsela *to cope, to manage*
chiamare *to call*
la chiamata *call*
il coraggio *courage, nerve*
la costanza *constancy, perseverance, regularity*
dedicare *to dedicate, to devote*
la dote *talent, gift* (**le doti** *talents*)
fa *ago*
forte *strong, loud, heavy*
la fortuna *luck*
funzionare *to function, to work*
giocare *to play*
l'impegno *commitment*
importante *important, essential*
lasciare *to leave*
la linea *line*
il malinteso *misunderstanding*
mandare *to send*
il modo *manner, style, way*
naturale *natural*
obbligare *to oblige to, to obligate*
occupato/a *occupied, busy*
ogni tanto *every so often*
la pallacanestro *basketball*
la partita *game, match*
la passione *passion*
il pezzo *piece, part*
possibile *possible*
il/la principale *boss*
il/la professionista *professional*
protestare *to protest*
riconoscere *to recognize*
riuscire *to succeed*
lo scambio *exchange, trade*
sentire *to hear*
la telefonata *telephone call*
il turno *shift*
l'ufficio postale *post office*
vedersi *to see each other*

2. REWRITE THE SENTENCES REPLACING *BISOGNARE* + VERB WITH THE EQUIVALENT CONSTRUCTION *CI* + *VOLERE*.

Example:

Per entrare, bisogna avere diciotto anni *(it's necessary to be 18-years-old)*. →
Per entrare, ci vogliono diciotto anni.

a. Per fare questo lavoro, bisogna avere la macchina.

→ ....

b. Bisognerà avere molte ore.

→ ....

c. Con quel freddo *(cold)*, bisognava avere il maglione.

→ ....

3. TRANSLATE THESE SENTENCES INTO ENGLISH.

a. Ci vogliono delle scarpe. →..

b. Ci vorrà un anno. →..

c. Con quanti amici venite? → ....

d. Che bella città! →..

19 4. LISTEN TO THE RECORDING AND FILL IN THE MISSING WORDS.

a. – .... chi parla?

b. – Ciao, ... Carlo.

c. – Non posso stare al telefono a lungo, aspetto una .... importante.

d. – Se vuoi .... e ti richiamo più tardi.

18. INFORMATION TECHNOLOGY AND THE INTERNET

INFORMATICA E INTERNET

AIMS	TOPICS
• CONVERSING ABOUT COMPUTERS AND THE INTERNET • ASKING FOR INFORMATION ABOUT INFORMATION TECHNOLOGY • CORRESPONDING BY EMAIL	• MORE ON DEMONSTRATIVE AND RELATIVE PRONOUNS • THE PRONOUN *CHI* • THE PRESENT CONDITIONAL ('WOULD')

ADVICE (pl.) ABOUT *(on the)* **A NEW COMPUTER**

Ms Magri: Hello, I'd like *(would-want)* some information (pl.) about the computer that I've just bought.

Clerk: Of course, ma'am, what information would you like *(desire)*?

Ms Magri: Have *(Bring)* patience: you [should] know [that] I don't understand anything *(not of-it I-understand nothing)* about IT.

Clerk: Don't worry *(Not yourself you-worry)*, ma'am. An IT expert would not come here *(at all)*: she would have nothing to learn from a shop assistant because she would already know everything, don't you think *(believe)*?

Ms Magri: Let's say that I would like *(to-me it-would-please)* to be a bit less inept *(clumsy)* when I use a PC, that's all. For example, my son made me buy a cordless mouse, but I can't manage *(not I-succeed)* to use it because first it has to be installed, and I don't have the installation CD.

Clerk: Pardon me, but who told you that it had to be installed?

Ms Magri: [It was] *(precisely)* my son [who] told me, who *(himself of-it)* understands it [well] enough … maybe!

Clerk: Be careful *(Do attention)*, because not [everyone] who gives advice (pl.) is always truly [an] expert, with all [due] respect to your son. In short, if you need [anything], come here *(to us)* and we will explain everything to you.

Ms Magri: Yes, but I can hardly come *(not I-can at-all)* all the way here *(end here)* each time that I have a problem: I would always be here!

Clerk: For us it would be a *(would-make)* pleasure to see you: that's what we're here for! But if *(If then)* you don't want to go to any trouble *(not yourself you-want to-inconvenience)*, on our website, in the menu, there is a heading *(entry)* 'online assistance': you click on it and a window will open *(itself it-opens)* where you can write all your questions. Handy, isn't it?

Ms Magri: Yes, it would all seem very easy, at least in theory *(words)* …

Clerk: All those who have used *(done)* it have been very satisfied. To get back to your mouse, there's almost never a CD *(attached)*, the computer connects to it automatically. In any case, the installation of many programs is now done *(as-of-now one does)* online. It would be impossible to do otherwise *(differently)*, because today small laptop PCs and tablets no longer have a CD drive *(reader)*.

Ms Magri: Mine has everything! I paid rather a high price *(I-have paid rather expensive)*, in order to be sure to have a device that works *(appliance functioning)* …

Clerk: And you did the right thing *(have done well)*, ma'am! As the saying goes *(As says the proverb)*, '[He] who spends more, spends less'!

20 CONSIGLI SUL NUOVO COMPUTER

Signora Magri: Buongiorno, vorrei alcune informazioni sul computer che ho appena comprato.

Commesso: Certo signora, che informazioni desidererebbe?

Signora Magri: Porti pazienza, sa, io di informatica non ci capisco niente.

Commesso: Non si preoccupi, signora. Un esperto in informatica non verrebbe mica qui: non avrebbe niente da imparare da un commesso di negozio perché saprebbe già tutto, non crede?

Signora Magri: Diciamo che mi piacerebbe essere un po' meno maldestra quando uso il PC, ecco. Per esempio, mio figlio mi ha fatto comprare un mouse wireless, ma non riesco a usarlo perché prima deve essere installato, e non ho il CD di installazione.

Commesso: Ma scusi, chi Le ha detto che deve essere installato?

Signora Magri: Me l'ha detto proprio mio figlio, che se ne intende abbastanza… forse!

Commesso: Faccia attenzione, perché non sempre chi dà consigli è veramente esperto, con tutto il rispetto per suo figlio. Insomma, se ha bisogno venga qui da noi e Le spiegheremo tutto.

Signora Magri: Sì, ma non posso mica venire fin qui ogni volta che ho un problema: sarei sempre qui!

Commesso: Ma a noi farebbe piacere vederLa, siamo qui per questo! Se poi non si vuole scomodare, sul nostro sito Internet, nel menù, c'è la voce "assistenza on line": Lei ci clicca su e si apre una finestra dove può scrivere tutte le Sue domande. Pratico, no?

Signora Magri: Sì, sembrerebbe tutto molto facile, almeno a parole…

Commesso: Tutti quelli che l'hanno fatto sono stati molto contenti. Per tornare al Suo mouse, non c'è quasi mai un CD allegato, il computer ci si connette automaticamente. In ogni caso l'installazione di tanti programmi ormai si fa on line. Sarebbe impossibile fare diversamente, perché oggi i piccoli PC portatili e i tablet, non hanno più il lettore di CD.

Signora Magri: Il mio ha tutto! L'ho pagato piuttosto caro, per essere sicura di avere un apparecchio funzionante…

Commesso: E ha fatto bene signora! Come dice il proverbio, "chi più spende meno spende"!

UNDERSTANDING THE DIALOGUE
COMPUTERS AND INFORMATION TECHNOLOGY

The general term **l'infomatica** can refer to *information technology, computer science* or *data processing*. Many IT terms are borrowed from English: **il computer** (or **il PC**), **il mouse**, **il tablet**, **wireless**, **l'internet**, etc. Don't forget that foreign loanwords are the same in the singular and plural in Italian: **il computer/i computer**, **il mouse/i mouse**, etc. Some other useful terms in this area include **l'indirizzo email** *email address*, **alto debito** *high speed*, **il computer portatile** *laptop* and **le reti sociali** *social networks*.

SOME LINGUISTIC DIFFERENCES

→ The equivalent of 'I'd like ...' in Italian is **vorrei** ('I would want') or **desidererei** ('I would desire') *I would like*. These are the conditional forms of verbs with the meaning *to want*.

→ Note that **consigli** *advice* (from **il consiglio** *a piece of advice, suggestion*) and **informazioni** (from **l'informazione** *a piece of information*) are plural in Italian: so the corresponding verb is as well!

→ Remember that double negatives can be used in Italian: **Non ci capisco niente.** ('Not of-it I-understand nothing.') *I don't understand anything about it.*

→ Reflexive verbs are often used to express feelings, as in **Non si preoccupi.** ('Not yourself you-worry.') *Don't worry.* As we've seen, they are also used to convey an impersonal or passive meaning (to avoid having to identify an active subject): **si apre una finestra** *a window opens*, **il computer ci si connette** *the computer connects to it*, **si fa on line** *it is done online*.

→ Note the useful expression **non riesco** ('I don't succeed') *I can't manage ...*

CULTURAL NOTE

Italy has not yet fully achieved the digital revolution. While the network infrastructure is progressively expanding, today only half the population has internet access from a fixed line (however, this tripled between 2000 and 2010). Only one out of three Italians own a computer, with the result that Italy has one of the highest rates in Europe of going online via a smartphone. So there is still some way to go before Italy reaches the levels of internet access elsewhere in Europe, such as the Netherlands, where more than 80% of the population has access to an internet connection.

◆ GRAMMAR
MORE ON DEMONSTRATIVE AND RELATIVE PRONOUNS

• We have already seen the demonstrative pronouns **questo** (**questa, questi, queste**) *this (one), these* and **quello** (**quella, quelli, quelle**) *that (one), those* (lesson 6). These must agree in gender and number with what is being referred to.
Quelli che l'hanno fatto sono stati molto contenti. *Those who have done it have been very satisfied.*
• The masculine singular pronoun **quello** can equally be used as a neutral *that* referring to something general and not specifically defined: **Quello che si sente dire.** *That which one hears said.*
• Another neutral term is **ciò** *this* or *that*, referring to something abstract or unspecified: **con tutto ciò** *for all that, in spite of everything*, **con tutto ciò...** *and with that ...*, **Ciò è vero.** *That's true.*
• A reminder that the relative pronoun can be **che** or **cui** + preposition (see lesson16): **Ciò di cui abbiamo bisogno.** *That which we need.*

THE PRONOUN *CHI*

• As we've seen, **chi** is the question word *who*.
Chi Le ha detto questo? *Who told you that?*
• When used as a relative pronoun, it has the same meaning as **quello che** *the one who*. So **chi** in this context translates to *he who, she who, one who, those who*:
La gente ascolta chi dà consigli. *People listen to those who give advice.*
Chi è stato in Italia... *Those who have been to Italy ...*
• With the above meaning, **chi** often appears in proverbs:
Chi più spende, meno spende. ('One who spends more, spends less.') *Buy cheap, buy twice.*
Chi vivrà vedrà. ('One who will live will see'.) *Time will tell.*
Ride bene chi ride ultimo. ('Laughs well one-who laughs last.') *He who laughs last laughs longest.*

▲ CONJUGATION
THE PRESENT CONDITIONAL

The conditional mood is used to express a desire, to make a polite request or query, or to talk about a hypothetical situation. The present conditional corresponds to the

English *would* + verb. Here are some examples:
Vorrei alcune informazioni. *I would like some information.*
Mi piacerebbe un panino. *I would like a sandwich.*
Avrei ma devo lavorare. *I would go but I have to work.*

In Italian the conditional is a simple (one-word) tense formed with conjugation endings. As in the future tense, the first group (**-are**) and second group (**-ere**) have the same conjugation. The third group (**-ire**) varies slightly, as its conjugation ending starts with an **i**. Here are the regular conditional conjugations:

	-are verbs	**-ere** verbs	**-ire** verbs
	parlare *to speak*	**prendere** *to take*	**finire** *to finish*
io	**parlerei** *I would speak*	**prenderei**	**finirei**
tu	**parleresti**	**prenderesti**	**finiresti**
lui, lei, Lei	**parlerebbe**	**prenderebbe**	**finirebbe**
noi	**parleremmo**	**prenderemmo**	**finiremmo**
voi	**parlereste**	**prendereste**	**finireste**
loro, Loro	**parlerebbero**	**prenderebbero**	**finirebbero**

• In the conditional, any irregularities occur in the verb stem – the conjugation endings are always regular. The irregularity in the stem is the same as in the future tense and is found in all persons. For example, the present conditional of **volere** *to want* is **vorrei, vorresti, vorrebbe, vorremmo, vorreste, vorrebbero**.

EXERCISES

1. FILL IN THE CORRECT DEMONSTRATIVE PRONOUN (PAY ATTENTION TO AGREEMENT!) + RELATIVE PRONOUN IN EACH SENTENCE.

Example: Volevi un vestito rosso *(red dress)* e l'hai comprato. →
Hai comprato quello che volevi.

a. Mi hai chiesto il libro di storia *(history book)* e te l'ho portato *(have brought it)*.
Ti ho portato .... mi hai chiesto.

b. Siamo andati in quella città. Tu ce l'avevi consigliata *(had recommended it)*.
Siamo andati in .... tu ci avevi consigliata.

c. Avete incontrato quegli amici. Ve li avevo presentati io.
Avete incontrato .... vi avevo presentato.

VOCABULARY

l'apparecchio *appliance, device*
l'assistenza *assistance*
cliccare *to click*
connettere *to connect*
contento/a *happy, glad, satisfied*
diversamente *differently, otherwise*
l'esperto *expert* (**esperto/a** *expert,* adj.)
facile *easy, simple*
la finestra *window*
funzionante *functioning, working*
impossibile *impossible*
l'informatica *information technology, computer science*
installare *to install*
l'installazione *installation*
intendersi *to know a lot about something* (**intendere** *to understand*)
il lettore *reader, player* (e.g. CD player) (in reference to a person, a female who reads is **la lettrice**)
maldestro/a *clumsy, awkward, inept*
il menù (or **menu**) *menu* (both in the IT sense and a restaurant menu)
ormai *by now, at this point*
la parola *word, speech* (**le parole** *words, remarks*)
la pazienza *patience*
pratico/a *practical*
il programma *programme* (**i programmi** *programmes*)
il proverbio *proverb, saying*
il rispetto *respect*
riuscire *to succeed, to manage to do something*
sicuro/a *sure*
il sito *site, website*
spendere *to spend*
spiegare *to explain*
spostarsi *to move*
la voce *voice, entry or item in a list*
veramente *truly, really*

2. REWRITE THESE SENTENCES USING THE PRONOUN *CHI* (WHICH ALWAYS REQUIRES AGREEMENT IN THE MASCULINE SINGULAR, I.E. 'HE WHO').

Example: Non mi piacciono le persone che parlano troppo.→
Non mi piace chi parla troppo.

a. Esco *(I go out)* solo con le persone che mi sono simpatiche.

→ ....

b. Quelli che sono andati in quella scuola parlano bene italiano.

→ ....

c. Le persone che non hanno diciotto anni non possono guidare la macchina *(drive a car)*.

→ ....

3. TRANSLATE THESE CONDITIONAL SENTENCES.

a. We would like. → ....

b. They would be. → ....

c. You (pl.) would have.→ ....

d. You (sing inf.) would know.→ ....

4. REWRITE THESE PRESENT-TENSE SENTENCES IN THE CONDITIONAL.

Example: Voglio un'informazione. → Vorrei un'informazione.

a. Mi piace andare in Italia. → ....

b. Mi può dire che ore sono? → ....

c. Possiamo arrivare un po' più tardi? → ....

19.
WRITING AN EMAIL

SCRIVERE UNA MAIL

AIMS

- READING AND WRITING EMAILS
- VOCABULARY RELATED TO MOBILE PHONES AND EMAILS

TOPICS

- FORMING ADVERBS
- THE PRESENT TENSE OF THE IRREGULAR VERB *SAPERE*
- THE PAST CONDITIONAL

EMAIL

<u>Natalia:</u> Federico, can I use your computer to send an email?

<u>Federico:</u> Sure, but why don't you send it with your mobile phone?

<u>N:</u> *(It)* I would have *(done)* willingly, but my phone is not connecting to the network today. In fact, at the moment it's not even letting me *(picking up for)* telephone: see the icon on the screen? There's no signal *(field)*. Yesterday it was also working *(going)* slowly: in fact, extremely slowly, I would say …

<u>F:</u> Mine is getting [a signal] perfectly: look, it's been *(is)* connected since this morning with no *(without)* problem.

<u>N:</u> It's been happening *(To-me it-occurs)* often since I changed operator. Before it never used to happen to me. I would have preferred to stay with the first one, but this one offered me a new phone. 'Offered', so to speak, seeing that I will pay for it with my subscription for two years.

<u>F:</u> Here you go, my PC is free, go ahead and send *(send by-all-means)* your email.

<u>N:</u> I have to reply to Luisa, who has written to me to let me know *(alert-me)* that tomorrow morning there's a meeting with the new sales manager. Did you know about it?

<u>F:</u> No, I don't know anything about it; they should have told me *(they-would-have needed to-tell-me-it)*.

<u>N:</u> So I['ll] forward the *(his/her)* email to you, that way you [can] read it as well. [Can you] give me your email address?

<u>F:</u> From your email inbox, just *(it-suffices-to)* type the first letters of my name in the address field and you'll see that it *(to-you)* appears automatically *(on its own)*.

<u>N:</u> Here's the text of Luisa's email: 'Hello all, Thursday, 15 February at 9:00, you are requested to be present at the meeting with Mr Biraghi, the new sales manager. Best regards, Luisa Mengoni.' However, I can't go *(there)*, I have [an] appointment with an important customer.

<u>F:</u> Explain *(Write)* it to her, otherwise *(if not)* she will make such a fuss *(a sack of stories)*: you know how Luisa is.

<u>N:</u> I'll *(I-do)* 'reply to all', so our *(the)* colleagues also know *(it)*: 'Hello, unfortunately tomorrow I won't be able to be there, having already arranged *(fixed)* another appointment some time ago.' I'm also asking for confirmation of receipt *(notice of reading)*, that way is *(I-am)* safer. Do you think *(say)* that it would have been better *(the case)* to send it as a registered email?

<u>F:</u> Come on *(Give)*, don't exaggerate, it's not *(at-all)* for the president of the republic!

21 POSTA ELETTRONICA

Natalia: Federico, posso usare il tuo computer per mandare una mail?

Federico: Sì, certo, ma perché non la mandi con il cellulare?

Natalia: L'avrei fatto volentieri, ma il mio cellulare oggi non si connette alla rete. Anzi, in questo momento non prende neanche per telefonare: vedi l'icona sullo schermo? Non c'è campo. Anche ieri andava lentamente, anzi, lentissimamente direi…

Federico: Il mio prende perfettamente, guarda, è connesso da stamattina senza problemi.

Natalia: Mi succede spesso da quando ho cambiato operatore, prima non mi era mai successo. Avrei preferito restare con quello di prima, ma questo mi ha regalato un telefono nuovo. "Regalato" si fa per dire, visto che lo pagherò con l'abbonamento per due anni.

Federico: Ecco, il mio PC è libero, manda pure la tua mail.

Natalia: Devo rispondere a Luisa che mi ha scritto per avvertirmi che domattina c'è una riunione con il nuovo responsabile delle vendite, tu lo sapevi?

Federico: No, non ne so niente; avrebbero dovuto dirmelo.

Natalia: Allora ti inoltro la sua mail, così la leggi anche tu. Mi dai il tuo indirizzo e-mail?

Federico: Dalla tua casella di posta elettronica, basta digitare le prime lettere del mio nome nella stringa dell'indirizzo, e vedrai che ti appare da solo.

Natalia: Ecco il testo della mail di Luisa: "Buongiorno a tutti, giovedì 15 febbraio alle ore 9 siete pregati di essere presenti all'incontro con il dott. Biraghi, nuovo responsabile delle vendite. Cordiali saluti, Luisa Mengoni." Io però non ci posso andare, ho appuntamento con un cliente importante.

Federico: Scriviglielo, se no farà un sacco di storie, sai com'è Luisa.

Natalia: Faccio "rispondi a tutti", così anche i colleghi lo sapranno: "Buongiorno, purtroppo domani non potrò essere presente avendo già da tempo fissato un altro appuntamento." Chiedo anche l'avviso di lettura, così sono più sicura. Dici che sarebbe stato il caso di mandarla in posta certificata?

Federico: Dai, non esagerare, non è mica per il presidente della repubblica!

UNDERSTANDING THE DIALOGUE
MORE MOBILE PHONE AND INTERNET VOCABULARY

In Italy, the expressions regarding mobile phone reception are **Il telefono prende / non prende.** *The phone is getting/not getting service.* **C'è / Non c'è campo.** *There is/isn't a signal.* The term **l'operatore** is used for *service provider*. If you want to legally track the delivery of an email, you can send it by **la posta elettronica certificata (P.E.C.)** *registered email*.

SI FA PER DIRE

The expression **si fa per dire** ('one does to speak') translates to *so to speak*, *so they say*, conveying the meaning that what has just been cited is not really true. It has the same effect as adding quote marks around a statement: **il telefono 'regalato'**.

UN SACCO DI

In colloquial spoken Italian, **il sacco di** *a sack of* is used to mean *a whole lot of, loads, tons*: **Quando parte, porta sempre un sacco di cose inutili.** *When he goes away, he always takes loads of useless things*. The term **un sacco** can also be used on its own to mean *a lot*: **Gli piace un sacco.** *He likes it a lot*. **La pizza mi piace un sacco.** *I like pizza a lot.*

GRAMMAR
ADVERBS

• Adverbs are used to describe a verb, an adjective or another adverb. An example is *She ate quickly*.
• They are often formed by adding the suffix **-mente** *-ly* to the feminine singular adjective: e.g. **lento** *slow* → **lenta** (f.) → **lentamente** *slowly*; **perfetto** *perfect* → **perfetta** (f.) → **perfettamente** *perfectly*, etc.
• If an adjective ends in **-le**, the final **-e** is dropped before the suffix **-mente**: **personale** *personal* → **personalmente** *personally*; **piacevole** *pleasant* → **piacevolmente** *pleasantly*.
• Some adverbs don't end in this suffix, but simply in **-i**, such as **volentieri** *gladly, willingly*, **tardi** *late*, **fuori** *outside*, etc.
• Some adjectives can be used as adverbs without changing form at all, such as **forte** *loud, strong* (adj.), *loudly, hard* (adv.).

• Like adjectives, adverbs can be intensified with **-issimo/a**: **lentissimamente** *very slowly*, **fortissimo** *very loudly*, **benissimo** *very well*.

▲ CONJUGATION
THE VERB *SAPERE*

Note that **sapere** *to know* is highly irregular in the present tense: **so, sai, sa, sappiamo, sapete, sanno**.

THE PAST CONDITIONAL

This tense corresponds to *would have* + past participle (in English this is the conditional perfect). It is a compound tense formed with the auxiliary verb **avere** or **essere** conjugated in the present conditional followed by a past participle:

	-are verbs	**-ere** verbs	**-ire** verbs
	andare *to go*	**vendere** *to sell*	**finire** *to finish*
io	**sarei andato/a** *I would have gone*	**avrei venduto** *I would have sold*	**avrei finito** *I would have finished*
tu	**saresti andato/a**	**avresti venduto**	**avresti finito**
lui, lei, Lei	**sarebbe andato/a**	**avrebbe venduto**	**avrebbe finito**
noi	**saremmo andati/e**	**avremmo venduto**	**avremmo finito**
voi	**sareste andati/e**	**avreste venduto**	**avreste finito**
loro, Loro	**sarebbero andati/e**	**avrebbero venduto**	**avrebbero finito**

• Don't forget that **essere** and **avere** use themselves as auxiliary verbs in the perfect tenses: **sarei stato** *I would have been*, etc.; **avrei avuto** *I would have had*, etc. Only when the auxiliary verb is **essere** does the past participle need to agree with the subject: **sarei stata** *I would have been* (one female), **saremmo andate** *we would have been* (more than one female): **Mia sorella sarebbe stata molto felice di conoscerti, ma oggi non poteva venire.** *My sister would have been very happy to meet you, but today she couldn't come.* BUT **Mia sorella avrebbe avuto molte cose da dirti, ma oggi non poteva venire.** *My sister would have had a lot to say to you, but today she was unable to come.*

• As we've mentioned, many past participles are irregular. Go back to lesson 10 to review these from time to time so you can recognize and use them more easily, for example, in the perfect tenses.

EXERCISES

1. REWRITE THESE PRESENT CONDITIONAL SENTENCES IN THE PAST CONDITIONAL.

a. Con il mio operatore queste cose non succederebbero. (auxiliary **essere**)

....

b. In treno viaggeremmo molto più comodi *(comfortable)*. (auxiliary **avere**)

....

c. Carla preferirebbe andarci lunedì. (auxiliary **avere**)

....

d. Carla ci andrebbe più volentieri lunedì. (auxiliary **essere**)

....

2. FORM ADVERBS FROM THESE ADJECTIVES.

a. strano → ....

b. professionale → ....

c. solito → ....

d. fortunato → ....

3. TRANSLATE THESE SENTENCES.

a. We would have liked ('wanted'). → ....

b. They (f.) would have been. → ....

c. He would have been able to. → ....

d. You (f. pl.) would have come. → ....

4. REWRITE THE SENTENCES, REPLACING *MOLTO* + ADVERB WITH THE *-ISSIMO/A/I/E* FORM OF THE ADVERB.

a. Camminavamo *(We were walking)* molto lentamente. →

....

b. Parla sempre molto forte. → ....

c. La nostra macchina va molto piano *(slowly)*. → ....

d. Siete arrivati molto tardi. → ....

VOCABULARY

l'abbonamento *subscription*
apparire *to appear*
avvertire *to alert, to inform, to let know, to warn*
l'avviso di lettura *confirmation of receipt*
il campo *field, signal*
la casella *mailbox, inbox*
certificato/a *certified*
cordiale *cordial, warm, friendly*
digitare *to type, to key in* (on a computer or phone)
esagerare *to exaggerate*
fissare *to fix, to establish, to set*
l'icona *icon*
l'incontro *encounter, meeting, gathering*
inoltrare *to forward, to transmit*
la mail *email*
il momento *moment*
neanche *not even*
l'operatore *operator, provider*
pregare *to request, to plead*
regalare *to offer as a gift*
la rete *network*
la repubblica *republic*
rispondere *to respond, to reply, to answer*
i saluti *greetings*
lo schermo *screen*
senza *without*
spesso *often, frequently*
stamattina *this morning*
la stringa *field* (for email address)
succedere *to happen, to occur*
telefonare *to telephone*
il testo *text*

21 ## 5. LISTEN TO THE RECORDING AND FILL IN THE MISSING WORDS.

a. Da qui non si può telefonare: non c'è ....

b. È vero, il mio cellulare non si .... alla rete.

c. Con il mio vecchio operatore non mi è mai .... di avere problemi di connessione.

d. Il nuovo operatore mi ha .... un cellulare nuovo.

20. GIVING PRACTICAL INSTRUCTIONS

DARE ISTRUZIONI PRATICHE

AIMS

- EXPLAINING A PROBLEM AND ASKING FOR HELP
- DESCRIBING HOW SOMETHING WORKS
- GIVING INSTRUCTIONS
- HELPING SOMEONE FIND SOMETHING

TOPICS

- THE VERBS FOR 'TO KNOW'
- THE VERBS FOR 'TO REMEMBER' AND 'TO FORGET'
- AGREEMENT WITH THE PAST PARTICIPLE
- MODAL VERBS

A PROBLEM GETTING INTO THE OFFICE

Elena: Hello Giovanni, excuse me for disturbing *(if I-disturb)* you so late, but I'm having a problem getting into the office.

Giovanni: But what *(there)* are you doing at the office at this hour?

E: Unfortunately, I had to come back because I forgot the report on our project with *(the)* Sweden, and I have to present it tomorrow morning at the conference in Milan. I couldn't come earlier, [as] I had a commitment; now I really have to get in and there's an alarm: how do I do it?

G: You don't know the code by heart?

E: No... I've noted it on my tablet, which *(and it)* I've forgotten at home.

G: You've forgotten your tablet at home, you don't know the code by heart, and you're locked *(closed)* outside of the office at 9:30 at night; you are really something *(a phenomenon)*, you know? Memorizing a few little things, for example *(type)*, [your] telephone number, car license plate number, social security number and so on *(like-this as)*, isn't in the end that difficult *(to-learn-them)*, is it?

E: So [will] you give it to me or not, this code?

G: Okay. Are you in front of the main entrance?

E: Yes, just in front of the keypad [for entering] the alarm code.

G: So you press once *(one time)* on the button with the asterisk, okay?

E: Right, done it; and then?

G: Key in the code: hash key, 1, 5, 5, 1, 3, A, B, then press OK twice *(two times)*.

E: That's it, now I've entered. Sorry, now wait a moment before hanging up: I want to be sure of finding the folder. All the project folders are in the cabinet in Sandro's office, right?

G: Yes, or at least that's where *(it's there that)* the secretary should have put them.

Elena: Darn, the door is locked *(closed by key)*!

G: Don't panic *(Not-any panic)*, come on *(give)*: the key should be in the metal cabinet in the corridor.

E: Thank goodness! Is it the key with the number 6?

G: Yes: be careful because the door is a bit hard to open. Turn the key halfway *(do half turn of key)* then lift the handle a little and pull hard. You'll see that it opens.

E: Now you're not going to tell me *(Not it-is that now to-me you-tell)* that I have to get a screwdriver and take apart *(dismantle)* the lock? No, it's opened: now I'm looking in the third drawer on the left ...

G : No, it's the second on the right.

E: Ah yes: there's the folder! I'm exhausted! And tomorrow morning I have to go to Milan to meet the Swedish customers. Last month as well it was me that had to go there because they didn't want to come all the way here. Thank you, Giovanni!

G: Good luck *(In mouth of-the wolf)*!

22 UN PROBLEMA PER ENTRARE IN UFFICIO

Elena: Pronto, Giovanni, scusa se ti disturbo così tardi, ma ho un problema per entrare in ufficio.

Giovanni: Ma che ci fai in ufficio a quest'ora?

Elena: Purtroppo sono dovuta tornare perché ho dimenticato la relazione sul nostro progetto con la Svezia e la devo presentare domattina al convegno di Milano. Non sono potuta venire prima, avevo un impegno, ora devo entrare per forza e c'è l'allarme, come faccio?

Giovanni: Ma non sai il codice a memoria?

Elena: No... L'ho segnato sul mio tablet e me lo sono dimenticato a casa.

Giovanni: Ti sei dimenticata il tablet a casa, non sai il codice a memoria e sei chiusa fuori dall'ufficio alle nove e mezza di sera; sei proprio un fenomeno, sai? Un po' di cosine a memoria, tipo numero di telefono, targa della macchina, codice fiscale e così via non è poi così difficile impararle, no?

Elena: Allora me lo dai o no questo codice?

Giovanni: Va bene: sei davanti all'ingresso principale?

Elena: Sì, proprio di fronte alla tastiera del codice di allarme.

Giovanni: Allora premi una volta sul tasto con l'asterisco, okay?

Elena: Sì, ecco fatto; e dopo?

Giovanni: Digita il codice: cancelletto uno cinque cinque uno tre AB, poi premi due volte OK.

Elena: Ecco, sì, ora sono entrata. Scusa, adesso aspetta un attimo prima di riattaccare, voglio essere sicura di trovare la cartellina. Tutte le cartelline dei progetti sono nell'armadietto nell'ufficio di Sandro, vero?

Giovanni: Sì, o almeno è lì che li avrebbe dovuti mettere la segretaria.

Elena: Accidenti, la porta è chiusa a chiave!

Giovanni: Niente panico, dai, la chiave dovrebbe essere nell'armadietto di metallo nel corridoio .

Elena: Meno male! È la chiave con il numero sei?

Giovanni: Sì, fai attenzione perché la porta è un po' dura da aprire: fa' mezzo giro di chiave poi solleva un po' la maniglia e tira forte, vedrai che si apre.

Elena: Non è che adesso mi dici che devo prendere un cacciavite e smontare la serratura? No, si è aperta, adesso guardo nel terzo cassetto a sinistra…

Giovanni: No, è il secondo a destra.

Elena: Ah sì: ecco la cartellina! Sono sfinita! E domattina devo andare a Milano ad incontrare i clienti svedesi. Anche il mese scorso ci sono dovuta andare io perché loro non sono voluti venire fin qui. Grazie, Giovanni!

Giovanni: In bocca al lupo!

UNDERSTANDING THE DIALOGUE
THE VERBS FOR 'TO KNOW'

There are two verbs for *to know* in Italian: **sapere** *to know a fact or how to do something* and **conoscere** *to be familiar with* (as well as *to meet someone*). In some contexts, **sapere** can be used with the latter meaning: e.g. **Non sai il codice a memoria.** *You don't know the code by heart.* **Sa benissimo l'inglese.** *He knows English well.* Note that **sapere** is irregular in the present tense (see lesson 19).

THE VERBS FOR 'TO REMEMBER' AND 'TO FORGET'

The verbs **ricordarsi** *to remember* and **dimenticarsi** *to forget* are reflexive. **Mi sono dimenticato che avevo un appuntamento importante.** *I forgot* ('myself I-have forgotten') *that I had an important appointment.* (reflexive verbs require the auxiliary verb **essere** in the perfect tenses); **Ricordati che domani abbiamo un appuntamento.** *Remember* ('yourself') *that tomorrow we have a date.*

IN BOCCA AL LUPO!

This expression is used to wish someone *good luck* without saying **buona fortuna**, which the superstitious believe brings bad luck. It literally means 'in the wolf's mouth': the reply is **crepi il lupo** 'may the wolf snuff it'. Poor wolf!

CULTURAL NOTE

Every Italian individual and company has **un codice fiscale** *fiscal code*, which consists of 16 digits and letters. It is used for all types of administrative procedures, from taxes to social security, and serves as an identification number. Introduced in 1973, it is so useful on a daily basis that many always carry their **tessera sanitaria** *social security card*, which includes **il codice fiscale**.

GRAMMAR
AGREEMENT WITH THE PAST PARTICIPLE

- As we've seen, the past participle agrees with the subject when the auxiliary verb is **essere**: **Carla e Luisa sono andate al mare.** *Carla and Luisa went to the seaside.* This is not the case when the auxiliary verb is **avere**: **Carla e Luisa hanno fatto una gita al mare.** *Carla and Luisa did a day trip to the sea.*
- However, with the auxiliary verb **avere**, if the direct object pronoun precedes the

verb, the past participle must agree with the object: **Le ho viste in riva al mare.** *I saw them* (f.) *at the seaside.*
• There's an example of the previous rule in the dialogue: **La segretaria li avrebbe dovuti mettere.** *The secretary should have put them [there].* (the past participle **dovuto**, from **dovere**, is in the plural to agree with the direct object **li**). This occurs because the direct object comes before the verb.
• With reflexive verbs, the past participle always agrees with the subject: **Elena si è dimenticata / si è ricordata di noi.** *Elena has forgotten / has remembered us*. **Ci siamo lavati i denti.** ('Ourselves we-have cleaned the teeth.') *We brushed our teeth.* Note that the same is true in indirect constructions such as **farsi male a** *to hurt*: **Mi sono fatta male alla mano.** *I* (f.) *hurt my hand.* ('Myself I-have done badly to the hand.')

▲ VERBS
MODAL VERBS

• Modal verbs are auxiliary verbs used with other verbs to convey likelihood, ability, permission, possibility or obligation. The four modal verbs in Italian are **dovere** *should, must*, **potere** *can*, **sapere** *to know how* and **volere** *to want to*, which are typically conjugated and followed by an infinitive:
Devo andare a Milano. *I must/should go to Milan*.
Non possiamo venire da voi. *We can't come to your place*.

• In the perfect tenses, the auxiliary required by the infinitive should be used:
Sono dovuto andare a Milano. *I had to go to Milan.* (the verb **andare** takes **essere** as an auxiliary)
Ho dovuto imparare il tedesco. *I had to learn German.* (the verb **imparare** takes **avere** as an auxiliary)

• The rule that the past participle needs to agree with the subject when the auxiliary verb is **essere** also applies to modal verbs:
Paolo e Luigi sono dovuti andare a Milano. *Paolo and Luigi had to go to Milan*.
Elena e Luisa sono dovute andare a Milano. *Elena and Luisa had to go to Milan*.

• When modal verbs are used on their own without another verb, they take the auxiliary verb **avere** (**sapere** and **volere** are often used as independent verbs).
Hai saputo che Sandro ha traslocato? *Did you know that Sandro has moved?*
Sì, l'ho saputo. *Yes, I knew that*.
Questo cambiamento, l'ha voluto il direttore. *The director wanted this change*.

• In fact, even when modal verbs are used with another verb that requires **essere** as the auxiliary, sometimes **avere** is used. This is particularly the case with **sapere**, even if this usage is not strictly correct:

Non ha saputo venire da sola. / Non è saputa venire da sola.
She didn't know how to come on her own.
Abbiamo dovuto partire alle cinque. / Siamo dovuti partire alle cinque.
We had to leave at 5:00.

EXERCISES

1. COMPLETE THE SENTENCES WITH THE PAST PARTICIPLE OF THE VERB IN PARENTHESES. (PAY ATTENTION TO AGREEMENT!)

a. Ti (m.) sei .... le mani prima di venire a tavola *(table)*? (lavarsi)

b. Le mie cugine *(cousins)* hanno .... in tutto il mondo. (viaggiare)

c. Ci (m.) siamo .... l'appuntamento. (dimenticarsi)

d. Carla, siamo in ritardo e tu non ti sei ancora .... le scarpe! (mettere)

2. COMPLETE THE SENTENCES BY PUTTING THE VERB IN THE PRESENT PERFECT.

a. Carla non .... aprire la porta. (sapere)

b. Mio fratello .... cambiare città per trovare lavoro. (dovere)

c. Ci (m.) dispiace, non .... arrivare prima. (potere)

d. Mia sorella non .... venire fin qui. (sapere)

3. TRANSLATE THESE SENTENCES.

a. They (m.) put on their shoes. →..

b. They (f.) brushed their *(cleaned the)* teeth. → ....

c. We (m.) forgot our appointment. → ....

d. She remembered you (informal sing.). → ....

22 4. LISTEN TO THE RECORDING AND FILL IN THE MISSING WORDS.

a. Non posso entrare perché c'è l'..........................

b. Ma come? Non sai il .... a memoria?

c. Devi digitare il codice sulla .... dell'allarme.

VOCABULARY

l'allarme *alarm*
l'armadietto *cabinet, cupboard, locker* (**l'armadio** *closet, wardrobe*)
l'asterisco *asterisk*
il cacciavite *screwdriver*
il cancelletto *hash key, pound sign* (on a keyboard)
la cartellina *folder* (diminutive of **la cartella** *file, briefcase*)
il cassetto *drawer*
la chiave *key*
chiuso/a *closed, locked, shut*
il codice *code*
il convegno *conference*
duro/a *hard, difficult*
il fenomeno *phenomenon*
fuori *outside*
incontrare *to meet up with, to run into someone*
l'ingresso *entrance*
l'istruzione *instruction* (**le istruzioni** *instructions*)
il lupo *wolf*
la maniglia *handle*
a memoria *by heart, by memory* (**la memoria** *memory*)
il metallo *metal*
il numero *number*
il panico *panic*
premere *to press*
il progetto *project*
la relazione *report, relationship*
scorso/a *past, last*
il segretario / la segretaria *secretary*
la serratura *lock*
sfinito/a *exhausted, worn out*
smontare *to dismantle, to take apart*
sollevare *to raise, to lift*
svedese *Swedish*
la targa *license plate, number plate*
la tastiera *keypad, keyboard*
il tasto *key, button*
tirare *to pull*

IV

FREE

TIME

21. RESERVING A HOTEL ROOM

PRENOTARE UNA CAMERA D'ALBERGO

AIMS

- GOING TO A HOTEL OR A RESTAURANT
- CHOOSING FROM DIFFERENT OPTIONS
- SPECIFYING YOUR PREFERENCES

TOPICS

- *C'È / CI SONO* IN DIFFERENT TENSES
- THE IRREGULAR VERBS *PIACERE, SCEGLIERE, TENERE, VALERE*

A ROOM WITH A SEA VIEW

Mr Marchetti: Hello? Good morning, I'd like to reserve a room for the weekend *(end week)* of 14 May, is that possible?

Receptionist: One moment ... Do you want [a] single, double [with two beds] or a double bed?

Mr M: I'd like a room with a double bed and bathroom and with a view of the sea: are there any left *(there of-them are still)*?

R: We have a room with a double bed and bathroom, but not with a sea view, I'm sorry. But it *(this)* is a really nice room, you know? Spacious, light, with air-conditioning, television, minibar, and, of course, wifi for internet access.

Mr M: Okay, fine. But, pardon me, [there's] something that is very important to me *(to a thing I-hold a-lot)*: is it quiet? Last year, you gave me a room that overlooked *(gave on)* the street, and all night there were people that were passing by, shouting, laughing; there were even cars with music playing full blast *(at all volume)*. The one you're proposing to me is not as noisy as that, is it?

R: No, absolutely not! Well, let's say that a little bit *(little-something)* of traffic from the street can be *(it is)* heard, but in any case, this year we have *(made)* put in double glazing *(glass-panes)*, and it's a whole different story *(other thing)*!

Mr M: Let's hope so *(well)* ... And how much does this room cost *(come)*?

R: 100 euros a night: the price includes *(in-the price is included)* breakfast *(first meal)*, which is *(one does)* from 8:00 to 10:30 in our dining room. That [room] does have *(yes)* a view of the sea, do you remember it?

Mr M: Of course I remember it! Every year I choose your hotel for the quality of the food! I love your fritto misto *(fried mixed*, pl.*)* and your seafood spaghetti *(spaghetti*, pl. *of-the rock)*!

R: Thank you, sir, many [of our] guests choose us for this [reason].

Mr M: If you'll excuse me, between now and *(from here to)* May perhaps there will be cancellations, and thus maybe there will be a room with an ocean view available, right? In which case, could you call me?

R: Certainly. You are Mr ... ?

Mr M: Marchetti, Francesco. It's a reservation for three nights: the13th, 14th and 15th of *(13, 14 and 15)* May.

R: One instant while I note it down *(that it I-mark)*. Ah, I forgot: in fact *(reality)* there is *(would-be)* a room with a sea view, but we never offer it to anyone *(to no-one)* because it's small and has no *(without)* air-conditioning. If you want it *(If you there attach-importance)* ...

Mr M: No, I don't like *(not to-me they-appeal)* small rooms, and plus I suffer [in] the heat! For now I['ll] take this one, then if there is *(are)* news you [can] call me. Do I have to send a deposit?

R: Normally it would be required to send us an advance of 10%, but seeing as you're a regular *(usual)* guest, we trust *(ourselves we-trust of)* you.

Mr M: Thank you for your *(the)* confidence! Goodbye!

23 UNA CAMERA CON VISTA SUL MARE

Signor Marchetti: Pronto? Buongiorno, vorrei prenotare una camera per il fine settimana del 14 maggio, è possibile?

Receptionist: Un momento… La vuole singola, doppia o matrimoniale?

Signor Marchetti: Vorrei una matrimoniale con bagno e con vista sul mare; ce ne sono ancora?

Receptionist: Abbiamo una camera matrimoniale con bagno, ma non con vista sul mare, mi dispiace. Ma questa è una bellissima camera, sa? Spaziosa, luminosa, con l'aria condizionata, televisione, frigobar e naturalmente il wi-fi per la connessione Internet.

Signor Marchetti: Va bene, va bene. Però, mi scusi, ad una cosa tengo moltissimo: è silenziosa? L'anno scorso mi avete dato una camera che dava sulla strada, e tutta la notte c'era gente che passava, gridava, rideva, c'erano persino macchine con la musica a tutto volume. Quella che mi proponete non è così rumorosa, vero?

Receptionist: No, assolutamente no! Beh, diciamo che qualcosina del traffico della strada lo si sente, ma in ogni caso quest'anno abbiamo fatto mettere i doppi vetri, ed è tutta un'altra cosa!

Signor Marchetti: Speriamo bene… E quanto viene questa camera?

Receptionist: Cento euro a notte; nel prezzo è compresa la prima colazione, che si fa dalle otto alle dieci e trenta nella nostra sala ristorante. Quella sì, che ha la vista sul mare, se la ricorda?

Signor Marchetti: Certo che me la ricordo! Ogni anno scelgo il vostro albergo per la qualità della cucina! Adoro i vostri fritti misti e i vostri spaghetti allo scoglio!

Receptionist: Grazie, signore, molti clienti ci scelgono per questo.

Signor Marchetti: Ma scusi, da qui a maggio forse ci saranno delle disdette, e allora ci sarà magari una camera con vista sul mare libera, no? In quel caso mi potreste chiamare?

Receptionist: Certo; Lei è il signor…?

Signor Marchetti: Marchetti Francesco. È una prenotazione per tre notti, 13, 14 e 15 maggio.

Receptionist: Un attimo che lo segno. Ah, dimenticavo: in realtà ci sarebbe una camera con vista sul mare, ma non la proponiamo mai a nessuno perché è piccola e senza climatizzatore. Se Lei ci tiene…

Signor Marchetti: No, non mi piacciono le camere piccole, e poi soffro il caldo! Per ora prendo questa, poi se ci sono novità mi chiamate voi. Devo mandare una caparra?

Receptionist: Normalmente bisognerebbe mandarci un anticipo del dieci per cento, ma siccome Lei è un cliente abituale, ci fidiamo di Lei.

Signor Marchetti: Grazie per la fiducia! Arrivederci!

UNDERSTANDING THE DIALOGUE
SINGOLA, DOPPIA O MATRIMONIALE?

A hotel room (**una camera**) can be **singola**, with a single bed for one person, **doppia** with twin beds, or **matrimoniale**, a room with a double bed. Tall people will be happy as **letti matrimoniali** *double beds* are usually quite big in Italy. These can also be referred to as beds **a due piazze** ('with two places'), as opposed to single beds, **a una piazza** ('with one place'). There are also beds **a una piazza e mezza** ('with one place and half'), which are also known as **letti matrimoniali alla francese**, because in France couples sleep in smaller beds. If one person wants to book a room with a double bed, he or she would ask for **una camera matrimoniale uso singola** *a double room for one person* ('single use').

VENIRE MEANING *COSTARE*

The verb **venire** is often used instead of the verb **costare** *to cost* to ask for or indicate a price. **Quanto viene questa camera?** *How much is* ('comes') *this room?*

FIDARSI

This reflexive verb means *to trust, to have confidence*, and it is often followed by the preposition **di** and the name of or pronoun referring to the person who is trusted (in English we use the preposition *in* in this context): **Mi fido di te.** *I have confidence in you.* As it is a reflexive verb, the auxiliary verb is **essere** and the past participle in the perfect tenses always agrees with the subject: **Ci siamo fidati di te.** *We have confidence in you.*

CULTURAL NOTE

Italians cherish their holidays, even though the economic crisis that the country has endured for over a decade means that many citizens no longer take the traditional three or four weeks off over the summer. Today, many content themselves with a few long weekends on the coast, or at most a week away from home. Compared to their European neighbours, Italians prefer to spend their vacations in their own country. It's relatively uncommon for them to choose a holiday abroad, apart from nearby low-cost countries such as Croatia and Slovenia. However, last-minute deals to faraway beach resorts are increasingly popular with young people. A typical vacation for an Italian is a family holiday in a relaxing spot that is suitable for children, for example, at the seaside resorts on the Adriatic or Tyrrhenian coasts. These are often located near towns with plenty of activities for adults as well, such as Rimini and Viareggio, with their buzzing night clubs and bars.

GRAMMAR
C'È / CI SONO

The table below gives the forms of **c'è** *there is*, **ci sono** *there are* (**Non ci sono camere libere.** *There are no rooms free.*) in the different tenses we've seen so far:

Present	Present perfect	Imperfect	Future	Future perfect	Present conditional	Past conditional
c'è	**c'è stato/a**	**c'era**	**ci sarà**	**ci sarà stato/a**	**ci sarebbe**	**ci sarebbe stato/a**
ci sono	**ci sono stati/e**	**c'erano**	**ci saranno**	**ci saranno stati/e**	**ci sarebbero**	**ci sarebbero stati/e**

So the meanings from left to right for the singular are *there is, there was/has been, there used to be, there will be, there will have been, there would be, there would have been*. Note that **ci** becomes **ce** before the pronoun **ne**: **ce ne sono** *there are some.*

CONJUGATION
SOME IRREGULAR VERBS

Here are some new frequently used verbs that are irregular in the present tense.

	piacere *to like*	**scegliere** *to choose*	**tenere** *to hold, to grasp*	**valere** *to be worth*
io	**piaccio**	**scelgo**	**tengo**	**valgo**
tu	**piaci**	**scegli**	**tieni**	**vali**
lui, lei, Lei	**piace**	**sceglie**	**tiene**	**vale**
noi	**piacciamo**	**scegliamo**	**teniamo**	**valiamo**
voi	**piacete**	**scegliete**	**tenete**	**valete**
loro, Loro	**piacciono**	**scelgono**	**tengono**	**valgono**

- The verbs **tenere** and **valere** are also irregular in the future and conditional e.g. **terrò** *I will hold*, **terrei** *I would hold* and **varrà** *it will be worth*, **varrebbe** *it would be worth*.
- Apart from **tenere**, these verbs also have irregular past participles: **piaciuto** (from **piacere**), **scelto** (from **scegliere**) and **valso** (from **valere**).

EXERCISES

1. COMPLETE THE SENTENCES WITH THE CORRECT FORM AND TENSE OF *C'È / CI SONO*.

a. Ho chiesto se .... una camera con vista sul mare, ma mi hanno detto che erano finite (*there were none left*, 'they-were finished').

b. In questo ristorante .... un'ottima *(excellent)* cucina.

c. Qui in giro *(Around here)* .... persone strane, non trovi?

d. L'anno prossimo .... una camera con vista sul mare.

2. COMPLETE THE SENTENCES WITH THE CORRECT PRESENT-TENSE FORM OF THE VERB GIVEN IN PARENTHESES.

a. Voglio una camera con vista sul mare, ci .... moltissimo. (tenere)

b. Carlo .... quell'albergo per la sua ottima cucina. (scegliere)

c. Mi .... *(it appeals to me)* mangiare la pizza alla sera. (piacere)

d. I quadri di quell'artista .... molti milioni. (valere)

3. TRANSLATE THESE SENTENCES.

a. He/she chooses. → ....

b. We have chosen. → ....

c. I didn't use to like the sea. → ....

d. I like Italian restaurants. → ....

23 4. LISTEN TO THE RECORDING AND FILL IN THE MISSING WORDS.

a. Buongiorno, vorrei .... una camera per il prossimo fine settimana.

b. Ora guardo se ci .... delle camere libere.

c. La vuole singola, doppia o ....?

d. Vorrei una camera con .... sul mare.

VOCABULARY

abituale *habitual, usual, regular*
l'albergo *hotel*
l'aria condizionata *air-conditioning (**l'aria** air)*
assolutamente *absolutely*
la caparra *deposit, down payment*
il climatizzatore *air-conditioning system*
la connessione *connection*
la disdetta *cancellation*
doppio/a *double*
la fiducia *trust, confidence*
il frigobar *minibar*
fritto/a *fried*
gridare *to shout, to yell*
luminoso/a *clear, light, bright*
matrimoniale *matrimonial*
misto/a *mixed*
la musica *music*
la/le novità *news*
persino *even, just, so much as*
prenotare *to reserve*
ridere *to laugh*
il ristorante *restaurant*
rumoroso/a *noisy, loud*
la sala *room* (larger room for collective activities)
scegliere *to choose*
lo scoglio *rock (**spaghetti allo scoglio** spaghetti with seafood)*
gli spaghetti *spaghetti* (pl.)
silenzioso/a *quiet, silent*
singolo/a *single, individual*
soffrire *to suffer*
spazioso/a *spacious*
sperare *to hope*
il vetro *glass, pane*
la vista *view*
il volume *volume*

22. AT THE TRAIN STATION OR AIRPORT

ALLA STAZIONE E ALL'AEROPORTO

AIMS

- TALKING ABOUT TRAVELLING BY TRAIN OR PLANE
- EXPRESSING CONCERN OR WORRY
- CALMING SOMEONE DOWN AND HELPING TO FIND A SOLUTION

TOPICS

- THE SUBJUNCTIVE MOOD
- MORE VERBS THAT ARE IRREGULAR IN THE PRESENT TENSE: *MORIRE, TACERE, TOGLIERE*

A STRESSED *(the stress of-the)* **TRAVELLER**

Alessandra: Excuse me, has the train for the airport already left?

Station master: Yes, one minute ago.

Alessandra: Oh no! What should *(And how)* I do now?

Station master: I believe *(that)* the next [one] leaves in half an hour.

Alessandra: That's *(It's)* too late! I will surely miss my *(the)* plane! You need *(One-needs)* to get to [the] airport an hour before *(the)* take-off for *(the)* check-in, the security checks and *(the)* boarding.

Station master: Unfortunately, there isn't an earlier one *(not there of-it are early)*: once *(one time)* there was one every 10 minutes, but now, with all the railway budget cuts, they are getting rid of *(they-remove)* all the trains [that are] low-cost and convenient for people, and the public service is dying little by little. And the travellers keep quiet and accept it all! Now that I think of it, the train that you missed was a regional [line], right?

Alessandra: Yes, it stopped *(itself was-stopping)* at all the stations. No, in almost all [of them]; it was a regional express *(rapid)*.

Station master: It seems to me that there is *(may be,* subjunctive*)* the next Intercity for Milan: that one also stops at the airport. It leaves in 10 minutes.

Alessandra: No! At this time there will be an endless line *(queue without end)* at the ticket window: I'll never manage to buy the supplement!

Station master: [Stay] calm, miss, there are automatic ticket machines that take both cash (pl.) and *(they-function both with the cash as with the)* credit and debit cards. I'm sorry that you are *(may-be,* subj.*)* so stressed, [but] in fact *(at bottom)* there's time, you can do it *(let's go)*!

Alessandra: What *(Thing)* do you want, it's travel anxiety *(the stress of-the traveller)* ... Thank you so much, I hope that there won't be (subj.) too many people at the ticket machines as well (...) That's it! I did it, I have my ticket: so *(and)* now where is the train?

Station master: It leaves from platform 3. You have seat 85 in carriage 4: it's the carriage at the end *(wagon of tail)*, the last [one].

Alessandra: Finally, the airport! I'll check *(I-look-at)* the departures board right away ... There it is! I have to go quickly *(in haste)* to gate G for boarding. My plane is coming from Palermo, it just landed and it takes off very shortly *(in very-little)*.

[Airline] employee: Excuse me, miss, your suitcase is too big to take *(to-be carried)* in [the] cabin. We have to tag it and put it in [the] hold: it's the rule.

Alessandra: But how [can that be]? This tiny bag? Never mind, I can *(will)* be separated from it for a few hours...

Employee: Don't worry, miss, relax *(yourself you-relax)*. The flight lasts only an hour and a half.

Alessandra: That's already too [long] for my taste *(tastes)*!

24 LO STRESS DEL VIAGGIATORE

Alessandra: Scusi, è già partito il treno per l'aeroporto?

Capostazione: Sì, un minuto fa.

Alessandra: Accidenti! E come faccio adesso?

Capostazione: Credo che il prossimo parta tra mezz'ora.

Alessandra: È troppo tardi! Di sicuro perderò l'aereo! Bisogna arrivare in aeroporto un'ora prima del decollo per il check-in, i controlli di sicurezza e l'imbarco.

Capostazione: Purtroppo non ce ne sono prima: una volta ce n'era uno ogni dieci minuti, ma ora, con tutti i tagli al bilancio delle ferrovie, tolgono tutti i treni economici e comodi per la gente, e il servizio pubblico muore a poco a poco. E i viaggiatori tacciono e accettano tutto! Ora che ci penso, il treno che ha perso Lei era un regionale, vero?

Alessandra: Sì, si fermava in tutte le stazioni; no, in quasi tutte, era un regionale veloce.

Capostazione: Mi sembra che ci sia il prossimo Intercity per Milano: quello si ferma anche all'aeroporto. Parte tra dieci minuti.

Alessandra: No! A quest'ora ci sarà una fila senza fine allo sportello, non ce la farò mai a comprare il supplemento!

Capostazione: Tranquilla, signorina, ci sono le biglietterie automatiche, che funzionano sia con i contanti che con le carte di credito e il bancomat. Mi dispiace che Lei sia così stressata, in fondo il tempo c'è, andiamo!

Alessandra: Cosa vuole, è lo stress del viaggiatore... Grazie mille, spero che non ci sia troppa gente anche alle biglietterie automatiche. (…) Ecco! Ce l'ho fatta, ho il biglietto, e adesso dov'è il treno?

Capostazione: Parte dal binario tre; Lei ha il posto 85 nella carrozza 4, è il vagone di coda, l'ultimo.

Alessandra: Finalmente all'aeroporto! Guardo subito il tabellone delle partenze… ecco! Devo andare in fretta al gate G per l'imbarco. Il mio aereo viene da Palermo, è appena atterrato e decolla tra pochissimo.

Impiegato: Scusi, signorina, il Suo bagaglio è troppo grande per essere portato in cabina. Dobbiamo etichettarlo e metterlo in stiva: è il regolamento.

Alessandra: Ma come! Questa piccolissima valigia? Pazienza, me ne separerò per qualche ora…

Impiegato: Non si preoccupi, signorina, si rilassi, il volo dura solo un'ora e mezza.

Alessandra: È già troppo, per i miei gusti!

UNDERSTANDING THE DIALOGUE
REGIONAL AND INTERCITY TRAINS

Whereas **il treno regionale** stops everywhere, **il regionale veloce** makes fewer stops, but there are quite a few even so … Trains such as the **Intercity** lines are faster and more comfortable, but the price is substantially higher. These include **la freccia rossa** *the red arrow* and **la freccia bianca** *the white arrow*, which are high-speed trains.

TWO USEFUL TERMS

→ The construction **sia … che** (or **sia … sia**) means *both … and* or *either … or*: **sia con i contanti, che con le carte di credito** *with both cash and credit cards.*

→ **tra** means *in, within* in relation to time: **tra dieci minuti** *in ten minutes.*

CULTURAL NOTE

Le FS (le Ferrovie dello Stato Italiane) ('the railways of the Italian state') is a state-owned company that manages the infrastructure and services of the Italian rail network. One of its subsidiaries is the state-owned **Trenitalia**, which is the main rail operator in Italy. The rail network has considerably improved over the last 30 years, and the legendary delays and disruptions of Italian trains are largely past history. High-speed trains such as the **Eurostar** and **Intercity** are used by many Italians, especially for business trips. Unfortunately, the trade-off for the speed and comfort of these trains is a relatively high ticket price, which means that the car remains the most common means of transport for breaks and family vacations. Passengers looking for a cheaper way to travel can take a regional train that is slower and makes a lot of stops (it's often called **il locale** *the local*, its former name). Today, privately owned train companies such as **Italo** operate services on certain lines for very reasonable prices, which may put pressure on the public transport system.

▲ CONJUGATION
THE SUBJUNCTIVE MOOD

The subjunctive mood is a verb form that is used much more frequently in Italian than in English. It is not a tense, but what is known as a grammatical mood. It is used mainly to express situations that are 'non-factual': that is, situations in which the speaker is unsure if something is possible or probable or to convey something that is hypothetical. (The verb form used for statements that express objective facts is called the indicative mood.)

This aspect of 'subjectivity' explains why the subjunctive is used after verbs such as **credere** *to believe*, **pensare** *to think*, **dubitare** *to doubt*, **immaginare** *to imagine*, etc., as well as verbs that express feelings or opinions: **temere** *to fear*, **rallegrarsi** *to be pleased*, **essere contento/a** *to be happy*, etc. The most frequent use of the subjunctive is in subordinate clauses, usually after the word **che** *that*, when there is a change of subject.

Credo che il prossimo parta tra mezz'ora.
I believe that the next one leaves in half an hour.
Mi fa piacere che Carlo venga domani.
I am pleased that Carlo is coming tomorrow.
Mi dispiace che oggi faccia brutto tempo.
I'm sorry that today the weather is bad.

As the use of the subjunctive is a bit tricky for English speakers – and even for Italians – we'll keep things simple at this stage. For now, just try to recognize its forms and start to get familiar with how it is used. Note that the subjunctive mood has different tenses. Here is the present subjunctive for the irregular verbs **avere** and **essere**, and the regular conjugations for the three verb groups:

			-are verbs	**-ere** verbs	**-ire** verbs
	avere	**essere**	**parlare**	**prendere**	**offrire**
io	**abbia**	**sia**	**parli**	**prenda**	**offra**
tu	**abbia**	**sia**	**parli**	**prenda**	**offra**
lui, lei, Lei	**abbia**	**sia**	**parli**	**prenda**	**offra**
noi	**abbiamo**	**siamo**	**parliamo**	**prendiamo**	**offriamo**
voi	**abbiate**	**siate**	**parliate**	**prendiate**	**offriate**
loro, Loro	**abbiano**	**siano**	**parlino**	**prendano**	**offrano**

• The closest English translation for the subjunctive is, for example, *that I have, that I be, that I speak, that I take, that I offer*. But as in the example sentences shown above, the present indicative is most commonly used in English in these cases.
• Many **-ire** verbs have a spelling change in which **-isc-** is inserted between the verb stem and the conjugation ending in all singular forms, as well as the third-person plural: e.g. (**finire**) **finisca**, **finisca**, **finisca**, **finiamo**, **finiate**, **finiscano**.

• Most irregular verbs form the present subjunctive by adding the conjugation endings to the verb stem of the first-person present indicative in all singular forms, as well as the third-person plural, while the first- and second-person plural (**noi** and **voi**) use the regular verb stem. For example, **venire** *to come*: **venga** *that I come*, **venga**, **venga**, **veniamo**, **veniate**, **vengano**.

MORE IRREGULAR VERBS

Here are three more frequently used verbs that are irregular in the present indicative.

	morire *to die*	**tacere** *to keep quiet*	**togliere** *to remove*
io	**muoio** *I am dying*	**taccio** *I keep quiet*	**tolgo** *I remove*
tu	**muori**	**taci**	**togli**
lui, lei, Lei	**muore**	**tace**	**toglie**
noi	**moriamo**	**tacciamo**	**togliamo**
voi	**morite**	**tacete**	**togliete**
loro, Loro	**muoiono**	**tacciono**	**tolgono**

The past participles are **morto** *died* (from **morire**), **taciuto** *kept quiet* (from **tacere**), and **tolto** *removed, taken away* (from **togliere**).

EXERCISES

1. COMPLETE WITH THE CORRECT FORM OF THE PRESENT SUBJUNCTIVE.

a. Mi dispiace che tu non .... da noi. (venire)

b. Ci sembra che voi .... troppo. (mangiare)

c. Spero che lei non .... il treno. (perdere)

d. Credo che Carla e Paolo .... l'aereo delle dodici e trenta. (prendere)

2. REWRITE THE SENTENCES IN THE PERSON GIVEN IN PARENTHESES.

Example: Credo che lei sia spagnola (loro). Credo che loro siano spagnole.

a. Spero che loro vadano al mare. (tu) →..

b. Credo che lei sia inglese. (voi) → ....

c. Mi fa piacere che tu venga a Milano. (voi) → ....

d. Non so a che ora lei finisca di lavorare. (voi) → ....

VOCABULARY

l'aereo *airplane*
l'aeroporto *airport*
a poco a poco *little by little*
atterrare *to land*
automatiche *automatic*
il bagaglio *baggage, luggage*
la biglietteria *ticket office, ticket counter, ticket machine*
il biglietto *ticket*
il binario *platform, rail, track*
la cabina *cabin*
il/la capostazione *station master*
la carrozza *railway carriage, car, wagon, coach*
il check-in *check-in* (at the airport)
comodo/a *convenient, comfortable*
il controllo *control, check, inspection*
decollare *to take off*
il decollo *take-off*
durare *to last* (a certain amount of time)
etichettare *to tag, to label* (**l'etichetta** *tag, label*)
fermarsi *to stop*
la ferrovia *railway*
la fila *queue, line*
finalmente *finally*
il gate *gate* (at the airport)
già *already*
il gusto *taste* (**i gusti** *tastes*)
l'imbarco *boarding*
in fretta *rapidly, in haste* (**la fretta** *haste, urgency*)
ogni *every, each*
la partenza *departure*
il posto *spot, place, seat*
regionale *regional*
il regolamento *regulations, rules* (sing.)
rilassarsi *to relax*
separare *to separate*
il servizio pubbico *public service*
la sicurezza *security*
la stazione *station*
la stiva *hold, cargo hold*
lo stress *stress*
stressato/a *stressed*
il supplemento *supplement, surcharge, additional charge*
il tabellone *notice board, timetable board*
il taglio *cut, incision, reduction* (**i tagli** *cuts*)
togliere *to remove, to take away*
il treno *train*
il vagone *railway carriage, car, wagon, coach*
la valigia *suitcase*
il viaggiatore / la viaggiatrice *traveller*
il volo *flight*

3. COMPLETE THE SENTENCES WITH THE CORRECT FORM OF THE IRREGULAR VERB SHOWN IN THE TENSE INDICATED.

a. Se mi sarà possibile, il mese prossimo .... da voi a Milano. (venire – future)

b. Quando che tu .... la porta, io potrò finalmente entrare a casa tua. (aprire – future perfect)

c. Le nostre vacanze al mare .... bellissime. (essere – present perfect)

d. Spero che Filippo .... bene. (scegliere – present subjunctive)

24 4. LISTEN TO THE RECORDING AND FILL IN THE MISSING WORDS.

a. Bisogna arrivare in aeroporto un'ora prima del .... per il check-in.

b. A quest'ora ci sarà una fila senza fine allo .... della biglietteria.

c. Il suo treno parte dal .... tre.

d. Non si preoccupi, signorina, si rilassi, il .... dura solo un'ora e mezza.

23. SPORTS AND FREE TIME

LO SPORT E IL TEMPO LIBERO

AIMS

- TALKING ABOUT SPORTS
- DISCUSSING YOUR STUDIES AND YOUR FAMILY

TOPICS

- THE PRESENT PERFECT SUBJUNCTIVE
- MORE VERBS THAT ARE IRREGULAR IN THE PRESENT INDICATIVE: *PRODURRE, SPEGNERE*

SPORTING GOODS

Paola: Hello, I'd like a pair of gym shoes. What *(thing)* do you recommend *(to me)*?

Salesperson: It depends, ma'am: we have tennis shoes, basketball [shoes], football [cleats], or even simply shoes for *(going)* running.

P: Yes, yes, exactly that! I need them *(to-me they-serve)* for my daily jog. The doctor has advised me to *(go)* run a bit every day. *(Of-them)* I bought a pair in a supermarket, but I don't think that it was *(has been,* subj.*)* a good purchase: I wore them only once and now my feet are hurting terribly!

S: I fear that they advised (subj.) you very badly!

P: What [would] you recommend instead?

S: For an amateur sporting activity like yours, let's say for fitness, I would suggest these *(to you)*: they are an excellent mid-range product. We produce them ourselves *(we same)*, through an Italian company that makes *(realizes)* our models. Nice, aren't they?

P: Oh yes! I would *(will)* wear these even to go for a walk!

S: I think your mobile phone may be (subj.) ringing, ma'am.

P : Oh, excuse me, usually I turn it off *(always)* when I go in a shop! – Hello? Yes, sorry, but I'm in a shop … yes, exactly, a sporting goods shop … Ah, okay, I['ll] buy it (f.) for you then. Bye! – That was my son, who needs a tracksuit *(all-in-one of physical fitness)* for the gym. You know, he's in *(he-does)* year 6 *(early middle),* and they have two hours of physical education a week.

S: What size does he wear?

P: I don't know, because he has grown so much in the last [few] months. I don't know if he still wears children's sizes.

S: Look, let's do *(like)* this: I['ll] give you an adult's small, [and] if that doesn't fit *(not goes well)*, you bring it back to me and we [will] change it [for you], okay?

P: Yes, thank you, that's very kind. Ah, give me a pair of shorts as well, and some cotton socks, still for him. Fortunately, his brother is already big and he buys *(himself them goes to buy)* his sporting goods on his own: it would be too complicated for me. He does loads of different sports, and for each [one] there is *(a)* different equipment: a kimono for judo, boxing gloves for Thai boxing, skis and boots for the hellish sports … Oh, pardon! I meant *(wanted to say)* 'winter sports'! The only sport that he doesn't do is swimming. That would be too simple: a swimsuit, a swim cap and a pair of goggles … and almost nothing to wash at home! In any case, at least he manages to buy himself stuff *(for to-buy-himself the stuff himself he-arranges)*: [as] for keeping it clean and organized *(in order)*, washed and ironed, a bit less!

25 ARTICOLI SPORTIVI

Paola: Buongiorno, vorrei un paio di scarpe da ginnastica; che cosa mi consiglia?

Commesso: Dipende, signora; abbiamo scarpe da tennis, da pallacanestro, da calcio, o anche semplicemente scarpe per andare a correre.

Paola: Sì, sì, proprio quelle! Mi servono per il mio jogging quotidiano. Il medico mi ha consigliato di andare a correre un po' ogni giorno. Ne ho comprato un paio in un supermercato, ma non credo che sia stato un buon acquisto: le ho messe solo una volta ed ora mi fanno terribilmente male i piedi!

Commesso: Temo che L'abbiano consigliata proprio male!

Paola: Lei, invece, che cosa mi consiglia?

Commesso: Per un'attività sportiva dilettantistica come la Sua, diciamo di fitness, Le consiglierei queste: sono un ottimo prodotto di media gamma. Le produciamo noi stessi, tramite una ditta italiana che realizza i nostri modelli. Belle, no?

Paola: Certo! Queste le metterò anche per andare a spasso!

Commesso: Credo che Le stia suonando il cellulare, signora.

Paola: Oh, mi scusi, di solito lo spengo sempre quando entro in un negozio! – Pronto? Sì, scusa ma sono in un negozio… sì, proprio di articoli sportivi… Ah, va bene, te la compro io allora. Ciao! – Era mio figlio, che ha bisogno di una tuta da ginnastica per la palestra; sa, fa la prima media, e hanno due ore alla settimana di educazione fisica.

Commesso: Che taglia porta?

Paola: Non so, perché è cresciuto tanto negli ultimi mesi, non so se porti ancora le taglie da bambino.

Commesso: Guardi, facciamo così: Le do una small da adulto, se non va bene me la riporta e la cambiamo; va bene?

Paola: Sì, grazie, è molto gentile. Ah, mi dia anche un paio di calzoncini e delle calze di cotone, sempre per lui. Per fortuna suo fratello è già grande e i suoi articoli sportivi se li va a comprare da solo: per me sarebbe troppo complicato. Fa un sacco di sport diversi, e per ognuno c'è un'attrezzatura diversa: il kimono per il judo, i guantoni per la boxe tailandese, gli sci e gli scarponi per gli sport infernali… Oh scusi! Volevo dire "gli sport invernali"! L'unico sport che non fa è il nuoto, sarebbe troppo semplice: un costume, una cuffia ed un paio di occhialini… e quasi niente da lavare a casa! Comunque almeno per comprarsi la roba si arrangia; per tenerla pulita e in ordine, lavata e stirata, un po' meno.

UNDERSTANDING THE DIALOGUE
ANDARE A SPASSO

The noun **lo spasso** *fun, amusement, enjoyment* is an old-fashioned word that is little used on its own today, but appears in idiomatic expressions such as **andare a spasso** *to go for a walk/stroll* and **essere a spasso** *to be unemployed.*

USING *STARE* IN THE SUBJUNCTIVE

Remember the uses of **stare** *to be* + verb? In these constructions, if the sentence is expressing something 'non-factual', hypothetical or subjective and there is a change in the subject of the verb in the subordinate clause (see the previous lesson), the verb **stare** is conjugated in the subjunctive.

→ **stare** + present participle *to be ...-ing* (to describe an action in progress, i.e. to be in the middle of doing something): **Non mi sembra che tu stia lavorando.** *It doesn't seem to me that you are* (present subjunctive) *working.*

→ **stare per** + infinitive *to be about to* + verb (to describe an imminent action): **Credo che tua sorella stia per arrivare qui.** *I think that your sister is about to* (present subjunctive) *get here.*

SOME VERBS THAT TAKE *ESSERE* AS THE AUXILIARY IN THE PERFECT TENSES

We've seen that most verbs of motion and all reflexive verbs use **essere** as the auxiliary. Some others include **crescere** *to grow* (**è cresciuto/a** *he/she has grown*, **dimagrire** *to lose weight* (**sono dimagrito/a** *I lost weight*), **ingrassare** *to gain weight* (**sono ingrassato/a** *I gained weight*), **invecchiare** *to age, to get old* (**sono invecchiati/e** *they have grown old*), **aumentare** *to increase* (**è aumentato/a** *it has increased*), **durare** *to last* (**è durato/a a lungo** *it has lasted a long time*). All these verbs convey a change over time. Don't forget that the past participle needs to agree with the subject: **Mia figlia è cresciuta.** *My daughter has grown.*

LA ROBA

This colloquial word means *stuff, things, 'the goods'.* It is always singular, so note that any adjectives and verbs used with it also need to be in the (feminine) singular. You might hear it used in idiomatic expressions such as **Roba da matti!** *That's crazy! It's unbelievable!* (**un matto** *a lunatic*, **matto/a** *crazy, insane*).

CULTURAL NOTE

Paola's younger son is in **prima media**, which is the equivalent of sixth grade or year 6 (10–11 years old). In Italy, **la scuola dell'obbligo** *compulsory schooling* goes from ages 6 to 16. It is divided into three stages: five years of **la scuola primaria** *primary school* (**la scuola dell'infanzia** *kindergarten*, for ages 3 to 5, is not compulsory), then three years of **la scuola media inferiore** *lower secondary school, middle school* (**prima, seconda** and **terza media** are the three grade levels, for ages 11 to 14), followed by five years of **la scuola media superiore** *upper secondary school, high school*. There are a number of types of upper secondary schools and degrees: **il liceo** offers an academic education with a specialization in a specific field of study (e.g. **classico** in classics, **scientifico** in science, **linguistico** in linguistics, **pedagogico** in education) or students can attend **un istituto tecnico** or **professionale** for a vocational degree. All five-year secondary schools grant access to the final exam, **la maturità**, which allows access to university.

CONJUGATION
THE PRESENT PERFECT SUBJUNCTIVE

• Remember that the present perfect is used to talk about a one-off event in the past in Italian. The present perfect subjunctive is used to express uncertainty in the present about something that occurred in the past. It is employed after present tense expressions that must be followed by the subjunctive (see the previous lesson to review this if you need to).

• The construction is typically the following: main clause (present indicative, describing what the subject thinks, believes, fears, etc. at the present time) + **che** + subordinate clause (present perfect subjunctive, describing a past event the speaker is uncertain about):

Non credo che sia stato un buon acquisto.
I don't think (indicative) *that it was* (subjunctive) *a good purchase*.

Penso che tu abbia fatto un errore.
I think (indicative) *that you have made* (subjunctive) *a mistake.*

• It is formed by conjugating the auxiliary verb in the present subjunctive + past participle. Here is an example with the irregular verb **scegliere** *to choose*:

abbia scelto *(that) I have chosen*	**abbiamo scelto** *(that) we have chosen*
abbia scelto *(that) you have chosen*	**abbiate scelto** *(that) you have chosen*
abbia scelto *(that) he/she has chosen*	**abbiano scelto** *(that) they have chosen*

• As with all perfect tenses, if the auxiliary verb is **essere**, the past participle needs to agree with the subject: (**dimagrire** *to lose weight*) **sia dimagrito/a** *(that) I, you, he, she lost weight*, **siamo dimagriti/e** *(that) we lost weight.*

MORE IRREGULAR VERBS

Here are two more frequently used verbs that are irregular in the present indicative.

	produrre *to produce*	**spegnere** *to turn off*
io	**produco** *I produce*	**spengo** *I turn off*
tu	**produci**	**spegni**
lui, lei, Lei	**produce**	**spegne**
noi	**produciamo**	**spegniamo**
voi	**producete**	**spegnete**
loro, Loro	**producono**	**spengono**

These verbs are also irregular in certain other tenses, for example:
produrrò *I will produce,* **producevo** *I used to produce,* **prodotto** *produced* (past participle), **spenga** *(that) I, you, he, she turn(s) off,* **spento** *turned off* (past participle)

EXERCISES

1. REWRITE THE SENTENCES USING THE PRESENT PERFECT SUBJUNCTIVE TO DESCRIBE AN 'UNCERTAIN' EVENT THAT TOOK PLACE IN THE PAST.

Example: Credo che il treno parta alle dodici e trenta. → Credo che il treno sia partito alle dodici e trenta.

a. Mi dispiace che tu non venga da noi.

→ ....

b. Ci sembra che voi mangiate troppo.

→ ....

c. Spero che lei non perda il treno.

→ ....

d. Credo che Carla e Paolo prendano l'aereo delle quattordici.

→ ....

VOCABULARY

l'adulto *adult*
arrangiarsi *to manage, to get by*
l'articolo *item, article*
(**gli articoli** *goods*)
l'attività *activity*
l'attrezzatura *equipment, gear*
il bambino / la bambina *child*
il calcio *football, soccer*
i calzoncini *shorts*
il costume *swimsuit*
il cotone *cotton*
la cuffia *swim cap*
dilettantistico/a *amateur, non-professional*
diverso/a *different, various*
l'educazione *education*
fisico/a *physical*
la gamma *range, selection*
la ginnastica *gym class, fitness, physical education*
i guantoni *boxing gloves*
(**il guanto** *glove*)
infernale *hellish*
invernale *wintry*
lavare *to wash*
il medico *doctor*
il modello *model*
il nuoto *swimming*
gli occhialini *swimming goggles*
l'ordine *order*
la palestra *gymnasium, training ground*
la pallacanestro *basketball*
il prodotto *product*
produrre *to produce*
pulito/a *clean, clear, tidy*
quotidiano/a *daily, everyday*
riportare *to bring back*
gli scarponi *boots* (for hiking or skiing)
lo sci *skiing*
semplicemente *simply*
sportivo/a *sporting, athletic*
stirare *to iron*
la taglia *size*
tailandese *Thai*
il tennis *tennis*
terribilmente *terribly*
la tuta *tracksuit, all-in-one*

2. REWRITE THESE SENTENCES SO THE PRESENT PERFECT SUBJUNCTIVE VERB IS IN THE PERSON INDICATED IN PARENTHESES.

Example: Credo che lei sia stata a Roma (loro). → Credo che loro siano stati a Roma.

a. Spero che loro siano andati a lavorare. (tu)

→ ....

b. Credo che lei abbia fatto un buon acquisto. (voi)

→ ....

c. Mi fa piacere che tu sia venuta a Milano. (voi)

→ ....

d. Mi sembra che lui abbia mangiato troppo. (loro)

→ ....

3. COMPLETE THE SENTENCES WITH THE CORRECT FORM OF THE IRREGULAR VERB SHOWN IN THE TENSE INDICATED.

a. Le Ferrovie dello Stato............................ molti treni su questa linea. (togliere – present perfect)

b. Non .... venire da te domani perché ho un problema alla macchina. (potere – present indicative)

c. Quando esco, ... sempre la luce. (spegnere – present indicative)

d. L'anno prossimo, la mia ditta .... molti elettrodomestici. (produrre – future)

25 4. LISTEN TO THE RECORDING AND FILL IN THE MISSING WORDS.

a. Vorrei un .... di scarpe da ginnastica per mio figlio.

b. Alle scuole medie vanno in .... due ore alla settimana per le lezioni di educazione fisica.

c. Devo comprare gli sci e gli scarponi per gli sport ....

24.
THE CINEMA AND THE THEATRE

IL CINEMA E IL TEATRO

AIMS	TOPICS
• MAKING ARRANGEMENTS TO GO OUT WITH FRIENDS • EXPRESSING PERSONAL TASTES • DISCUSSING DIFFERENT OPTIONS • TALKING ABOUT THE CINEMA AND THE THEATRE	• THE IMPERFECT AND PAST PERFECT SUBJUNCTIVE • MORE ON THE USAGE OF THE SUBJUNCTIVE

SOCIALLY ACTIVE OR ESCAPIST CINEMA?

Ludovico: What do you think about going *(To-you it-would-go to-go)* to the cinema tonight?

Simona: It depends on the film: you know *(well)* that I prefer the theatre.

L: Oh really? I thought *(that)* you liked *(to-you they-appeal,* subj.*)* both.

S: I'm not saying that I don't like cinema, but the theatre is another thing altogether *(all another thing)*. I like *(those)* theatres full of lights and chandeliers, velvet seats, the intermission in the foyer drinking a glass of sparkling wine ... I love the moment when *(in which)* the curtain opens, and on the stage the actors appear in [the] flesh *(and bone)*. You want to compare that *(put)* with the celluloid stars of the movies?

L: Imagine that *(But look)*! Who would've believed it *(would-have never said)*? It seems *(seemed)* to me that you've gone (subj.) to the cinema loads of times …

S: And I have *(gone there)*! But most *(the major part of-the)* times I leave disappointed, maybe because I'm expecting too much.

L: But *(yes)*, after all, going to the cinema should *(also)* be a diversion, shouldn't it?

S: Perhaps *(It-will-be)*, but I feel the need to make my brain work even in my free time. I don't like so-called escapist films, and I always try *(seek)* to go see socially active films that mean *(want to say)* something. Unfortunately, great Italian auteur cinema is dead, and the great masters of neorealism or Italian comedy are no more. And although I try *(seek)* not to be pessimistic, I don't see any current director[s] deserving of those big names.

L: In short, no cinema tonight …

S: No, not at all *(for charity)*! I didn't at all say that so you would change your mind *(so-that you change* [subj.] *idea)*! Rather, I'd like you to introduce me to *(to-me made* [subj.] *to-know)* a different director that I [will] really like (subj.)!

L: To tell [you] the truth, I wanted to suggest *(to you)* a romantic comedy with Sauro Perdone …

S: It wouldn't happen to be *(Not it-will-be at-all)* 'He who risks nothing, gains nothing'? It must be one of those mainstream films full of actors and TV personalities that imitate the style of TV shows, and plus *(in more)* with a lot of vulgarity and stupid jokes. No thanks!

L: Okay, I was sure of it …

S: I suggest *(to you)* instead 'Without a Past' by Paolo Correntino, which denounces the crimes of the mafia after the war.

L: Sounds light *(What cheerfulness)*! Okay, out of *(for)* friendship I['ll] go with you. At worst, I['ll] eat a kilo of popcorn [and] then go home …

26 CINEMA IMPEGNATO O CINEMA DI EVASIONE?

Ludovico: Ti andrebbe di andare al cinema stasera?

Simona: Dipende dal film; sai bene che preferisco il teatro.

Ludovico: Ah sì? Credevo che ti piacessero entrambi.

Simona: Non dico che il cinema non mi piaccia, ma il teatro è tutta un'altra cosa. Mi piacciono quelle sale piene di luci e di lampadari, le poltroncine di velluto, l'intervallo nel ridotto a bere un bicchiere di spumante; amo il momento in cui si apre il sipario e sul palcoscenico appaiono attori in carne ed ossa; vuoi mettere con le star di celluloide del cinema?

Ludovico: Ma guarda! Chi l'avrebbe mai detto! Mi sembrava che fossi andata al cinema un sacco di volte…

Simona: E ci sono andata! Ma la maggior parte delle volte esco delusa, forse perché mi aspetto troppo.

Ludovico: Ma sì, in fondo andare al cinema deve essere anche un passatempo, no?

Simona: Sarà, ma io sento il bisogno di fare funzionare il cervello anche nel mio tempo libero. Non mi piacciono i cosiddetti film d'evasione, e cerco sempre di andare a vedere film impegnati, che vogliano dire qualcosa. Purtroppo il grande cinema d'autore italiano è morto, e non ci sono più i grandi maestri del neorealismo o della commedia all'italiana. E nonostante io cerchi di non essere pessimista, non vedo nessun regista attuale degno di quei grandi nomi.

Ludovico: Insomma niente cinema stasera…

Simona: No, per carità! Non dicevo mica questo perché tu cambiassi idea! Anzi, mi piacerebbe che tu mi facessi conoscere un regista diverso, che mi piaccia davvero!

Ludovico: A dire la verità, volevo proporti una commedia sentimentale con Sauro Perdone…

Simona: Non sarà mica *Chi non risica non rosica*? Sarà uno di quei "cinepanettoni" pieni di attori e personaggi televisivi, che imitano lo stile degli sceneggiati, ed in più con tanta volgarità e battute stupide. No, grazie!

Ludovico: Va bene, ne ero sicuro…

Simona: Io ti proporrei invece *Senza passato* di Paolo Correntino, che denuncia i crimini della mafia nel dopoguerra.

Ludovico: Che allegria! Va bene, per amicizia vengo con te. Male che vada, mangio un chilo di popcorn poi me ne torno a casa…

UNDERSTANDING THE DIALOGUE

ENTRAMBI

entrambi (m.) / **entrambe** (f.) means *both* or *either*: **Mi piacciono entrambe le cose.** *Both things appeal to me. Either one appeals to me.*

THE SUBJUNCTIVE TO SHOW UNCERTAINTY

Hopefully you are starting to recognize the conjugated forms that indicate a verb is in the subjunctive. This will help you begin to get to grips with its use: as we see in this dialogue, it conveys a sense of uncertainty, subjectivity or doubt, as in **Non dico che il cinema non mi piaccia.** *I'm not saying that I don't like* (present subjunctive) *cinema*. Here its use conveys ambiguity about Simona's point of view, which is reinforced by the double negation: it is unclear whether she likes films or not. Or in the last line, **male che vada** *at worst* ('badly that it-goes' [present subjunctive]), the use of the subjunctive expresses the possibility (but not the certainty) that something will go badly.

SARÀ...

Sarà implies **sarà vero**, with the meaning *perhaps it's true*.

NIENTE

The adverb **niente** before a noun translates to *no*: **Ho mangiato un primo, un secondo, e niente caffè.** *I had a starter, a main course and no coffee.*

CULTURAL NOTE

Italian neorealism developed in the years after World War II, through the films of directors such as Vittorio De Sica (**Ladri di biciclette** *Bicycle Thieves*, 1948), Roberto Rossellini (**Roma città aperta** *Rome, Open City*, 1945) and Luchino Visconti (**La terra trema** *The Earth Trembles*, 1948). Marked by its political and social activism and showing the lives of working people hit hard by the recent conflict, neorealism aimed to depict real life and used non-professional actors. The classic period of Italian comedy produced films that were certainly more commercial than the neorealist masterpieces, but are artistic in their own right. From the 1950s, directors such as Pietro Germi (**Divorzio all'italiana** *Divorce Italian Style*, 1962), Mario Monicelli (**I soliti ignoti** *Persons Unknown*, 1958) and Dino Risi (**I mostri** *The

Monsters, 1963) painted a portrait of Italian society with strokes of dark humour. Their actors, including Ugo Tognazzi, Alberto Sordi, Marcello Mastroianni and Vittorio Gassmann, made these films famous around the world. In the 1990s, Vittorio De Sica's son Christian De Sica created mainstream comedy films, dubbed **il cinepanettone**, which were made to please the crowds. This nickname comes from the Christmas cake **il panettone**, as these comedies are typically released during the holidays when more people go to the movies.

GRAMMAR AND CONJUGATION
THE IMPERFECT AND PAST PERFECT SUBJUNCTIVE

IMPERFECT SUBJUNCTIVE

• The imperfect subjunctive is used to express uncertainty in the past about an event that took place or was expected to occur at the same time as the action in the main clause. It appears after past tense expressions that take the subjunctive (e.g. **credevo che...** / *I believed that ...*, **pensavo che...** / *I thought that ...*). Here is the imperfect subjunctive for the irregular verbs **avere** and **essere**, and the regular conjugations for the three verb groups:

			-are verbs	**-ere** verbs	**-ire** verbs
	avere	essere	parlare	prendere	finire
io	avessi	fossi	parlassi	prendessi	finissi
tu	avessi	fossi	parlassi	prendessi	finissi
lui, lei, Lei	avesse	fosse	parlasse	prendesse	finisse
noi	avessimo	fossimo	parlassimo	prendessimo	finissimo
voi	aveste	foste	parlaste	prendeste	finiste
loro, Loro	avessero	fossero	parlassero	prendessero	finissero

• These translate to *that I had, that I were, that I spoke, that I took, that I finished*.

• Only a few verbs are irregular in the imperfect subjunctive. Most are regular: that is, they are formed by adding the conjugations above to the verb stem, e.g. **andare**: **andassi, andassi, andasse, andassimo, andaste, andassero**.

PAST PERFECT SUBJUNCTIVE

• The past perfect subjunctive expresses uncertainty in the past about earlier past events. It appears after past tense expressions that take the subjunctive. It is formed by conjugating the auxiliary verb in the imperfect subjunctive + past participle.

• For example, here is the past perfect subjunctive of **scegliere** *to choose*: **avessi scelto** *(that) I had chosen,* **avessi scelto, avesse scelto, avessimo scelto, aveste scelto, avessero scelto**.

USAGE EXAMPLES

• If the main clause is in the past tense and the action in the subordinate clause happened at the same time, the imperfect subjunctive is used: **Pensavo que tu facessi un errore.** *I thought that you made a mistake.*

• If the action in the subordinate clause occurred earlier than the action in the main clause, the past perfect subjunctive is used: **Pensavo che tu avessi fatto un errore.** *I thought that you had made a mistake.*

• If the verb in the main clause is in the conditional, the imperfect subjunctive must be used: **Se avessi più soldi, comprerei una casa.** *If I had more money, I would buy a house.*

<table>
<tr><td>main clause</td><td>subordinate clause</td><td>main clause</td><td>subordinate clause</td></tr>
<tr><td colspan="4">in the present</td></tr>
<tr><td colspan="2">Spero che tu stia bene.</td><td colspan="2">Spero che tu sia stato bene.</td></tr>
<tr><td>present indicative</td><td>present subjunctive</td><td>present indicative</td><td>present perfect subj.</td></tr>
<tr><td colspan="2">I hope that you are well.</td><td colspan="2">I hope that you have been well.</td></tr>
<tr><td colspan="4">in the past</td></tr>
<tr><td colspan="2">Speravo che tu stessi bene.</td><td colspan="2">Speravo che tu fossi stato bene.</td></tr>
<tr><td>imperfect indicative (or other past tense)</td><td>imperfect subjunctive</td><td>imperfect indicative (or other past tense)</td><td>past perfect subj.</td></tr>
<tr><td colspan="2">I hoped that you were well.</td><td colspan="2">I hoped that you had been well.</td></tr>
</table>

MORE USES OF THE SUBJUNCTIVE

• The subjunctive is used in clauses that express a hypothetical goal, after terms such as **perché** *so that* or **affinché** *in order that*: **Non dicevo questo perché tu cambiassi idea.** *I wasn't saying that so that you would change your mind.*

• Or after **che** when there is a change in subject: **Cerco di andare a vedere film che vogliano dire qualcosa.** *I try to go see films that mean something.* Note the nuance that Simona is not talking about an actual film, but an ideal that she seeks.

• The subjunctive is also found in subordinate clauses after terms such as **benché** or **nonostante** *although, despite*: **Nonostante io cerchi di non essere pessimista...** *Even though I try* (present subjunctive) *not to be pessimistic ...*

VOCABULARY

l'allegria *cheerfulness, gaiety*
l'amicizia *friendship*
l'autore / l'autrice *author, artist, creator, auteur*
la battuta *joke*
il bicchiere *glass*
la carità *charity*
in carne ed ossa *in the flesh* (**la carne** *flesh, meat;* **l'osso** *bone;* **le ossa** *bones)*
la celluloide *celluloid*
il cervello *brain*
la commedia *comedy*
il crimine *crime (***i crimini** *crimes)*
degno/a *worthy, deserving*
deluso/a *disappointed, let down*
denunciare *to denounce, to decry*
il dopoguerra *postwar period*
l'evasione *escapism*
imitare *to imitate*
impegnato/a *politically or socially active, involved, committed*
l'intervallo *intermission*
il lampadario *chandelier*
il maestro *master* (**i maestri** *masters)*
il neorealismo *neorealism*
il palcoscenico *stage*
il passatempo *diversion, pastime, hobby*
il passato *the past*
il personaggio *personality, celebrity (***i personaggi** *personalities)*
pessimista *pessimistic*
la poltroncina *seat* (diminutive of **la poltrona**)
il/la regista *director*
il ridotto *foyer, entrance hall*
la sala *hall, theatre*
lo sceneggiato *TV show, televised drama* (**gli sceneggiati** *TV shows)*
sentimentale *sentimental, emotional*
il sipario *curtain*
lo spumante *sparkling wine*
stasera *tonight*
lo stile *style*
stupido/a *stupid, dumb*
il teatro *theatre*
televisivo/a *television* (adj.)
il velluto *velvet, velour*
la volgarità *vulgarity, obscene language*

EXERCISES

1. REWRITE EACH SENTENCE IN THE PAST TENSE USING THE IMPERFECT OR PAST PERFECT SUBJUNCTIVE.

a. Spero che veniate da me. Speravo ....

b. Sono contento che tu sia arrivata così presto. Ero contento ....

c. Ci sembra che siate stati molto chiari. Ci sembrava ....

d. Dubito che dicano la verità. Dubitavo ....

2. REWRITE EACH SENTENCE, PUTTING THE VERB IN THE SUBORDINATE CLAUSE IN THE PERSON INDICATED IN PARENTHESES.

a. Speravo che loro fossero andati a lavorare. (tu)

→ ....

b. Credevo che lei avesse fatto un buon acquisto. (voi)

→ ....

c. Mi faceva piacere che tu fossi venuta a Milano. (voi)

→ ....

d. Mi sembrava che lui avesse mangiato troppo. (loro)

→ ....

3. TRANSLATE THESE PHRASES INTO ITALIAN.

a. They will do. → ....

b. You (informal sing.) would choose. → ....

c. We do. → ....

d. You (pl.) will see. → ....

e. You (pl.) would see. → ....

26 ## 4. LISTEN TO THE RECORDING AND FILL IN THE MISSING WORDS.

a. Preferisci il cinema o il teatro? – Mi piacciono ....

b. Non mi piacciono i film commerciali, preferisco il cinema d'........................

c. Volevo andare al cinema, ma ho cambiato .... : niente cinema, resto a casa.

d. Quel film è di un .... molto bravo: ha ottime recensioni *(reviews)* sui giornali.

25. ARRANGING AN OUTING WITH FRIENDS

ORGANIZZARE UNA GITA TRA AMICI

AIMS	TOPICS
• DECIDING ON PLANS FOR A DAY OUT • TALKING ABOUT OUTDOOR ACTIVITIES AND PICNICS	• THE MAIN PREPOSITIONS • THE PAST CONDITIONAL TO CONVEY A POSSIBLE FUTURE OUTCOME

OUTING ON *(of)* EASTER MONDAY

Renato: At last, Easter weekend: *(ourselves)* we can rest for three days!

Aurora: In fact *(To tell the truth)*, we told *(had told to)* Susanna and *(to)* Federico that we would go *(would have gone to do)* with them on an Easter Monday outing.

R: Ah yes! But it's also rest[ful] to go amble through the woods in the hills after a week in the city traffic.

A: Yes, but where [shall] we go?

R: We had thought of Mt Lario, as from the summit there is *(one sees)* a beautiful view. Furthermore, it's a rather short hike: in three hours at most *(maximum)* we'll be at the top *(up there)*.

A: You call that short?! Keep in mind that we also need to come down *(Watch that then is-needed also to-descend)*! And with all that you men eat and drink on picnics, the descent will be difficult!

R: Speaking of which, we have to go do the shopping to make the sandwiches.

A: I already made them this morning, and not just *(other than)* sandwiches! Federico wanted us to buy *(that we buy,* subj.*)* two roast chickens *(on-the spit)* and chips, as well as wine. Imagine how you'll be in shape afterwards to get down Mt Lario!

R: And who is bringing paper plates and glasses, cutlery (pl.) and *(little)* napkins?

A: We agreed *(we had rested of agreement)* that they would bring *(would have brought)* them, but I prefer not to rely on it *(not to-trust)* so I've grabbed them as well. We'll prepare the backpacks the night before … Rather, have you thought about the route *(itinerary)*?

R: Yes, I remember it well, we must've been there 20 times … We['ll] go by car to Cantini Piazza *(large square)*, from there we['ll] climb by foot to the Mazzini shelter, and there, instead of continuing on the plateau, we['ll] take the path through the woods: the one that goes to Tana Valley. At Nena Pass, we'll cut *(one cuts)* to the right and arrive *(one arrives)* directly at Mt Lario.

A: But isn't that way too long *(like-this not it one lengthens too-much)*? From Mazzini shelter there's a very convenient shortcut for Nena Pass, without going through the woods: that path is in the shade and [can] be awfully cold.

R: I was sure that you wouldn't want *(wouldn't have wanted)* to go through the woods, with the excuse of the cold: admit *(say)* rather that you're scared *(have fear)* of vipers, because we saw one once 10 years ago. But I like the forest precisely because it's cool and full of squirrels, marmots and lovely little animals.

A: Okay, so let's do that path on the way there, but you'll see that on the way back we'll shorten it, since with all that you'll have eaten, you'll definitely want to take the shortcut. Moreover, if it's cold in the forest, it risks blocking your digestion!

27 GITA DI PASQUETTA

Renato: Finalmente il fine settimana di Pasqua: ci possiamo riposare per tre giorni!

Aurora: A dire il vero, avevamo detto a Susanna e a Federico che saremmo andati a fare con loro la gita di Pasquetta.

Renato: Certo! Ma è riposo anche andare a passeggiare per i boschi in collina, dopo una settimana nel traffico della città.

Aurora: Sì, ma dove andiamo?

Renato: Avevamo pensato al monte Lario, perché dalla cima si vede un bellissimo panorama, poi è una camminata abbastanza corta, al massimo in tre ore saremo lassù.

Aurora: Chiamala corta! Guarda che poi bisogna anche scendere! E con tutto quello che mangiate e bevete voi uomini ai picnic, la discesa sarà dura!

Renato: A proposito, dobbiamo andare a fare la spesa per fare i panini.

Aurora: L'ho già fatta io stamattina, ed altro che panini! Federico ha voluto che comprassimo due polli allo spiedo e le patatine, e anche il vino! Figurati come sarete in forma poi per scendere dal monte Lario.

Renato: E chi porta piatti e bicchieri di carta, posate e tovagliolini?

Aurora : Eravamo rimasti d'accordo che li avrebbero portati loro, ma preferisco non fidarmi e li ho presi anch'io. Prepareremo gli zaini la sera prima… Piuttosto, hai pensato all'itinerario?

Renato: Sì, me lo ricordo bene, ci saremo stati venti volte… Andiamo in macchina fino al piazzale Cantini, da lì saliamo a piedi al rifugio Mazzini e là, invece di continuare sull'altopiano prendiamo il sentiero tra i boschi, quello che va in Val Tana; al passo della Nena, si taglia a destra e si arriva dritti al monte Lario.

Aurora: Ma così non la si allunga troppo? Dal rifugio Mazzini c'è una scorciatoia comodissima per il passo della Nena, senza passare per i boschi: quel sentiero è all'ombra e ci fa un freddo terribile.

Renato: Ero sicuro che non saresti voluta passare per i boschi, con la scusa del freddo: di' piuttosto che hai paura delle vipere, perché una volta dieci anni fa, ne abbiamo vista una... A me invece il bosco piace proprio perché è fresco e pieno di scoiattoli, di marmotte e di animaletti bellissimi.

Aurora: Va bene, facciamo pure quella strada all'andata, ma vedrai che al ritorno l'accorceremo, perché con tutto quello che avrete mangiato, vorrete per forza prendere la scorciatoia. E poi, se nel bosco fa freddo, rischia di bloccarvi la digestione!

UNDERSTANDING THE DIALOGUE
AN IDIOMATIC EXPRESSION WITH *CHIAMARE*

As in English, in Italian the verb **chiamare** *to call* can be used to beg to differ with what someone says. **Ho mangiato pochi spaghetti.** *I only ate a bit of spaghetti.* **Chiamali pochi! Ne avrai mangiato mezzo chilo!** *You call that a little! You must have eaten a kilo of it!*

UOMO (SING.), *UOMINI* (PL.)

The plural of **l'uomo** *man, human being* is irregular: **gli uomini** *men, humans*.

CULTURAL NOTE

Easter Monday is also known as **il lunedì dell'Angelo**, after the angel that announced the resurrection of Jesus Christ, according to the Bible. Colloquially, Italians call it **Pasquetta** ('Little Easter'), and on this day people traditionally organize picnics in the countryside. It isn't uncommon to see dozens of families in fields eating **panini** ... and a lot of other delicious foods!

GRAMMAR
THE PAST CONDITIONAL TO CONVEY A POSSIBLE FUTURE EVENT

• The past conditional corresponds to the English *would have ... -ed*. It is formed by conjugating the auxiliary verb in the present conditional + past participle:
Avremmo mangiato tutto! *We would have eaten everything!*
• An important usage difference in Italian is that with a past tense, the past conditional must be used to talk about a possible future outcome (in English, the present conditional is used in this case): **Avevamo detto che saremmo andati a fare una gita.** *We had said that we would go* ('would have gone') *on an outing.*

THE MAIN PREPOSITIONS

We've seen quite a few different prepositions. Now is a good time to review the most important ones (see the table on the next page). One thing to note is that the prepositions used after verbs can vary from those used in English: e.g. **dire a qualcuno** *to tell someone* (the preposition **a** is required after this verb to introduce the object). Other examples include **andare a passeggiare** *to go walking*, **rischiare di bloccare** *to risk blocking* (some verbs require **a** or **di** before a following infinitive).

<table>
<tr><th>a</th><th>di</th><th>da</th><th>in</th></tr>
<tr><td>Direction of movement:
Vado a Roma.
I'm going to Rome.
Vado a lavorare.
I'm going to work.</td><td>Ownership:
la macchina di Giulia
Giulia's car</td><td>Origin and distance:
Vengo da Milano.
I come from Milan.
Abito a tre chilometri da Milano. *I live 3 km from Milan.*
Siamo lontani da Torino? *Are we far from Turin?*</td><td>Expressions describing location:
Abito in Italia.
I live in Italy.</td></tr>
<tr><td>Stating a location:
Abito a Roma.
I live in Rome.</td><td>Description:
un libro di storia
a book of stories, a storybook</td><td>To introduce the agent of the action in the passive voice:
È stato visto da tutti. *It was seen by everyone.*</td><td>Expressions describing how long an action took:
L'ho fatto in due ore. *I did it in two hours.*</td></tr>
<tr><td rowspan="4">Expressions describing location:
vicino a *near to*
davanti a *in front of*
di fronte a *opposite to, facing*
in mezzo a *in the middle of*
intorno a *around, near*
di fianco a *alongside of, next to*</td><td>Content:
una tazza di caffè
a cup of coffee</td><td>A container:
una tazza da caffè
a coffee cup</td><td rowspan="2">Expressions describing quantity:
Veniamo in due.
Two of us are coming.</td></tr>
<tr><td>After adverbs:
prima di *first of*
invece di *instead of*</td><td>*since, for*
Ti aspetto da due ore. *I've been waiting for you for two hours.*</td></tr>
<tr><td>In expressions:
Credo di no.
I don't believe so.
Dico di sì. *I say yes.*</td><td>*at someone's place*
Vieni a mangiare da noi? *Are you coming to eat at ours?*</td><td rowspan="2">To introduce a means:
Sono venuta in treno.
I came by train.</td></tr>
<tr><td>In time expressions:
di giorno, di sera, di domenica *in the daytime, in the evening, on Sunday*</td><td>Goal of an action:
È una cosa da fare. *It's something that has to be done.*</td></tr>
</table>

con	su	per	tra, fra
with **Abito con Paolo.** *I live with Paolo.* **Lavora con cura.** *He works with attention.*	*on* **L'ho dimenticato sul tavolo.** *I forgot it on the table.*	*for* to express a cause or an aim: **Sono tornato a casa per il gran freddo.** *I came home because it was very cold.* **Sono venuto per questo.** *I came because of that.*	*between* **fra me e te** *between you and me*
Means/method: **Sono arrivata con il treno delle due e mezzo.** *I arrived on the 2:30 train.*	Approximation: **un giovane sui vent'anni** *a young man about 20 years of age*	Destination: **Ho preso il treno per Roma.** *I took the train to Rome.*	*among* **fra noi tutti** *among us all*
		Movement in a defined area: **Passeggiamo per la città.** *We strolled around the city.*	*in* (referring to time): **Vengo tra due ore.** *I'm coming in two hours.*

EXERCISES

1. FILL IN THE SENTENCES WITH THE MOST APPROPRIATE PREPOSITION (OR CONTRACTED PREPOSITION + ARTICLE).

a. .... che ora parte il tuo treno?

b. Vivo .... la mia famiglia.

c. Abita e lavora .... Inghilterra.

d. Siamo partiti molto presto, ... cinque.

e. Sono partito con degli amici, eravamo .... cinque.

f. Sono stato molto tempo lontano .... Italia.

g. Vieni a cenare .... noi, abitiamo qui vicino.

h. Questo film è stato realizzato .... un bravissimo regista.

i. Sto partendo ora da casa, arriverò.............. un'ora.

VOCABULARY

accorciare *to shorten*
allungare *to lengthen*
l'altopiano *plateau*
l'andata *outward voyage, the way there*
l'animale *animal* (**gli animali** *animals;* **animaletti** *little animals)*
bloccare *to block, to impede*
il bosco *forest (***i boschi** *woods)*
la camminata *walk, hike*
la carta *paper*
la cima *summit, peak*
la collina *hill*
corto/a *short*
la digestione *digestion*
la discesa *descent*
la forma *shape, physical condition*
fresco/a *cool*
la gita *outing, excursion*
l'itinerario *route, itinerary*
lassù *up there*
la marmotta *marmot*
il monte *mountain*
l'ombra *shade*
l'ora *hour (***le ore** *hours)*
il panino *sandwich* (**i panini** *sandwiches)*
il panorama *view, landscape*
passeggiare *to stroll, to amble*
il passo *mountain pass*
le patatine *chips, fries* (**la patata** *potato)*
la paura *fear*
il piatto *plate (***i piatti** *plates)*
il piazzale *large square*
il picnic *picnic*
il pollo *chicken* (the meat)
le posate *cutlery* (pl.) *(***la posata** *piece of cutlery)*
il rifugio *shelter*
rimanere d'accordo *to agree*
riposarsi *to rest*
il riposo *rest, break*
il ritorno *return trip, the way back*
lo scoiattolo *squirrel*
la scorciatoia *shortcut*
la scusa *excuse, justification*
il sentiero *path*
lo spiedo *spit, skewer*
tagliare *to cut*
terribile *terrible, awful*
il tovagliolo *napkin, serviette* (**i tovagliolini** diminutive of **i tovaglioli** *napkins, serviettes)*
il vino *wine*
la vipera *viper, poisonous snake*
lo zaino *backpack, rucksack*

2. REWRITE THE SENTENCES IN THE PAST TO EXPRESS A POSSIBLE FUTURE OUTCOME (THIS REQUIRES THE PAST CONDITIONAL IN ITALIAN).

a. Decidiamo che faremo una gita insieme.

→ Avevamo deciso ....

b. È sicuro che andrà a Napoli.

→ Era sicuro ....

c. Mi dicono che partiranno per l'America.

→ Mi dicevano ....

d. Racconta *(He/she recounts)* che studierà all'estero *(overseas)*.

→ Raccontava che ....

27 ## 3. LISTEN TO THE RECORDING AND FILL IN THE MISSING WORDS.

a. Dalla .... del monte Lario si vede un bellissimo panorama.

b. Per fare prima *(faster)*, invece di prendere il sentiero normale, prenderemo

una ....

c. Faremo una strada all' .... ed una diversa *(different one)* al ritorno.

26. VISITING AN ART EXHIBITION

VISITARE UNA MOSTRA D'ARTE

AIMS	TOPICS
• TALKING ABOUT ART • EXPRESSING ARTISTIC TASTES AND OPINIONS • MAKING 'IF ... ' HYPOTHESES	• TENSE SEQUENCE IN 'IF' SENTENCES • MORE VERBS THAT ARE IRREGULAR IN THE PRESENT INDICATIVE: *DISTRARRE*, ETC.

THE LIFE OF AN ARTIST

Caterina: This exhibition is really wonderful. [It's] lucky *(that)* we came, isn't it?

Alessandro: Fortunately *(that)* we knew about it; who knows how many exhibitions *(ourselves)* we've missed due to *(for)* lack of information.

Caterina: If we read (subj.) the papers more often, maybe we would be better *(more)* informed.

Alessandro: It's true: even this time, if we hadn't read (subj.) the newspaper by chance at the café, we wouldn't have known about it

Caterina: Or as *(to-the)* usual, we would have learned about it a month after the closing, and we would've said: what a shame *(what sin)*!

Alessandro: Besides *(Of-the rest)*, if I read the newspaper in the morning at the office, or even just if I am distracted [for] a minute, my boss calls me every name in the book *(of-it he-says of all the colours)*! And in the afternoon, when I get *(return)* home, who wants *(has desire)* to start *(put-oneself)* reading?

Caterina: Come on, let's not talk about depressing *(sad)* things, let's enjoy *(benefit-ourselves)* these marvels! In any case, if you hear *(will-come to know)* about other exhibitions like this, will you tell me about it and *(there)* we will go for sure. This painter truly knows how to do everything: portraits, landscapes, still life, even abstract paintings, though I always prefer figurative painting.

Alessandro: In the last *(preceding)* room, there were also his sculptures, both bas-relief and 360° statues.

Caterina: He appeals to me above all as a painter: he has a very full *(rich)* palette, with broad brush strokes that leave a thick layer *(depth)* of colour on the canvas, [resulting in] a really exciting painting, don't you think *(find)*?

Alessandro: Also in his sculptures, it seems that he attacks (subj.) the block of marble with his chisel, and in any case he always leaves it rough, without polishing it, like a testimony of his struggle with the material.

Caterina: When he started *(At-the his beginnings)*, he was criticized a lot, you know, because he was considered a conservative artist, precisely because of his strong connection with the tradition of the great Renaissance and Italian Baroque artists. Those *(They)* were the years of conceptual art and Arte Povera, when the 'death of art' was declared and they *(one)* criticized the humble work of the artist in his or her studio, the hours spent making sketches and studies on paper with a simple pencil or going at [the crack of] dawn to the countryside with a canvas and easel to look for subjects to paint from real llife.

Alessandro: It seems like you're talking (subj.) about the life of a martyred saint!

Caterina: But do you realize *(yourself you-render account of)* how many sacrifices the life of an artist involves *(is made)*?

Alessandro: Look, if it's like that, then I'm not so bad [off] at the office: my boss is starting to seem *(to-me becomes-again)* nice!

28 VITA D'ARTISTA

Caterina: Questa mostra è davvero bellissima; meno male che siamo venuti, vero?

Alessandro: Meno male che l'abbiamo saputo; chissà quante mostre ci siamo persi per mancanza di informazione.

Caterina: Se leggessimo più spesso i giornali, forse saremmo più informati.

Alessandro: È vero: anche questa volta, se non avessimo letto il giornale per caso al bar, non l'avremmo saputo.

Caterina: O come al solito l'avremmo imparato un mese dopo la chiusura, e avremmo detto: che peccato!

Alessandro: Del resto, se leggo il giornale alla mattina in ufficio, o anche solo se mi distraggo un minuto, il mio capo me ne dice di tutti i colori! E al pomeriggio, quando torno a casa, chi ha voglia di mettersi a leggere?

Caterina: Dai, non parliamo di cose tristi, godiamoci queste meraviglie. In ogni caso, se verrai a sapere di altre mostre come questa, me lo dirai e ci andremo di sicuro. Questo pittore sa fare proprio di tutto: ritratti, paesaggi, nature morte, persino quadri astratti, anche se io preferisco sempre la pittura figurativa.

Alessandro: Nella sala precedente c'erano anche sue sculture, sia bassorilievi che statue a tutto tondo.

Caterina: A me piace soprattutto come pittore: ha una tavolozza veramente ricchissima, con larghe pennellate che lasciano sulla tela un grosso spessore di colore: una pittura davvero emozionante, non trovi?

Alessandro: Anche nelle sculture sembra che aggredisca il blocco di marmo con lo scalpello, ed in ogni caso lo lascia sempre grezzo, senza lucidarlo, come una testimonianza della sua lotta con la materia.

Caterina: Ai suoi esordi è stato tanto criticato, sai, perché era considerato un artista conservatore, proprio per il suo legame forte con la tradizione dei grandi artisti del Rinascimento e del barocco italiano. Erano gli anni dell'arte concettuale e dell'arte povera, in cui si proclamava la morte dell'arte e si criticava il lavoro umile dell'artista nel suo studio, le ore passate a fare schizzi e studi su carta con una semplice matita o ad andare all'alba per la campagna con tela e cavalletto a cercare soggetti da dipingere dal vero.

Alessandro: Sembra che tu stia parlando della vita di un santo martire!

Caterina: Ma ti rendi conto di quanti sacrifici è fatta la vita di un artista?

Alessandro: Guarda, se è così non sto poi così male in ufficio: il mio capo mi ridiventa simpatico!

UNDERSTANDING THE DIALOGUE
MORE USES OF REFLEXIVE VERBS

Sometimes verbs are used reflexively in Italian to deliberately exaggerate the meaning, as in **ci siamo persi una mostra** *we missed an exhibition* (from **perdersi**). It's also possible to say **abbiamo perso una mostra** (from **perdere**), which means the same thing but is more neutral. The usual meaning of **perdersi** is *to get lost, to lose one's way*: **ci siamo persi** *we got lost*. When verbs are used reflexively to amplify the meaning, they are always followed by a direct object: **Godiamoci queste meraviglie.** *Let's enjoy these marvels.* (from **godersi**) or **Mi faccio una bella vacanza.** *I'm having an amazing holiday.* (from **farsi**).

VENIRE A SAPERE

Translating literally as 'to come to know', this verb phrase means *to be aware, to find out, to hear*. **Come lo sei venuto a sapere?** *How did you find out about it?*

CULTURAL NOTE

L'arte povera ('poor art') was an artistic movement that emerged at the end of the 1960s in Italy. It was a reaction against the principles and techniques of academic art, with artists choosing to use commonplace or mundane materials such as wood, iron, earth, and often industrial waste materials, to attack the values of established institutions and contemporary society. While in some ways the art resembles Art Brut or outsider art, **l'arte povera** was not the work of inexperienced or self-taught makers, but on the contrary a highly intellectualized movement of elite avant-garde artists, such as Michelangelo Pistoletto, Giovanni Anselmo and Giulio Paolini.

GRAMMAR
TALKING ABOUT HYPOTHETICAL SITUATIONS WITH 'IF'

Let's look at the tense sequence in **se** (*if …*) sentences in Italian.

• To describe a hypothetical situation in the present, the **se** clause must be in the imperfect subjunctive, and the main clause in the present conditional:

Se leggessimo i giornali, saremmo più informati.

imperfect subjunctive — present conditional

If we read the newspapers, we would be better informed.

past indicative — present conditional

• To describe a hypothetical situation in the past, the **se** clause is in the past perfect subjunctive, and the main clause is in the past conditional:

Se non avessimo letto il giornale, non l'avremmo saputo.

past perfect subjunctive — past conditional

If we had not read the newspaper, we wouldn't have known about it.

past perfect indicative — conditional perfect

• If a hypothetical situation is presented as something factual (so is not really a hypothesis), the present indicative is used in both clauses:

Se leggo il giornale in ufficio, il mio capo me ne dice di tutti i colori.

present indicative — present indicative

If I read the newspaper at the office, my boss calls me every name in the book.

present indicative — present indicative

• To describe a possible future situation, several combinations of the present and future indicative can be used in the clauses: present/present, present/future (as in English) or future/future (which is not possible in English):

Se verrai a sapere di altre mostre, me lo dirai e ci andremo.

future indicative — future indicative — future indicative

If you find out about other exhibitions, tell me about it and we'll go.

present indicative — imperative — future indicative

▲ CONJUGATION
MORE VERBS THAT ARE IRREGULAR IN THE PRESENT TENSE

In this dialogue, we encountered a new verb that is irregular in several tenses: **distrarre** *to distract*. We saw it used in the reflexive form **mi distraggo** *I am distracted* (from **distrarsi** *to be distracted*). This verb conjugates like other verbs ending in **-trarre**, for example: **trarre** *to pull, to draw*, **attrarre** *to attract, to lure*, **contrarre** *to contract*, **sottrarre** *to subtract*. Here are the forms of **distrarre** in the present indicative:

io	**distraggo**	**noi**	**distraiamo**
tu	**distrai**	**voi**	**distraete**
lui, lei, Lei	**distrae**	**loro, Loro**	**distraggono**

• Verbs ending in **-trarre** are also irregular in the future (e.g. **distrarrò** *I will distract*), in the conditional (e.g. **distrarrei** *I would distract*) and in the present subjunctive (e.g. **distragga** *(that) I/you/he/she distract*).

• The past participle is **distratto**, and the present participle is **distraendo**.

EXERCISES

1. FILL IN THE SENTENCES WITH THE MOST APPROPRIATE PREPOSITION (OR CONTRACTED PREPOSITION + ARTICLE).

a. Abitiamo .... Italia.

b. Vivete .... Milano.

c. Vivo qui .... tre anni e questa città mi piace molto.

d. La mia casa è proprio di fronte .... museo archeologico.

2. COMPLETE THESE 'IF' SENTENCES BY CONJUGATING THE VERB IN PARENTHESES IN THE CORRECT FORM.

a. Se .... per Roma, veniamo di certo da voi. (passare)

b. Se .... comprare una macchina nuova, lo faranno di sicuro. (potere)

c. Se ....ricco, mi comprerei una macchina sportiva. (essere)

d. Se .... quel film entrambi, ora potremmo parlarne. (vedere)

3. TRANSLATE THESE SENTENCES INTO ITALIAN.

a. If you (informal sing.) want to talk to me, I'll come to your place.

→ ....

b. If I had known about it, I wouldn't have come.

→ ....

c. If you (informal pl.) go to France next year, we'll come with you.

→ ....

d. If you (informal sing.) were here, we could talk about it.

→ ....

4. COMPLETE THE 'IF' SENTENCES BY CONJUGATING THE VERB IN PARENTHESES.

a. Se mi scriverai, io di certo ti .... (rispondere)

b. Se mi avessi scritto, io di certo ti .... (rispondere)

c. Se foste venuti a quella mostra, ... dei quadri bellissimi. (vedere)

d. Se abitaste più vicini a casa nostra, noi .... più spesso da voi. (venire)

VOCABULARY

aggredire *to attack*
l'alba *dawn*
l'arte *art*
l'artista *artist* (**gli artisti/e** *artists*)
astratto/a *abstract*
barocco/a *Baroque, ornate*
il bassorilievo *bas-relief*
il blocco *block*
la campagna *countryside*
il capo *boss, head*
il cavalletto *easel*
chissà *who knows*
la chiusura *closing, closure*
concettuale *conceptual*
conservatore *conservative*
considerare *to consider*
criticare *to criticize*
dipingere *to paint*
emozionante *exciting, moving*
l'esordio *beginning*
figurativo/a *figurative*
godersi *to enjoy oneself*
    (**godere** *to enjoy*)
grezzo/a *rough, coarse, crude*
largo/a *wide, broad* (**larghe**, pl.)
il legame *connection, link*
la lotta *struggle, battle*
lucidare *to polish*
la mancanza *lack, shortage*
il marmo *marble*
il/la martire *martyr*
la materia *material*
la matita *pencil*
la morte *death*
la mostra *exhibition*
la natura morta *still life*
    (**la natura** *nature*)
il paesaggio *landscape*
    (**i paesaggi** *landscapes*)
il peccato *sin, crime, shame*
la pennellata *brush stroke*
la pittura *painting*
povero/a *poor*
proclamare *to declare, to proclaim*
ricco/a *rich, lavish, abundant*
    (**ricchissimo/a** *very rich*)
il Rinascimento *the Renaissance*
il ritratto *portrait*
il sacrificio *sacrifice*
il santo / la santa *saint*
lo scalpello *chisel*
lo schizzo *sketch*
    (**gli schizzi** *sketches*)
la scultura *sculpture*
    (**le sculture** *sculptures*)
il soggetto *subject*
    (**i soggetti** *subjects*)
lo spessore *thickness, depth*
la statua *statue*
lo studio *studio, workshop*
la tavolozza *palette*
la tela *canvas*
la testimonianza *testimony*
tondo/a *round*
    (**a tutto tondo** *all-round, 360°*)
la tradizione *tradition*
triste *sad, gloomy, depressing*
umile *humble, modest*
la voglia *desire*
    (**avere voglia** *to want*)

28 ## 5. LISTEN TO THE RECORDING AND FILL IN THE MISSING WORDS.

a. Io e mio marito ci siamo .... molte mostre per mancanza di informazione.

b. L'abbiamo imparato un mese dopo la chiusura, e ci siamo detti: che .... !

c. C'è chi ama *(There are those who love)* l'arte astratta, ma io preferisco la pittura ....

d. Se mi .... anche solo un minuto, il mio capo me ne dice di tutti i colori!

27. AT THE RESTAURANT

AL RISTORANTE

AIMS	TOPICS

AIMS

- CHOOSING AND ORDERING FROM A RESTAURANT MENU
- TALKING ABOUT YOUR TASTES IN FOOD
- UNDERSTANDING THE NAMES OF DISHES

TOPICS

- THREE TYPES OF 'IF' SENTENCES DESCRIBING A HYPOTHETICAL SITUATION

AT A LOCAL RESTAURANT

Elena: This trattoria is really lovely! Look, even the forks, knives and spoons look like *(they-seem)* objects of art! How did you hear about it *(it you-have known)*?

Roberto: I read a review in *(on)* a food magazine *(magazine of cuisine)*.

E: I didn't know that you read (subj.) cooking magazines!

R: Oh, you know, it's a bit [of] a trend: people are *(one is)* talking about it so much that I became curious *(to-me has come the curiosity)*. I started to watch TV shows [about food], then I tried to cook a few dishes following the recipe. But to tell [you] the truth, it appeals to me more to go to *(in-the)* good restaurants like this [one]! What *(of-it)* do you say we have a look *(give a glance)* at the menu? I wouldn't want the waiter to arrive *(that the waiter arrive,* subj.*)* and we aren't *(that we not be,* subj.*)* ready to order.

E: Sure! What do you recommend as a starter? What did your magazine say?

R: Look, usually if a review suggests a particular speciality, I always get it, but this time it talked only about an excellent liver Vicenza-style, and nothing about first courses. So order what *(Take by-all-means that which)* you like, then we'll judge as well, as if we were (subj.) two journalists who have to write a review *(exactly)*.

E: In any case, if the newspaper recommended (subj.) a dish that I don't like, I wouldn't get it! I have rather simple tastes: I['ll] get the penne Bolognese.

R: I prefer farfalle with rabbit *(sauce of hare)*. It might even be *(If-only it's)* real wild game. They opened the hunting season *(the hunt)* just last week.

E: How awful *(What horror)*! I am for the abolition of this barbarity! You see? If your paper had recommended (subj.) a game-based dish, I surely wouldn't have followed its advice!

R: Okay, okay, calm down … I['ll] get a noodle soup *(soup in broth)* if you want … So I imagine that as [a] main, you won't want the stew of wild boar?

E: No way *(But not-even for dream)*! And plus I'm not hungry enough to eat a second course as well. Usually I have *(I-lunch with)* a plate of pasta for lunch.

R: Do you want *(that we-take,* subj.*)* an hors-d'œuvre, perhaps vegetarian?

E: No, no, your game has spoiled *(to-me has made pass)* my appetite … On the other hand, I'm thirsty: shall we get *(we-make bring)* a bottle of mineral water?

R: Do you want *(it)* sparkling or still?

E: Whatever *(As)* you want.

R: Which wine [shall] we choose? Usually one drinks red with meat and white with fish, but you don't eat either one or the other …

E: I don't drink, thank you. I am teetotal.

R: How jolly *(What gaiety)*! And perhaps instead of *(at-the place of-the)* dessert, a bit of baking soda to [help us] digest?

29 IN TRATTORIA

Elena: Questa trattoria è bellissima! Guarda: perfino le forchette, i coltelli e i cucchiai sembrano oggetti d'arte! Come l'hai conosciuta?

Roberto: Ho letto la recensione su una rivista di cucina.

Elena: Non sapevo che leggessi riviste di cucina!

Roberto: Oh, sai, è un po' una moda: se ne parla tanto che mi è venuta la curiosità. Ho cominciato a guardare delle trasmissioni alla televisione, poi ho provato a cucinare qualche piatto seguendo la ricetta. Ma per dire la verità, mi piace di più andare nei buoni ristoranti come questo! Che ne dici di dare un'occhiata al menù? Non vorrei che il cameriere arrivasse e che noi non fossimo pronti a ordinare.

Elena: Certo! Che cosa mi consigli come primo? Che cosa raccontava la tua rivista?

Roberto: Guarda, di solito, se una recensione consiglia una specialità in particolare, io la prendo sempre, ma questa volta parlava solo di un'ottimo fegato alla vicentina, e niente sui primi. Prendi pure quello che ti piace, poi giudicheremo anche noi, come se fossimo due giornalisti che devono scrivere una recensione, appunto.

Elena: In ogni caso, se il giornale consigliasse un piatto che non mi piace, io non lo prenderei! Ho dei gusti abbastanza semplici: prendo le penne al ragù.

Roberto: Io preferisco le farfalle al sugo di lepre. Magari è vera cacciagione. Hanno aperto la caccia proprio la settimana scorsa.

Elena: Che orrore! Io sono per l'abolizione di questa barbarie! Vedi? Se il tuo giornale avesse consigliato un piatto a base di cacciagione, io non avrei di certo seguito il suo consiglio!

Roberto: Va bene, va bene, calmati… Prendo una minestra in brodo, se vuoi… Quindi immagino che come secondo non vorrai lo spezzatino di cinghiale…

Elena: Ma neanche per sogno! E poi non ho abbastanza fame per mangiare anche il secondo. Di solito io pranzo con un piatto di pasta.

Roberto: Vuoi che prendiamo un antipasto, magari vegetariano?

Elena: No, no, la tua cacciagione mi ha fatto passare l'appetito… In compenso ho sete, facciamo portare una bottiglia d'acqua minerale?

Roberto: La vuoi gasata o naturale?

Elena: Come vuoi tu.

Roberto: Quale vino scegliamo? Di solito si beve rosso con la carne e bianco con il pesce, ma tu non mangi nè l'una nè l'altro…

Elena: Io non bevo, grazie, sono astemia.

Roberto: Che allegria! E magari al posto del dolce un po' di bicarbonato per digerire?

UNDERSTANDING THE DIALOGUE
EATING OUT IN ITALY

Italian food is world-famous and is very often good wherever you choose to eat. There are a range of options for eating out: a **ristorante** is a restaurant with more upscale cuisine, a **trattoria** is a family-run restaurant with local dishes, and an **osteria** has simple, regional food. The latter two typically feature homemade local cooking. Some restaurants offer a fixed-price set of courses (**il menù fisso** or **il menù turistico**). The menu (**il menù**) is divided into courses: **l'antipasto** *hors-d'œuvre, appetizer*, **il primo** *starter, first course*, which is almost always pasta or soup (another word for **il primo** is **la minestra** *soup*: the dialogue mentions **la minestra in brodo** which is noodles in broth), **il secondo** *main course* (meat or fish), and, last but not least, **il dolce** *dessert*.

COME SE...

After **come se**, the verb must be in the imperfect or past perfect subjunctive, as in other hypothetical 'if' sentences. In the present: **Me lo chiedi come se fosse una cosa facile!** *You ask me that as if it were* (imperfect subjunctive) *something easy!* In the past: **Parlava fortissimo, come se fossimo stati lontani.** *He was speaking very loudly, as if we were* (past perfect subjunctive) *far away*.

NÈ... NÈ

The conjunction **nè** *neither, nor* is used in the phrase **nè l'una nè l'altro** *neither one nor the other*. However, note that in Italian, it can also be used in a sentence with a negative verb, so in that case translates to *either ... or*: **Tu non mangi nè l'una nè l'altro.** *You don't eat either one or the other.*

CULTURAL NOTE

There are more than 200 different types of Italian pasta, each of which takes its name from its shape or its origins. For example, **penne** (from **la penna** *quill*), **farfalle** (from **la farfalla** *butterfly*), **orecchiette** (from **l'orecchio** *ear*), **linguine** (from **la lingua** *tongue*), **reginette** (from **la regina** *queen*), **cavatappi** *corkscrew*, **conchiglie** (from **la conchiglia** *shell*), **creste di gallo** *rooster's crest*, **fisarmoniche** (from **la fisarmonica** *accordion*), **lumache** (from **la lumaca** *snail*), and even **strozzapreti** ('strangle-priests'), a pasta said to be designed to choke gluttonous clergymen!

GRAMMAR
THREE TYPES OF 'IF …' SENTENCES

In an 'if' sentence describing a hypothetical situation, the main clause states a possible outcome that depends on a condition given in the subordinate clause (the 'if' clause):

subordinate clause	main clause
Se domani farà bello	**andremo al mare.**
It it's ('will be') *nice tomorrow,*	*we'll go to the sea.*

In this lesson's dialogue, the conversation includes three types of 'if' sentence, in which the tense sequence varies according to the degree of probability that the outcome will occur (or did occur), according to the speaker:

→ **Se una recensione consiglia una specialità in particolare, io la prendo sempre.** *If a review recommends a particular speciality, I always get it.* Roberto simply states what he does (present indicative) when a certain situation arises (present indicative).

→ **Se il giornale consigliasse un piatto che non mi piace, io non lo prenderei!** *If the paper recommended a dish I don't like, I wouldn't get it!* Elena says what she wouldn't do (present conditional) if something was to happen (imperfect subjunctive, as it describes a possibility that may not occur).

→ **Se il tuo giornale avesse consigliato un piatto a base di cacciagione, io non avrei di certo seguito il suo consiglio!** *If your paper had recommended a game-based dish, I surely wouldn't have followed its advice!* Elena describes a possibility that didn't happen in the past (past perfect subjunctive) and what she wouldn't have done as a result (past conditional).

Let's have a closer look at these three types of 'if' sentences:

1. The hypothesis is real or highly probable

This is a simple supposition, presented in a neutral way without taking a position on the probability of the outcome. In this case, the indicative mood (present or future tense) is used in both clauses:

subordinate clause	main clause
Se fai presto	**arriverai in tempo.**
present indicative	future indicative
If you do it quickly,	*you'll arrive in time.*

2. The hypothesis is possible but not certain

The speaker making the hypothesis is not sure if the outcome will occur. In this case, the verb in the subordinate clause is in the imperfect subjunctive and the verb in the main clause is in the present conditional:

subordinate clause	main clause
Se facessi presto	**arriveresti in tempo.**
imperfect subjunctive	present conditional
If you were to do it quickly,	*you would arrive in time.*

3. The hypothesis (condition or outcome) is impossible or unattainable

• In the present: The situation is unachievable (or totally imaginary) in the present or the future. The verb in the subordinate clause is in the imperfect subjunctive, and the verb in the main clause is in the present conditional:

subordinate clause	main clause
Se io fossi in te	**non accetterei la sua proposta.**
imperfect subjunctive	present conditional
If I were you,	*I would not accept his/her offer.*

• In the past: Neither the condition nor the outcome occurred. The verb in the subordinate clause is in the past perfect subjunctive, and the verb in the main clause is in the past conditional (the conditional perfect in English):

subordinate clause	main clause
Se avessi fatto presto	**saresti arrivato in tempo.**
past perfect subjunctive	conditional perfect
If you had done it quickly,	*you would have arrived in time.*

EXERCISES

1. FILL IN THE SENTENCES WITH THE MOST APPROPRIATE PREPOSITION (OR CONTRACTED PREPOSITION + ARTICLE).

a. È molto bravo *(capable/clever)*, lavora .... molta cura.

b. Siamo andati .... un ristorante cinque stelle *(star)*.

c. Mi piace leggere riviste .... cucina.

d. Ieri hanno guardato un bel film ....televisione.

VOCABULARY

l'abolizione *abolition*
abstemo/a *teetotal*
l'appetito *appetite*
la barbarie *barbarity, savagery*
il bicarbonato *baking soda*
la bottiglia *bottle*
il brodo *broth, bouillon*
la caccia *hunt, hunting*
la cacciagione *wild game*
calmarsi *to calm oneself*
il cameriere / la cameriera *waiter / waitress*
il campo *field, area of expertise*
la carne *meat*
il cinghiale *wild boar*
il coltello *knife* (**i coltelli** *knives)*
consigliare *to advise, to recommend, to suggest*
il cucchiaio *spoon* (**i cucchiai** *spoons)*
cucinare *to cook*
la curiosità *curiosity*
digerire *to digest*
la fame *hunger* (**avere fame** *to be hungry)*
il fegato *liver*
la forchetta *fork* (**le forchette** *forks)*
gasato/a *carbonated, fizzy*
giudicare *to judge*
in particolare *in particular*
la lepre *hare*
magari *if only, I wish, perhaps*
il menù *menu*
minerale *mineral*
la moda *fashion, style, trend, fad*
nè ... nè *neither ... nor*
l'occhiata *glance, glimpse*
l'oggetto *object* (**gli oggetti** *objects)*
ordinare *to order*
l'orrore *horror*
il piatto *dish, plate*
raccontare *to recount*
il ragù *meat sauce*
la ricetta *recipe*
la rivista *magazine*
la sete *thirst* (**avere sete** *to be thirsty)*
il sogno *dream*
la specialità *speciality*
lo spezzatino *stew*
il sugo *sauce, gravy, juice*
la trasmissione *broadcast, programme*
la trattoria *family-run local restaurant*
vegetariano/a *vegetarian*
la verità *truth*
il vino *wine*

e. La recensione non diceva niente .... primi di questa trattoria.

f. Avete mai mangiato le penne .... ragù?

g. .... solito, pranzo con un piatto di pasta e nient'altro *(nothing else)*.

2. COMPLETE THE 'IF' SENTENCES BY CONJUGATING THE VERBS IN PARENTHESES IN THE APPROPRIATE TENSE AND PERSON.

a. Te lo prometto: se domani lo .... gliene .... di sicuro. (io – incontrare – parlare)

b. Se io .... in te, ... meno. (essere – lavorare)

c. Se invece di perdere sempre il vostro tempo a giocare voi .... di più,

.... ottimi risultati a scuola. (studiare – avere)

d. L'anno scorso, se invece di perdere il vostro tempo a giocare voi ....

di più, ... ottimi risultati a scuola. (studiare – avere)

3. TRANSLATE THESE SENTENCES INTO ENGLISH.

a. Se potrò venire da voi, verrò di sicuro.

→ ....

b. Ho scelto questa macchina perché mi piace molto.

→ ....

c. Non fai nessuno sport, ma dovresti.

→ ....

d. Salgono sulla cima della montagna.

→ ....

29 4. LISTEN TO THE RECORDING AND FILL IN THE MISSING WORDS.

a. Come .... prendo spaghetti al ragù.

b. Poi come .... uno spezzatino.

c. Ho letto una recensione di questa trattoria su una .... di cucina.

d. Con questo caldo non ho molta fame, ma ho ....

28. GOING SHOPPING

FARE SHOPPING

AIMS	TOPICS
• TALKING ABOUT CLOTHES AND FASHION • GOING TO A SHOPPING CENTRE • SHARING DIFFERING OPINIONS AND EXPRESSING PREFERENCES	• REVIEW EXERCISES

AT THE SHOPPING CENTRE

Marco: I hate these horrible shopping centres, where you walk *(one walks)* under the neon lights for kilometres and spend half [your] salary buying useless things. Meanwhile, outside it's beautiful weather, splendidly sunny *(there's a sun magnificent)*, the *(little)* birds are singing on the trees and we're in here *(here inside)* suffocating.

Elsa: Oh Marco, what [a] grouch! Just because once a month I ask you to come with me to do a bit of shopping. My colleagues' husbands *(there)* go without making all this fuss *(all these stories)* … Let's take *(We-go-up with)* the escalator *(stairs moving)* to the second floor, I want to go see the new Maletton collection, I always find the clothes really cute.

M: We could also take the elevator: I'm already carrying a tonne of bags and sacks …

E: Come on, come up this way *(by here)* with me, grump *(unpleasant)*! I want to go in that shop right there *(precisely)* because last year it had *(there I-have seen)* very colourful little summer dresses, long skirts [that were] a bit 'gypsy' and patterned tank tops. Look, this leather jacket would look good on you *(to-you would-go well)*: don't you like it?

M: *(But)* Just imagine! The James Dean studded leather jacket! Can you picture me walking around wearing that thing *(But me there you-see on stroll with that thing on)*?

E: Of course I can picture you! You would be a bit less gloomy: you always seem [like you're] dressed for a funeral *(dressed in mourning)* …

M: Come on, look at the clothes for you: it's you who wants to redo your wardrobe, not me!

E: You're right. I want to try on these long-sleeved T-shirts. Where are the changing rooms?

M: There they are, they're over there at the back, but there's an insane queue!

E: How does this look on me *(to-me is this)*? You don't think it's *(that it-be,* subj.*)* too big for me?

M: Yes, maybe it's better to try *(that you-try,* subj.*)* a smaller size. I['ll] go get it for you *(in-the department)*. Here, this one looks *(is)* really good on you, it's perfect. You look *(are)* very pretty dressed like that.

E: Huh, what [a] compliment! Your bad mood is over *(To-you has passed the bad-mood)* about coming *(having come)* with me to the shopping centre ?

M: Yes, well, actually *(at bottom)* I like keeping *(making)* you company. Plus, I *(to-you it)* confess: while I was going to get you the T-shirt, I looked out the window and it's raining. When the weather's bad, it's better to be indoors. Maybe even the *(little)* birds, if they were able to (subj.), would willingly come *(to do)* shopping when it rains!

30 NEL CENTRO COMMERCIALE

Marco: Odio questi orridi centri commerciali, dove si cammina sotto le luci al neon per chilometri e si spende mezzo stipendio comprando cose inutili. Intanto fuori fa bel tempo, c'è un sole magnifico, gli uccellini cantano sugli alberi e noi siamo qui dentro a soffocare.

Elsa: Uffa, Marco, che brontolone! Solo perché una volta al mese ti chiedo di accompagnarmi a fare un po' di compere; i mariti delle mie colleghe ci vanno senza fare tutte queste storie... Saliamo con le scale mobili al secondo piano, voglio andare a vedere la nuova collezione di Maletton, ci trovo sempre vestiti carinissimi.

Marco: Potremmo anche prendere l'ascensore: sto già portando una tonnellata di borse e sacchetti...

Elsa: Dai, sali di qua con me, antipatico! Voglio andare in quel negozio proprio perché l'anno scorso ci ho visto dei vestitini estivi coloratissimi, gonne lunghe un po' zingaresche e canottiere fantasia. Guarda, questo giubbotto di pelle ti andrebbe bene: non ti piace?

Marco: Ma figurati! Il "chiodo" alla James Dean! Ma mi ci vedi, in giro con quel "coso" addosso?

Elsa: Certo che ti ci vedo! Saresti un po' meno lugubre, sembri sempre vestito a lutto...

Marco: Dai, guarda i vestiti per te: sei tu che vuoi rifarti il guardaroba, mica io!

Elsa: Hai ragione; voglio provarmi queste magliette a manica lunga. Dove sono le cabine di prova?

Marco: Eccole, sono là in fondo, ma c'è una fila pazzesca!

Elsa: Come mi sta questa? Non trovi che sia troppo grande per me?

Marco: Sì, forse è meglio che provi una taglia più piccola, te la vado a prendere io nel reparto. Ecco, questa ti sta benissimo, è perfetta; sei molto carina vestita così.

Elsa: Uh, che complimento! Ti è passato il malumore per essere venuto con me nel centro commerciale?

Marco: Sì, dai, in fondo mi fa piacere farti compagnia. E poi, te lo confesso: mentre andavo a prenderti la maglietta, ho guardato dalla finestra e sta piovendo. Quando fa brutto, è meglio stare al chiuso. Forse anche gli uccellini, se potessero, verrebbero volentieri a fare shopping, quando piove!

UNDERSTANDING THE DIALOGUE
SOME IDIOMATIC EXPRESSIONS

- → We've now seen the interjection **dai** in a number of lessons. It's time to explain this very commonly used term. It is the **tu** imperative of the verb **dare** *to give*, so literally **Dai!** means *Give!* It can convey different things, but typically it is used in the sense of *Come on!* to urge someone to do (or not to do) something: **Dai, non ti arrabbiare!** *Come on, don't get angry!* As it is an informal **tu** command, it should only be used in casual contexts, not in formal conversations.
- → Another commonly used **tu** imperative (of **figurarsi** *to imagine*) is **Figurati!** which means *Just imagine!*
- → A reminder of how to talk about the weather in Italian: **fa bel tempo** *it's nice weather*, **fa brutto** *it's bad weather*.
- → To say that something looks good on someone, you can use **andare bene** or **stare bene**: **Questo giubbotto di pelle ti andrebbe bene.** *This leather jacket would look good on you.* **Come mi sta questa?** *How does this one look on me?* **Questa ti sta benissimo.** *This one looks great on you.*

IL "COSO"

The colloquial masculine term **il coso** means *thingy, whatsit*, and it is commonly used in everyday speech to refer to something inspecific or to belittle something, as in the dialogue, where Marco refers to the leather jacket as **un coso...** (the proper term is the feminine noun **la cosa** *thing*). Another widely used colloquial term for this is **la roba** *stuff, things*. **Che roba è?** *What is that stuff?*

CULTURAL NOTE

Like elsewhere in Europe, **i centri commerciali** *shopping centres* started to appear in Italy (initially in northern Italy) at the beginning of the 1970s. Most consisted of a giant supermarket with a variety of other shops around it. It wasn't until the 1980s that shopping centres began to spread more widely across the country. At last count there were 969 of these, employing more than 300,000 people. Altogether they receive 1,800,000,000 visitors per year, the equivalent of each Italian going to one on average 32 times a year (almost three times a month). However, Italian villages, towns and cities also still have a variety of small, family-owned shops and boutiques as well as traditional workshops where craftspeople such as shoemakers, tailors or upholsterers sell their wares and services.

VOCABULARY

addosso *on*
l'albero *tree* (**gli alberi** *trees)*
antipatico/a *unpleasant*
l'ascensore *elevator, lift*
camminare *to walk*
la canottiera *tank top, sleeveless T-shirt*
cantare *to sing*
carino/a *cute, pretty, lovely, charming*
il chiodo *nail, spike* (also, *studded leather jacket*)
la collezione *collection*
coloratissimo/a *very colourful*
le compere *shopping*
il complimento *compliment*
confessare *to confess*
estivo/a *summer, summery* (adj.)
fantasia *patterned, print, design*
il giubbotto *jacket*
grande *large, big*
il guardaroba *wardrobe, closet*
intanto *meanwhile, in the meantime*
inutile *useless, pointless*
lugubre *gloomy*
il lutto *mourning, bereavement*
magnifico/a *extraordinary, magnificent*
il malumore *bad mood*
la manica *sleeve* (**le maniche** *sleeves)*
mentre *while*
il neon *noon*
odiare *to hate*
orrido/a *horrible, awful*
pazzesco/a *insane, crazy*
la pelle *leather, skin*
perfetto/a *perfect*
il piano *floor, storey*
piovere *to rain*
provare *to try*
il reparto *department*
rifare *to redo*
le scale mobili *escalator*
soffocare *to suffocate*
il sole *the sun*
la tonnellata *tonne*
gli uccellini *little birds* (**l'uccello** *bird)*
il vestito *dress, suit, clothes*
zingaresco/a *gypsy*

EXERCISES

1. COMPLETE THE SENTENCES WITH THE MOST APPROPRIATE PREPOSITION FROM THE FOLLOWING LIST (EACH CAN ONLY BE USED ONCE): *A, DI, PER, CON, IN.*

a. Ho preso il treno .... mezzogiorno.

b. Ho telefonato .... tuo fratello per dirgli di venire da me.

c. I tuoi genitori hanno fatto tanti sacrifici .... te.

d. A quarant'anni, Carlo vive ancora .... sua madre.

e. Siamo vissuti *(lived)* a lungo .... Inghilterra.

2. COMPLETE THE SENTENCES WITH THE MOST APPROPRIATE CONTRACTED PREPOSITION + ARTICLE.

a. Siamo entrati .... sua bellissima casa.

b. Siete saliti .... cima della collina.

c. Questo prodotto viene .... Francia.

d. La grammatica .... italiano mi sembra difficile.

e. Mi piace il canto .... uccelli.

3. REWRITE THESE SENTENCES IN THE PLURAL.

a. La grande città non può essere silenziosa.

→ ....

b. La sua mano era grande e forte.

→ ....

c. Il mio amico sceglie una scuola difficile.

→ ....

d. Vorrebbe un uovo *(egg)* fresco. → ....

e. Avresti potuto incontrare un compagno *(partner)* simpatico.

→ ....

f. Affitterà un monolocale ampio *(studio ample)* e spazioso.

→ ....

30 4. LISTEN TO THE RECORDING AND WRITE THESE NUMBERS IN WORDS.

a. 14 → ....

b. 93 → ....

c. 130 → ....

d. 84 → ....

e. 11 → ....

f. 172 → ....

g. 888 → ....

30 5. LISTEN TO THE RECORDING AND WRITE THESE ORDINAL NUMBERS IN WORDS.

a. 34° → ....

b. 67° → ....

c. 12° → ....

d. 602° → ....

e. 1000° → ....

f. 15° → ....

g. 8° → ....

6. TRANSLATE THESE SENTENCES INTO ITALIAN.

a. Next year my parents are going to visit the Italian cities.

→ ....

b. He would have liked *(wanted)* to go there, but he wasn't able to.

→ ....

c. Ma'am, you (**Lei**) had told us that you would arrive at 5:00.

→ ....

d. We should have risen *(ourselves)* early to go to our grandparents'.

→ ....

e. They will offer you (**tu**) a rental apartment.

→ ....

f. You (**voi**) were watching a film when Carlo called you.

→ ....

g. If I had not asked (subj.) him about it, he wouldn't *(it)* have told me.

→ ....

h. Listening to you (**tu**) speak, I understood right away that you were not from here.

→ ....

i. Take (**tu**) my car, go there and tell *(it to)* him.

→ ....

7. PUT THESE IMPERFECT INDICATIVE VERBS IN THE FUTURE TENSE.

a. facevamo → ....

b. bevevi → ....

c. proponevate → ....

d. sapevo → ....

e. volevano → ....

f. veniva → ....

g. potevamo → ....

8. PUT THESE PRESENT PERFECT VERBS IN THE PRESENT CONDITIONAL.

a. ho fatto → ....

b. siete rimasti → ....

c. abbiamo visto → ....

d. sono venute → ....

e. ha vissuto → ....

f. hanno tenuto → ....

g. hai dato → ....

9. COMPLETE THESE SENTENCES WITH THE CORRECT PRESENT SUBJUNCTIVE FORM OF THE VERB GIVEN IN PARENTHESES.

a. Credo che Luisa .... troppi dolci. (mangiare)

b. Pensate che io .... troppo? (parlare)

c. Spero che Carlo .... con cura. (lavorare)

d. Non è possibile che voi .... a queste storie! (credere)

e. Speriamo che Filippo ci .... presto! (scrivere)

f. Mi sembra che il treno .... alle dodici e trenta. (partire)

g. È meglio che tu non gli .... la porta. (aprire)

10. COMPLETE THE SENTENCES WITH THE CORRECT FORM OF THE PAST PERFECT SUBJUNCTIVE.

a. Marta pensa che io non le creda.

→ Marta pensa che ieri io non le ....

b. Sono contento che Lea venga a casa mia.

→ Sono contento che ieri Lea .... a casa mia.

c. Giorgio teme *(fears)* che suo figlio mangi troppi dolci.

→ Giorgio teme che ieri suo figlio .... troppi dolci.

APPENDICES

EXERCISE ANSWERS

NOTE

On the following pages, you'll find the answers to the exercises in the lessons. The exercises accompanied by audio are indicated by the icon, along with the number of the corresponding track on the streaming platform. The exercise recordings are found on the same track as the lesson dialogue, following just after it.

PRONUNCIATION, P. 15

	[k]	[ch]	[sh]	[g]	[j]
parchi	x				
porci		x			
giardino					x
prosciutto			x		
fischiare	x				
piccolo	x				
lasciare			x		
lanciare		x			
lunghissimo				x	

PRONUNCIATION, P. 16

Firenze – canzone – Federico – cantavano – cantavamo – felicità – macchina – fantastico – raccontatemelo – raccontamelo

1. INTRODUCTIONS AND GREETINGS

1. a. la **b.** gli **c.** il **d.** l' **e.** le

2.

Masculine singular	Masculine plural	Feminine singular	Feminine plural
il vicino siciliano	i vicini siciliani	la vicina siciliana	le vicine siciliane
il ragazzo bello	i ragazzi belli	la ragazza bella	le ragazze belle

03 **3. a.** chiamo **b.** sono – piacere **c.** da **d.** Sono **e.** arrivederci **f.** prossima

4. a. sono **b.** siamo **c.** siete **d.** sono, sei **e.** è

2. TALKING ABOUT YOURSELF

1. a. una **b.** dei **c.** uno **d.** una **e.** degli **f.** delle

2. a. abbiamo **b.** ha **c.** avete **d.** hai

04 **3. a.** a **b.** accomodati **c.** lavoro **d.** Faccio **e.** Quanti **f.** Ho

4.

Masculine singular	Masculine plural	Feminine singular	Feminine plural
uno scandinavo	degli scandinavi	una scandinava	delle scandinave
un ragazzo bravissimo	dei ragazzi bravissimi	una ragazza bravissima	delle ragazze bravissime

3. ADDRESSING OTHERS (*TU* OR *LEI*)

1. a. disturbo **b.** desidera **c.** passano – arrivano **d.** desiderate **e.** chiamo – chiami

2.

Masculine singular	Masculine plural	Feminine singular	Feminine plural
l'insegnante canadese	gli insegnanti canadesi	l'insegnante canadese	le insegnanti canadesi
il francese gentile	i francesi gentili	la francese gentile	le francesi gentili

05 **3. a.** dov'è **b.** Sono – da **c.** bisogno **d.** desidera **e.** da

4. a. nella **b.** sulla **c.** dall' **d.** al **e.** colla

4. ASKING FOR INFORMATION AND EXPLANATIONS

1. a. Non abitiamo a Bologna.
b. Non riflettete un po'.
c. Non vendono scarpe.
06 **2. a.** Vuole vedere le scarpe nere?
b. Hai capito la nostra offerta?
c. C'è un posto libero vicino a te?
3. a. i prezzi convenienti **b.** le offerte eccezionali **c.** i clienti fortunati
4. a. la cliente siciliana
b. la commessa gentile
c. la vicina canadese
5. a. chiudono **b.** vede **c.** rifletto
d. prendiamo

5. ADMINISTRATIVE PROCEDURES

1. a. le mie amiche greche **b.** le città ricche **c.** i tuoi amici simpatici
2. a. le studentesse simpatiche
b. la dottoressa canadese
c. la principessa siciliana
3. a. preferiamo **b.** parte **c.** capisce
d. soffri
4. a. mio **b.** le vostre **c.** la sua
d. la tua
07 **5. A** come Ancona, **S** come Savona, **S** come Salerno, **I** come Imola, **M** come Milano, **I** come Imola, **L** come Livorno: **ASSIMIL**

6. DESCRIBING PEOPLE

1. a. le tue foto piccole **b.** questi maglioni rossi **c.** quei bei bar
d. quegli studenti magri **e.** i tuoi cappelli gialli **f.** quelle estati calde
2. a. Questo – quella **c.** Quella
c. questa **d.** quel
3. a. sta – Sto **b.** vanno **c.** do
d. faccio
08 **4. a.** caldo – freddo **b.** spiaggia – mare **c.** sinistra **d.** faccio – vacanza

7. DAILY ACTIVITIES

09 **1. a.** quattrocentoquattro
b. novantuno
c. millenovecentocinquantasette
d. ventidue **e.** settantatré
2. a. Cenano alle diciannove e trenta (alle sette e mezza). **b.** Ci svegliamo alle sette e un quarto (e quindici).
c. Faccio la doccia alle nove e venti.
d. Vado in piscina alle diciassette e trenta (alle cinque e mezza).
3. a. rimango **b.** ci sediamo – beviamo
c. vuole – può **d.** sa – può **e.** dovete
4. a. che **b.** di **c.** come **d.** che

8. LOOKING FOR AN APARTMENT

10 **1. a.** quarantaquattresimo **b.** ottocentoquarantacinquesimo **c.** quinto **d.** settantatreesimo **e.** sedicesimo

2. a. molto bella / bellissima **b.** il più caro **c.** la più buona / la migliore **d.** molto piccolo / piccolissimo

3. a. esco **b.** vieni **c.** salgono **d.** dite

10 **4. a.** stanze – piano **b.** ci – solo **c.** camera – fondo **d.** propongo – condividere

9. ARRANGING TO MEET A FRIEND

1.

Masculine	Feminine
l'attore famoso	l'attrice famosa
lo scrittore americano	la scrittrice americana
il dottore simpatico	la dottoressa simpatica
i pittori milanesi	le pittrici milanesi

2.

Singular	Plural
l'uovo fresco	le uova fresche
il mio braccio	le mie braccia
il muro della casa	I muri della casa
la nostra mano	le nostre manı

3. a. veniamo **b.** propone **c.** deve **d.** Stiamo

11 **4. a.** andando **b.** imparando **c.** leggendo **d.** facendo

10. ASKING FOR DIRECTIONS

1. a. le **b.** mi **c.** lo **d.** li
2. a. Ho studiato l'italiano per il mio lavoro. **b.** Luisa e Carla sono partite presto per evitare il traffico. **c.** Avete ringraziato il vigile per l'informazione.
12 **3. a.** ho letto **b.** è stata **c.** avete visto **d.** abbiamo chiesto

11. DOING THE SHOPPING

1. a. te **b.** voi **c.** loro **d.** lei
2. a. Facevate la spesa al supermercato. *You did the shopping at the super-market. / You used to do/ were doing the shopping at the supermarket.* **b.** Bevevano solamente acqua. *They drank only water. / They used to drink/were drinking only water.* **c.** Non diceva niente. *He/she said nothing. / He/she used to say/was saying nothing.* **d.** Eri a Firenze? *Have you been to Florence? / Were you/did you used to be in Florence?*
3. a. Bevevi. **b.** Mangiavano. **c.** Dicevate. **d.** Prendevamo. **e.** Finivo.

12. GOING TO THE DOCTOR

1. a. prendi **b.** Andiamo **c.** venga **d.** sentite **e.** leggere
2. a. Andiamoci. **b.** Prendine tre. **c.** Non farlo. **d.** Fallo.
3. a. Mia sorella è andata/andava in vacanza al mare. **b.** Abbiamo bevuto/ Bevevamo caffè per non dormire. **c.** Marco e Luca si sono preoccupati/si preoccupavano troppo. **d.** Hai preso/ Prendevi la mia macchina ogni mattina.
14 **4. a.** medicine **b.** cucchiaio **c.** peggiorare

13. GOING TO THE BANK

1. a. apriremo **b.** firmerà **c.** chiuderà **d.** arriveranno
2. a. potrai **b.** verrò **c.** dovrete **d.** vedremo
3. a. Gli parleremo. **b.** Ci andrete. **c.** Lo firmerà, signore. **d.** Lo dovranno fare.
15 **4. a.** prelevare **b.** firmare **c.** bolletta

14. MAKING A CLAIM (AT THE POST OFFICE)

1. a. Ce l'avete mandato. **b.** Gliela chiedo. **c.** Ve ne parliamo. **d.** Glielo verseranno.
2. a. Sto per fare un lavoro difficile.
b. Stai per spiegarmi la tua situazione.
c. Stavamo per arrivare a casa sua.
d. Stanno per andare a lavorare.
3. a. Non me l'ha detto. **b.** Ce li mettete. **c.** Ve ne hanno parlato.
d. Glielo compreremo.
4. a. Ce li hanno dati. **b.** Ve le hanno prese. **c.** Glieli hanno letti.
d. Me l'hanno comprata.

15. A JOB INTERVIEW

1. a. parlartene **b.** chiedervela
c. preparartela **d.** Portateceli.
2. a. A quest'ora dormiranno.
b. Sarà già arrivata a casa.
c. Avrai preso il raffreddore.
d. Non parleranno italiano.
3. a. Diglielo. **b.** Mettetevelo.
c. Dicendotelo ... **d.** Dagliela.
4. a. sarò tornato **b.** avremo ricevuto
c. avranno trovato **d.** avrete finito

16. ATTENDING A WORK MEETING

1. a. Ti spiego il problema per cui sono venuto. **b.** Ti ho portato il libro che mi avevi prestato. **c.** Voglio vedere il lavoro di cui mi avete tanto parlato.
2. a. La mia casa in montagna è stata affittata da turisti francesi. **b.** L'inglese è parlato da molti. **c.** Roma è visitata da turisti di tutto il mondo.
3. a. *This work must be done.* **b.** *It wasn't spoken about.* **c.** *A person doesn't get much sleep.* ('One sleeps little.') **d.** *It's a city one must see.*
4. a. è stata scritta **b.** è stata fondata
c. è stato capito

17. ON THE PHONE

19 **1. a.** A che ora arriva l'autobus?
b. Che cosa volete mangiare?
c. Quali sono le tue città preferite?
2. a. Per fare questo lavoro, ci vuole la macchina. **b.** Ci vorranno molte ore.
c. Con quel freddo, ci voleva il maglione.
3. a. *Shoes are required. / One needs shoes.* **b.** *A year will be needed.* **c.** *How many friends are you* (pl.) *coming with?*
d. *What a beautiful city!*
19 **4. a.** Pronto **b.** sono **c.** chiamata
d. riattacco

18. INFORMATION TECHNOLOGY AND THE INTERNET

1. a. quello che **b.** quella che **c.** quelli che

2. a. Esco solo con chi mi è simpatico. **b.** Chi è andato in quella scuola parla bene italiano. **c.** Chi non ha diciotto anni non può guidare la macchina.

3. a. Vorremmo. **b.** Sarebbero. **c.** Avreste. **d.** Sapresti.

4. a. Mi piacerebbe andare in Italia. **b.** Mi potrebbe dire che ore sono? **c.** Potremmo arrivare un po' più tardi?

19. WRITING AN EMAIL

1. a. Con il mio operatore queste cose non sarebbero successe. **b.** In treno avremmo viaggiato molto più comodi. **c.** Carla avrebbe preferito andarci lunedì. **d.** Carla ci sarebbe andata più volentieri lunedì.

2. a. stranamente **b.** professionalmente **c.** solitamente **d.** fortunatamente

3. a. Avremmo voluto. **b.** Sarebbero state. **c.** Avrebbe potuto. **d.** Sareste venute.

4. a. Camminavamo lentissimamente. **b.** Parla sempre fortissimo. **c.** La nostra macchina va pianissimo. **d.** Siete arrivati tardissimo.

21 **5. a.** campo **b.** connette **c.** successo **d.** regalato

20. GIVING PRACTICAL INSTRUCTIONS

1. a. lavato **b.** viaggiato **c.** dimenticati **d.** messa

2. a. ha saputo **b.** ha dovuto **c.** siamo potuti **d.** è saputa

3. a. Si sono messi le scarpe. **b.** Si sono lavate i denti. **c.** Ci siamo dimenticati il nostro appuntamento. **d.** Si è ricordata di te.

22 **4. a.** allarme **b.** codice **c.** tastiera

21. RESERVING A HOTEL ROOM

1. a. c'era **b.** c'è **c.** ci sono **d.** ci sarà

2. a. tengo **b.** sceglie **c.** piace **d.** valgono

3. a. Sceglie. **b.** Abbiamo scelto. **c.** Non mi piaceva il mare. **d.** Mi piacciono i ristoranti italiani.

23 **4. a.** prenotare **b.** sono **c.** matrimoniale **d.** vista

22. AT THE TRAIN STATION OR AIRPORT

1. a. venga **b.** mangiate **c.** perda **d.** prendano
2. a. Spero che tu vada al mare.
b. Credo che voi siate inglesi.
c. Mi fa piacere che voi veniate a Milano.
d. Non so a che ora voi finiate di lavorare.
3. a. verrò **b.** avrai aperto **c.** sono state **d.** scelga
4. a. decollo **b.** sportello **c.** binario **d.** volo

23. SPORTS AND FREE TIME

1. a. Mi dispiace che tu non sia venuto da noi. **b.** Ci sembra che voi abbiate mangiato troppo. **c.** Spero che lei non abbia perso il treno. **d.** Credo che Carla e Paolo abbiano preso l'aereo delle quattordici.
2. a. Spero che tu sia andato a lavorare. **b.** Credo che voi abbiate fatto un buon acquisto. **c.** Mi fa piacere che voi siate venuti a Milano. **d.** Mi sembra che loro abbiano mangiato troppo.
3. a. hanno tolto **b.** posso **c.** spengo **d.** produrrà
4. a. paio **b.** palestra **c.** invernali

24. THE CINEMA AND THE THEATRE

1. a. Speravo che veniste da me. **b.** Ero contento che tu fossi arrivata così presto. **c.** Ci sembrava che foste stati molto chiari. **d.** Dubitavo che dicessero la verità.
2. a. Speravo che tu fossi andato a lavorare. **b.** Credevo che voi aveste fatto un buon acquisto. **c.** Mi faceva piacere che voi foste venuti a Milano. **d.** Mi sembrava che loro avessero mangiato troppo.
3. a. Faranno. **b.** Sceglieresti. **c.** Facciamo. **d.** Vedrete. **e.** Vedreste.
26 **4. a.** entrambi **b.** autore **c.** idea **d.** regista

25. ARRANGING AN OUTING WITH FRIENDS

1. a. A **b.** con **c.** in **d.** alle **e.** in **f.** dall' **g.** da **h.** da **i.** tra
2. a. Avevamo deciso che avremmo fatto una gita insieme. **b.** Era sicuro che sarebbe andato a Napoli. **c.** Mi dicevano che sarebbero partiti per l'America. **d.** Raccontava che avrebbe studiato all'estero.
27 **3. a.** cima **b.** scorciatoia **c.** andata

26. VISITING AN ART EXHIBITION

1. a. in **b.** a **c.** da **d.** al

2. a. passiamo **b.** potranno **c.** fossi **d.** avessimo visto

3. a. Se vuoi parlarmi, vengo da te. **b.** Se l'avessi saputo, non sarei venuto. **c.** Se andrete in Francia l'anno prossimo, verremo con voi. **d.** Se tu fossi qui, potremmo parlarne.

4. a. risponderò **b.** avrei risposto **c.** avreste visto **d.** verremmo

28 **5. a.** persi **b.** peccato **c.** figurativa **d.** distraggo

27. AT THE RESTAURANT

1. a. con **b.** in **c.** di **d.** alla **e.** sui **f.** al **g.** Di

2. a. incontro – parlo **b.** fossi – lavorerei **c.** studiaste – avreste **d.** aveste studiato – avreste avuto

3. a. *If I can come to your place, I certainly will.* **b.** *I chose this car because I like it a lot.* **c.** *You don't do any sport, but you should.* **d.** *They are climbing on the peak of the mountain.*

29 **4. a.** primo **b.** secondo **c.** rivista **d.** sete

28. GOING SHOPPING

1. a. di **b.** a **c.** per **d.** con **e.** in

2. a. nella **b.** sulla **c.** dalla **d.** dell' **e.** degli

3. a. Le grandi città non possono essere silenziose. **b.** Le sue mani erano grandi e forti. **c.** I miei amici scelgono scuole difficili. **d.** Vorrebbero uova fresche. **e.** Avreste potuto incontrare compagni simpatici. **f.** Affitteranno monolocali ampi e spaziosi.

30 **4. a.** quattordici **b.** novantatré **c.** centotrenta **d.** ottantaquattro **e.** undici **f.** centosettantadue **g.** ottocentoottantotto

30 **5. a.** trentaquattresimo **b.** sessantasettesimo **c.** dodicesimo **d.** seicentoduesimo **e.** millesimo **f.** quindicesimo **g.** ottavo

6. a. L'anno prossimo i miei genitori andranno a visitare le città italiane. **b.** Avrebbe voluto andarci, ma non ha potuto. **c.** Signora, ci aveva detto che sarebbe arrivata alle cinque. **d.** Dovevamo alzarci presto per andare dai nostri nonni. **e.** Ti proporranno un appartamento in affitto. **f.** Stavate

guardando un film, quando Carlo vi ha chiamati. **g.** Se io non gliel'avessi chiesto, non me l'avrebbe detto.
h. Sentendoti parlare, ho capito subito che non eri di qui. **i.** Prendi la mia macchina, vacci e diglielo.
7. a. faremo **b.** berrai **c.** proporrete
d. saprò **e.** vorranno **f.** verrà
g. potremo
8. a. farei **b.** rimarreste **c.** vedremmo
d. verrebbero **e.** vivrebbe
f. terrebbero **g.** daresti
9. a. mangi **b.** parli **c.** lavori
d. crediate **e.** scriva **f.** parta **g.** apra
10. a. abbia creduto **b.** sia venuta
c. abbia mangiato

GRAMMATICAL APPENDIX

PRONUNCIATION

The Italian alphabet consists of 21 letters, which are pronounced as follows:

Letter	Pronunciation	Reference when spelling a word aloud
a	*[ah]*	Ancona
b	*[bee]*	Bologna, Bari
c	*[chee]*	Como
d	*[dee]*	Domodossola
e	*[ay]*	Empoli
f	*[ef-fe]*	Firenze
g	*[jee]*	Genova
h	*[ak-ka]*	hotel
i	*[ee]*	Imola, Imperia
l	*[el-leh]*	Livorno
m	*[em-meh]*	Milano
n	*[en-neh]*	Napoli
o	*[o]*	Otranto
p	*[pee]*	Palermo, Padova
q	*[koo]*	Quarto
r	*[erreh]*	Roma
s	*[esseh]*	Savona, Salerno
t	*[tee]*	Torino, Taranto
u	*[oo]*	Udine
v	*[vee]*	Venezia
z	*[dseta]*	Zara

The letters **j, k, w, x, y** do not exist in the Italian alphabet and so are rarely used, although they occur in loan words from other languages. In these cases, just use the name of the letter when spelling aloud: **i lunga** (j), **cappa** (k), **vu doppia** (w), **ics** (x), **ipsilon** or **i greca** (y).

NOTE

The following section includes an overview of some of the main grammatical points and verb forms introduced in this course. For more information, you can refer to the lessons indicated.

GRAMMAR

DEFINITE ARTICLE (LESSON 1)

	MASCULINE NOUN			FEMININE NOUN	
	Starting with a consonant (but see column 2)	Starting with **s** + consonant, **gn-, z-, ps-**	Starting with a vowel	Starting with a consonant	Starting with a vowel
SINGULAR	**il** **il** mio autobus	**lo** **lo** studente	**l'** **l'**autobus	**la** **la** vicina	**l'** **l'**amica
PLURAL	**i** **i** miei	**gli** **gli** studenti, **gli** autobus		**le** **le** vicine, **le** amiche	

INDEFINITE ARTICLE (LESSON 2)

	MASCULINE NOUN		FEMININE NOUN	
	Starting with a consonant (but see column 2) or a vowel	Starting with **s** + consonant, **gn-, z-, ps-**	Starting with a consonant	Starting with a vowel
SINGULAR	**un** **un** posto **un** amico	**uno** **uno** studente	**una** **una** studentessa	**un'** **un'**amica
	Starting with a consonant (but see column 2)	Starting with **s** + consonant, **gn-, z-, ps-** or a vowel	Starting with a consonant or a vowel	
PLURAL	**dei** **dei** colleghi	**degli** **degli** studenti, **degli** amici	**delle** **delle** ottime scuole, **delle** amiche	

CONTRACTED PREPOSITIONS + ARTICLES (LESSON 3)

	il	lo	l'	la	i	gli	le
a	al	allo	all'	alla	ai	agli	alle
di	del	dello	dell'	della	dei	degli	delle
da	dal	dallo	dall'	dalla	dai	dagli	dalle
in	nel	nello	nell'	nella	nei	negli	nelle
con	col	collo	coll'	colla	coi	cogli	colle
su	sul	sullo	sull'	sulla	sui	sugli	sulle

NOUNS/ADJECTIVES ENDING IN -O (LESSON 1)

	MASCULINE	FEMININE
SINGULAR	**-o** il sicilian**o** bell**o**	**-a** la sicilian**a** bell**a**
PLURAL	**-i** i sicilian**i** bell**i**	**-e** le sicilian**e** bell**e**

NOUNS/ADJECTIVES ENDING IN -E (LESSON 3)

	MASCULINE	FEMININE
SINGULAR	**-e** il canades**e** gentil**e**	**-e** la canades**e** gentil**e**
PLURAL	**-i** i canades**i** gentil**i**	**-i** le canades**i** gentil**i**

EXCEPTIONS FOR FORMING THE PLURAL

Some masculine nouns don't change in the plural: these include foreign loan words (**lo sport** *sport* → **gli sport** *sports*), words whose stress falls on the last syllable (**la città** *city* → **le città** *cities*), single-syllable words (**il re** *king* → **i re** *kings*), shortened words (**il cinema** *cinema* → **i cinema** *cinemas*) and words ending in **-i** (**l'analisi** *analysis* → **le analisi** *analyses*).

OTHER EXAMPLES OF FORMING THE FEMININE OR PLURAL

• Some masculine singular nouns that end in **-o** become feminine in the plural and end in **-a**: e.g. **l'uovo** *egg* (masc. sing.) → **le uova** *eggs* (fem. pl.) ; **il paio** *pair* → **le paia** *pairs*, etc.
• Some masculine singular nouns end in **-a** (these don't change form in the singular feminine): **il /la giornalista** *journalist*, **il / la collega** *colleague*. They do, however, have separate forms in the plural: **i giornalisti /le giornaliste** *journalists*.
• Some nouns form the feminine singular with **-essa**: this is the case for certain activities/professions (**lo studente** → **la studentessa** *student*, **il dottore**→ **la dottoressa** *doctor*), certain animals (**il leone** *lion* → **la leonessa** *lioness*), certain noble titles (**il conte** *count* → **la contessa** *countess*), etc.
• Some nouns form the feminine singular with **-trice**: this is the case for certain activities/professions such as **attore** → **attrice** *actor*, **pittore** → **pittrice** *painter*, **ricercatore** → **ricercatrice** *researcher*, etc.
• Note that **la mano** *hand* is a feminine noun ending in **-o**. Its plural is **le mani** *hands.*

MAKING COMPARISONS (LESSON 7)

• To compare nouns or pronouns, comparative adjectives (often formed by adding *-er* in English) are formed with **più...di** *more ... than* or **meno...di** *less ... than* (or the contracted form of the preposition **di** + article): **La giacca è più cara della gonna.** *The jacket is more expensive than the skirt.*
• To compare adverbs, verbs or adjectives, or if the comparative is preceded by a preposition or indicates a quantity, **che** is used: **Mi piace di più dormire che lavorare.** *I like sleeping more than working.*
• To say *as ... as*, **come** or (less frequently) **quanto** is placed before the second term being compared: **Gennaio è freddo come febbraio.** *January is as cold as February.*

INTENSIFYING ADJECTIVES AND THE SUPERLATIVE (LESSON 8)

• There are two main ways to intensify an adjective or adverb in Italian:

1. By adding the suffix **-issimo/a/i/e** (which needs to agree with the noun).
2. The adverb **molto** can be placed before the adjective or adverb.

• Superlative adjectives (*the most, the least*, or *the ...-est* in English) are formed with **il/la/i/le più/meno...di**. The construction is definite article + noun + **più** or **meno** + adjective: **la ragazza più alta della scuola** *the tallest girl in the school*.

SPECIFIC COMPARATIVE, SUPERLATIVE AND INTENSIFIED TERMS (LESSON 8)

ADJECTIVE	COMPARATIVE	SUPERLATIVE	INTENSIFIED FORM
buono *good*	**migliore** *better*	**il migliore** *the best*	**ottimo** *great*
cattivo *bad*	**peggiore** *worse*	**il peggiore** *the worst*	**pessimo** *terrible*
grande *big*	**maggiore** *bigger*	**il maggiore** *biggest*	**massimo** *greatest*
piccolo *small*	**minore** *smaller*	**il minore** *smallest*	**minimo** *least, slightest*

ADVERB	COMPARATIVE	INTENSIFIED FORM
bene *well*	**meglio** *better*	**ottimamente**, **molto bene** *excellently, very well*
male *badly*	**peggio** *worse*	**pessimamente**, **molto male** *terribly, very badly*

POSSESSIVE ADJECTIVES AND PRONOUNS (LESSON 5)

	OBJECT POSSESSED			
POSSESSOR	masc. sing.	fem. sing.	masc. pl.	fem. pl.
my/mine	**il mio**	**la mia**	**i miei**	**le mie**
your(s) (informal sing.)	**il tuo**	**la tua**	**i tuoi**	**le tue**
his/her(s)/its *your(s)* (formal sing.)	**il suo** **il Suo**	**la sua** **la Sua**	**i suoi** **i Suoi**	**le sue** **le Sue**
our(s)	**il nostro**	**la nostra**	**i nostri**	**le nostre**
your(s) (informal pl.)	**il vostro**	**la vostra**	**i vostri**	**le vostre**
their(s) *your(s)* (formal pl.)	**il loro** **il Loro**	**la loro** **la Loro**	**i loro** **i Loro**	**le loro** **le Loro**

DEMONSTRATIVE ADJECTIVES AND PRONOUNS (LESSON 6)

• **questo** *this (one)* refers to a noun in proximity to the speaker or the person being spoken to. It has the regular forms for an **-o** adjective (**questo/a/i/e**).
• **quello** *that (one)* refers to something more distant. When used as a pronoun, **quello** has just four forms (**quello/a/i/e**), but when used as an adjective (i.e. before a noun), it changes form as follows:

	MASCULINE NOUN			FEMININE NOUN	
	Starting with a consonant (but see column 2)	Starting with **s** + consonant, **gn, z, ps**	Starting with a vowel	Starting with a consonant	Starting with a vowel
SINGULAR	**quel** **quel cappello** *that hat*	**quello** **quello studente** *that student*	**quell'** **quell'amico** *that friend*	**quella** **quella foto** *that photo*	**quell'** **quell'amica** *that friend*
PLURAL	**quei** **quei cappelli**	**quegli** **quegli studenti,** **quegli amici**		**quelle** **quelle foto,** **quelle amiche**	

OBJECT PRONOUNS (WEAK FORMS) (LESSON 10)

Subject pronoun	Direct object pronoun	Indirect object pronoun
io *I*	**mi** *me*	**mi** *(to) me*
tu *you* (inf. sing.)	**ti** *you*	**ti** *(to) you*
lui *he*, **lei** *she*, **Lei** *you* (for. sing.)	**lo** *him, it* (m.), **la** *her, it* (f.) **La** *you* (formal)	**gli** *(to) him*, **le** *(to) her* **Lei** *you* (formal)
noi *we*	**ci** *us*	**ci** *(to) us*
voi *you* (inf. pl.)	**vi** *you*	**vi** *(to) you*
loro *they*	**li** *them* (m.), **le** *them* (f.)	**gli** *(to) them*

The feminine third-person singular is used to address someone (man or woman) in a formal context. So **Lei** and **La** refer to the formal *you*.

OBJECT PRONOUNS (STRONG FORMS) (LESSON 11)

Subject pronoun	Direct and indirect object pronouns (after a preposition)
io *I*	**(a) me** *(to) me*
tu *you* (inf. sing.)	**(a) te** *(to) you*
lui *he*, **lei** *she*, **Lei** *you* (for. sing.)	**(a) lui** *(to) him*, **(a) lei** *(to) her* **(a) Lei** *(to) you*
noi *we*	**(a) noi** *(to) us*
voi *you* (inf. pl.)	**(a) voi** *(to) you*
loro *they*	**(a) loro** *(to) them*

USING DIRECT AND INDIRECT OBJECTS TOGETHER (LESSON 14)

Indirect object pronouns	Direct object pronouns				
	lo	**la**	**li**	**le**	**ne**
mi	**me lo**	**me la**	**me li**	**me le**	**me ne**
ti	**te lo**	**te la**	**te li**	**te le**	**te ne**
gli, le **Le**	**glielo** **Glielo**	**gliela** **Gliela**	**glieli** **Glieli**	**gliele** **Gliele**	**gliene** **Gliene**
ci	**ce lo**	**ce la**	**ce li**	**ce le**	**ce ne**
vi	**ve lo**	**ve la**	**ve li**	**ve le**	**ve ne**
gli	**glielo**	**gliela**	**glieli**	**gliele**	**gliene**

RELATIVE PRONOUNS (LESSON 16)

• A relative pronoun is used to introduce a clause that gives more information about something previously mentioned in the main clause (e.g. *that, who, which,* etc.). The most common relative pronoun is **che**.
• If the relative pronoun follows a preposition, **cui** is used.
• The longer forms **il quale** (masc. sing.), **la quale** (fem. sing.), **i quali** (masc. pl.), **le quali** (fem. pl.) can also be used, though they are less frequent. If preceded by a preposition, this contracts with the article.

THE MAIN PREPOSITIONS

<table>
<tr><th>a</th><th>di</th><th>da</th><th>in</th></tr>
<tr>
<td>Direction of movement:
Vado a Roma.
I'm going to Rome.
Vado a lavorare.
I'm going to work.</td>
<td>Possession:
la macchina di Giulia
Giulia's car</td>
<td>Origin and distance:
Vengo da Milano.
I come from Milan.
Abito a tre chilometri da Milano.
I live 3 km from Milan.
Siamo lontani da Torino?
Are we far from Turin?</td>
<td>Expressions describing location:
Abito in Italia.
I live in Italy.</td>
</tr>
<tr>
<td>Stating a location:
Abito a Roma.
I live in Rome.</td>
<td>Description:
un libro di storia
a history book</td>
<td>To introduce the agent of the action in the passive voice:
È stato visto da tutti.
It was seen by everyone.</td>
<td>Expressions describing how long an action took:
L'ho fatto in due ore.
I did it in two hours.</td>
</tr>
<tr>
<td rowspan="4">Expressions describing location:
vicino a
near to
davanti a
in front of
di fronte a
opposite, facing
in mezzo a
in the middle of
intorno a
around
di fianco a
alongside of</td>
<td>Content:
una tazza di caffè
a cup of coffee</td>
<td>A container:
una tazza da caffè
a coffee cup</td>
<td rowspan="2">Expressions describing quantity:
Veniamo in due.
Two of us are coming.</td>
</tr>
<tr>
<td>After adverbs:
prima di
before, first of
invece di
instead of</td>
<td>since, for
Ti aspetto da due ore.
I've been waiting for you for two hours.</td>
</tr>
<tr>
<td>In expressions:
Credo di no.
I don't believe so.
Dico di sì.
I say yes.</td>
<td>at someone's place
Vieni a mangiare da noi?
Are you coming to eat at our place?</td>
<td rowspan="2">To introduce a means:
Sono venuta in treno.
I came by train.</td>
</tr>
<tr>
<td>In time expressions:
di giorno, di sera, di domenica
in the daytime, in the evening, on Sunday</td>
<td>Goal of an action:
È una cosa da fare.
It's something that has to be done.</td>
</tr>
</table>

con	su	per	tra, fra
with **Abito con Paolo.** *I live with Paolo.* **Lavora con cura.** *He works with attention.*	*on* **L'ho dimenticato sul tavolo.** *I forgot it on the table.*	*for* to express a cause or an aim: **Sono tornato a casa per il gran freddo.** *I came home because it was very cold.* **Sono venuto per questo.** *I came because of that.*	*between*: **fra me e te** *between you and me*
Means/method: **Sono arrivata con il treno delle due e mezzo.** *I arrived on the 2:30 train.*	Approximation: **un giovane sui vent'anni** *a young man about 20 years of age*	Destination: **Ho preso il treno per Roma.** *I took the train to Rome.*	*among*: **fra noi tutti** *among us all*
		Movement in a defined area: **Passeggiamo per la città.** *We strolled around the city.*	*in* (referring to time): **Vengo tra due ore.** *I'm coming in two hours.*

VERB CONJUGATIONS

ESSERE 'TO BE'

	Present indicative	Imperfect indicative	Imperative
io	**sono**	**ero**	
tu	**sei**	**eri**	**sii**
lui, lei, Lei	**è**	**era**	**sia**
noi	**siamo**	**eravamo**	**siamo**
voi	**siete**	**eravate**	**siate**
loro, Loro	**sono**	**erano**	

Future indicative	Present conditional	Present subjunctive	Imperfect subjunctive
sarò	**sarei**	**sia**	**fossi**
sarai	**saresti**	**sia**	**fossi**
sarà	**sarebbe**	**sia**	**fosse**
saremo	**saremmo**	**siamo**	**fossimo**
sarete	**sareste**	**siate**	**foste**
saranno	**sarebbero**	**siano**	**fossero**

- Past participle: **stato**
- Examples of some perfect tense forms: **sono stato** (present perfect indicative) (lesson 10), **ero stato** (past perfect indicative), **sarò stato** (future perfect indicative) (lesson 15), **sarei stato** (conditional perfect) (lesson 19), **sia stato** (present perfect subjunctive) (lesson 23).

C'È / CI SONO 'THERE IS/ARE'

Present indicative	Present perfect indicative	Imperfect indicative	Future indicative
c'è *there is*	**c'è stato/a** *there has been*	**c'era** *there was/used to be*	**ci sarà** *there will be*
ci sono *there are*	**ci sono stati/e** *there have been*	**c'erano** *there were/used to be*	**ci saranno** *there will be*

Future perfect indicative	Present conditional	Conditional perfect
ci sarà stato/a	**ci sarebbe**	**ci sarebbe stato/a**
ci saranno stati/e *there will have been*	**ci sarebbero** *there would be*	**ci sarebbero stati/e** *there would have been*

AVERE 'TO HAVE'

	Present indicative	Imperfect indicative	Imperative
io	**ho**	**avevo**	
tu	**hai**	**avevi**	**abbi**
lui, lei, Lei	**ha**	**aveva**	**abbia**
noi	**abbiamo**	**avevamo**	**abbiamo**
voi	**avete**	**avevate**	**abbiate**
loro, Loro	**hanno**	**avevano**	

Future indicative	Present conditional	Present subjunctive	Imperfect subjunctive
avrò	**avrei**	**abbia**	**avessi**
avrai	**avresti**	**abbia**	**avessi**
avrà	**avrebbe**	**abbia**	**avesse**
avremo	**avremmo**	**abbiamo**	**avessimo**
avrete	**avreste**	**abbiate**	**aveste**
avranno	**avrebbero**	**abbiano**	**avessero**

- Past participle: **avuto**
- Examples of some perfect tense forms: **ho avuto** (present perfect indicative) (lesson 10), **avevo avuto** (past perfect indicative), **avrò avuto** (future perfect indicative) (lesson 15), **avrei avuto** (conditional perfect) (lesson 19), **abbia avuto** (present perfect subjunctive) (lesson 23).

REGULAR *-ARE* VERBS (1ST GROUP): *PARLARE* 'TO TALK, TO SPEAK'

	Present indicative	Imperfect indicative	Imperative
io tu lui, lei, Lei noi voi loro, Loro	**parlo** **parli** **parla** **parliamo** **parlate** **parlano**	**parlavo** **parlavi** **parlava** **parlavamo** **parlavate** **parlavano**	 **parla** **parli** **parliamo** **parlate**

Future indicative	Present conditional	Present subjunctive	Imperfect subjunctive
parlerò **parlerai** **parlerà** **parleremo** **parlerete** **parleranno**	**parlerei** **parleresti** **parlerebbe** **parleremmo** **parlereste** **parlerebbero**	**parli** **parli** **parli** **parliamo** **parliate** **parlino**	**parlassi** **parlassi** **parlasse** **parlassimo** **parlaste** **parlassero**

- Past participle: **parlato**
- Examples of some perfect tense forms: **ho parlato** (present perfect indicative) (lesson 10), **avevo parlato** (past perfect indicative), **avrò parlato** (future perfect indicative) (lesson 15), **avrei parlato** (conditional perfect) (lesson 19), **abbia parlato** (present perfect subjunctive) (lesson 23).

REGULAR *-ERE* VERBS (2ND GROUP): *VENDERE* 'TO SELL'

	Present indicative	Imperfect indicative	Imperative
io	**vendo**	**vendevo**	
tu	**vendi**	**vendevi**	**vendi**
lui, lei, Lei	**vende**	**vendeva**	**venda**
noi	**vendiamo**	**vendevamo**	**vendiamo**
voi	**vendete**	**vendevate**	**vendete**
loro, Loro	**vendono**	**vendevano**	

Future indicative	Present conditional	Present subjunctive	Imperfect subjunctive
venderò	**venderei**	**venda**	**vendessi**
venderai	**venderesti**	**venda**	**vendessi**
venderà	**venderebbe**	**venda**	**vendesse**
venderemo	**venderemmo**	**vendiamo**	**vendessimo**
venderete	**vendereste**	**vendiate**	**vendeste**
venderanno	**venderebbero**	**vendano**	**vendessero**

- Past participle: **venduto**
- Examples of some perfect tense forms: **ho venduto** (present perfect indicative) (lesson 10), **avevo venduto** (past perfect indicative), **avrò venduto** (future perfect indicative) (lesson 15), **avrei venduto** (conditional perfect) (lesson 19), **abbia venduto** (present perfect subjunctive) (lesson 23).

REGULAR *-IRE* VERBS (3RD GROUP): *PARTIRE* 'TO LEAVE'

	Present indicative	Imperfect indicative	Imperative
io tu lui, lei, Lei noi voi loro, Loro	**parto** **parti** **parte** **partiamo** **partite** **partono**	**partivo** **partivi** **partiva** **partivamo** **partivate** **partivano**	 **parti** **parta** **partiamo** **partite**

Future indicative	Present conditional	Present subjunctive	Imperfect subjunctive
partirò **partirai** **partirà** **partiremo** **partirete** **partiranno**	**partirei** **partiresti** **partirebbe** **partiremmo** **partireste** **partirebbero**	**parta** **parta** **parta** **partiamo** **partiate** **partano**	**partissi** **partissi** **partisse** **partissimo** **partiste** **partissero**

- Past participle: **partito**
- Examples of some perfect tense forms: **sono partito/a** (present perfect indicative) (lesson 10), **ero partito/a** (past perfect indicative), **sarò partito/a** (future perfect indicative) (lesson 15), **sarei partito/a** (conditional perfect) (lesson 19), **sia partito/a** (present perfect subjunctive) (lesson 23).

-IRE VERBS WITH AN *-ISC-* SPELLING CHANGE

Many **-ire** verbs insert **-isc-** between the verb stem and the conjugation ending in all singular forms as well as the third-person plural, in the present indicative, present subjunctive and the imperative. Here is an example with **capire** *to understand*.

Present indicative	Present subjunctive	Imperative
capisco **capisci** **capisce** **capiamo** **capite** **capiscono**	**capisca** **capisca** **capisca** **capiamo** **capiate** **capiscano**	 **capisci** **capisca** **capiamo** **capite**

SOME COMMON IRREGULAR -*ARE* VERBS

andare *to go*	**dare** *to give*	**fare** *to do, to make*	**stare** *to be* (used to describe temporary states or locations and to form continuous tenses)
PRESENT INDICATIVE			
vado **vai** **va** **andiamo** **andate** **vanno**	**do** **dai** **dà** **diamo** **date** **danno**	**faccio** **fai** **fa** **facciamo** **fate** **fanno**	**sto** **stai** **sta** **stiamo** **state** **stanno**
• **tu** imperative: **vai** or **va'** • future: **andrò**, etc. • conditional: **andrei**, etc. • present subjunctive: **vada**, etc.	• **tu** imperative: **dai** or **da'** • future: **darò**, etc. • conditional: **darei**, etc. • present subjunctive: **dia**, etc.	• past participle: **fatto** • **tu** imperative: **fai** or **fa'** • imperfect: **facevo**, etc. • future: **farò**, etc. • conditional: **farei**, etc. • present subjunctive: **faccia**, etc. • imperfect subjunctive: **facessi**, etc.	• **tu** imperative: **stai** or **sta'** • imperfect: **facevo**, etc. • future: **starò**, etc. • conditional: **starei**, etc. • present subjunctive: **stia**, etc.

SOME COMMON IRREGULAR *-ERE* VERBS

bere *to drink*	**dovere** *to have to*	**potere** *to be able to*	**sapere** *to know*	**volere** *to want*	**proporre** *to propose*
PRESENT INDICATIVE					
bevo **bevi** **beve** **beviamo** **bevete** **bevono**	**devo** **devi** **deve** **dobbiamo** **dovete** **devono**	**posso** **puoi** **può** **possiamo** **potete** **possono**	**so** **sai** **sa** **sappiamo** **sapete** **sanno**	**voglio** **vuoi** **vuole** **vogliamo** **volete** **vogliono**	**propongo** **proponi** **propone** **proponiamo** **proponete** **propongono**
• past participle: **bevuto** • imperfect: **bevevo**, etc. • future: **berrò**, etc. • conditional: **berrei**, etc. • present subjunctive: **beva**, etc. • imperfect subjunctive: **bevessi**, etc.	• future: **dovrò**, etc. • conditional: **dovrei**, etc. • present subjunctive: **debba**, etc.	• future: **potrò**, etc. • conditional: **potrei**, etc. • present subjunctive: **possa**, etc.	• **tu** imperative: **sappi** • future: **saprò**, etc. • conditional: **saprei**, etc. • present subjunctive: **sappia**, etc.	• future: **vorrò**, etc. • conditional: **vorrei**, etc. • present subjunctive: **voglia**, etc.	• past participle: **proposto** • future: **proporrò**, etc. • conditional: **proporrei**, etc. • present subjunctive: **proponga**, etc.

piacere *to please, to appeal to*	**scegliere** *to choose*	**tenere** *to hold*	**valere** *to be worth*
PRESENT INDICATIVE			
piaccio **piaci** **piace** **piacciamo** **piacete** **piacciono**	**scelgo** **scegli** **sceglie** **scegliamo** **scegliete** **scelgono**	**tengo** **tieni** **tiene** **teniamo** **tenete** **tengono**	**valgo** **vali** **vale** **valiamo** **valete** **valgono**

• past participle: **piaciuto** • present subj.: **piaccia**, etc.	• past participle: **scelto** • present subj.: **scelga**, etc.	• future: **terrò**, etc. • conditional: **terrei**, etc. • present subj.: **tenga**, etc.	• past participle: **valso** • future: **varrò**, etc. • conditional: **varrei** • present subj.: **valga**, etc.

SOME COMMON IRREGULAR *-IRE* VERBS

dire *to tell, to say*	**salire** *to climb, to go up*	**uscire** *to leave, to go out*	**venire** *to come*
PRESENT INDICATIVE			
dico **dici** **dice** **diciamo** **dite** **dicono**	**salgo** **sali** **sale** **saliamo** **salite** **salgono**	**esco** **esci** **esce** **usciamo** **uscite** **escono**	**vengo** **vieni** **viene** **veniamo** **venite** **vengono**
• past participle: **detto** • **tu** imperative: **di'** • imperfect: **dicevo**, etc. • present subjunctive: **dica**, etc. • imperfect subjunctive: **dicessi**, etc.	• present subjunctive: **salga**, etc.	• present subjunctive: **esca**, etc.	• past participle: **venuto** • future: **verrò**, etc. • conditional: **verrei**, etc. • present subjunctive: **venga**, etc.

◆ TENSE SEQUENCE

TENSE SEQUENCE IN SUBJUNCTIVE SENTENCES (LESSON 24)

<table>
<tr><td>main clause</td><td>subordinate clause</td><td>main clause</td><td>subordinate clause</td></tr>
<tr><td colspan="4">in the present</td></tr>
<tr><td colspan="2">Spero che tu stia bene.</td><td colspan="2">Spero che tu sia stato bene.</td></tr>
<tr><td>present indicative</td><td>present subjunctive</td><td>present indicative</td><td>present perfect subj.</td></tr>
<tr><td colspan="2">I hope that you are well.</td><td colspan="2">I hope that you have been well.</td></tr>
<tr><td colspan="4">in the past</td></tr>
<tr><td colspan="2">Speravo che tu stessi bene.</td><td colspan="2">Speravo che tu fossi stato bene.</td></tr>
<tr><td>imperfect indicative (or other past tense)</td><td>imperfect subjunctive</td><td>imperfect indicative (or other past tense)</td><td>past perfect subj.</td></tr>
<tr><td colspan="2">I hoped that you were well.</td><td colspan="2">I hoped that you had been well.</td></tr>
</table>

TENSE SEQUENCE IN 'IF' SENTENCES (LESSON 27)

There are three types of 'if' sentences:

1. The hypothesis is real or highly probable

This is a simple supposition, presented in a neutral way without taking a position on the probability of the outcome. In this case, the indicative mood (present or future tense) is used in both clauses:

subordinate clause	main clause
Se fai presto	**arriverai in tempo.**
present indicative	future indicative
If you do it quickly,	*you'll arrive in time.*

2. The hypothesis is possible but not certain

The speaker making the hypothesis is not sure if the outcome will occur. In this case, the verb in the subordinate clause is in the imperfect subjunctive and the verb in the main clause is in the present conditional:

subordinate clause	main clause
Se facessi presto	**arriveresti in tempo.**
imperfect subjunctive	present conditional
If you were to do it quickly,	*you would arrive in time.*

3. The hypothesis (condition or outcome) is impossible or unattainable

• In the present: The situation is unachievable (or totally imaginary) in the present or the future. The verb in the subordinate clause is in the imperfect subjunctive, and the verb in the main clause is in the present conditional:

subordinate clause	main clause
Se io fossi in te	**non accetterei la sua proposta.**
imperfect subjunctive	present conditional
If I were you,	*I would not accept his/her offer.*

• In the past: Neither the condition nor the outcome occurred. The verb in the subordinate clause is in the past perfect subjunctive, and the verb in the main clause is in the past conditional (the conditional perfect in English):

subordinate clause	main clause
Se avessi fatto presto	**saresti arrivato in tempo.**
past perfect subjunctive	conditional perfect
If you had done it quickly,	*you would have arrived in time.*

Created by: Céladon Éditions
www.celadoneditions.com
Graphic designer: Sarah Boris
Italian reviewer: Luciana Marchesi
English translations and editing: Elise Bradbury
Sound engineer: Léonard Mule @ Studio du Poisson Barbu

Legal deposit: January 2021
Publication number: 4346
ISBN: 978-2-7005-8177-5
www.assimil.com

Printed in Czech Republic by PBtisk